THE CONSTITUTION OF THE UNITED STATES OF AMERICA

This is the second edition of Professor Tushnet's excellent short critical introduction to the history and current meaning of the United States' Constitution. It is organised around two themes: first, the US Constitution is old, short, and difficult to amend. These characteristics have made constitutional 'interpretation', especially by the US Supreme Court, the primary mechanism for adapting the Constitution to ever-changing reality. Second, the Constitution creates a structure of political opportunities that allows political actors, including political parties, to pursue the preferred policy goals even to the point of altering the very structure of politics. Politics, that is, often gives meaning to the Constitution. Deploying these themes to examine the structure of the national government, federalism, judicial review, and individual rights, the book provides basic information about, and deeper insights into, the way the US constitutional system has developed and what it means today.

D0061183

Constitutional Systems of the World
General Editors: Peter Leyland, Andrew Harding and Benjamin L Berger
Associate Editors: Grégoire Webber and Rosalind Dixon

In the era of globalisation, issues of constitutional law and good governance are being seen increasingly as vital issues in all types of society. Since the end of the Cold War, there have been dramatic developments in democratic and legal reform, and post-conflict societies are also in the throes of reconstructing their governance systems. Even societies already firmly based on constitutional governance and the rule of law have undergone constitutional change and experimentation with new forms of governance; and their constitutional systems are increasingly subjected to comparative analysis and transplantation. Constitutional texts for practically every country in the world are now easily available on the internet. However, texts which enable one to understand the true context, purposes, interpretation and incidents of a constitutional system are much harder to locate, and are often extremely detailed and descriptive. This series seeks to provide scholars and students with accessible introductions to the constitutional systems of the world, supplying both a road map for the novice and, at the same time, a deeper understanding of the key historical, political and legal events which have shaped the constitutional landscape of each country. Each book in this series deals with a single country, or a group of countries with a common constitutional history, and each author is an expert in their field.

Published volumes

The Constitution of the United Kingdom; The Constitution of the United States;
The Constitution of Vietnam; The Constitution of South Africa; The Constitution of Japan;
The Constitution of Germany; The Constitution of Finland;
The Constitution of Australia; The Constitution of the Republic of Austria;
The Constitution of the Russian Federation; The Constitutional System of Thailand;
The Constitution of Malaysia; The Constitution of China; The Constitution of Indonesia;
The Constitution of France; The Constitution of Spain; The Constitution of Mexico;
The Constitution of Canada; The Constitutional Systems of the Commonwealth Caribbean;
The Constitution of Israel; The Constitution of Singapore

Forthcoming volumes

The Constitution of Belgium; The Constitution of Taiwan; The Constitutional Systems of the
Independent Central Asian States; The Constitution of Romania; The Constitution of the
United Kingdom (third edition)

Link to series website
http://www.hartpub.co.uk/series/csw

See also the new series

Constitutional Systems of the World: Thematic Studies

Central-Local Relations in Asian Constitutional Systems

The Constitution of the United States of America

A Contextual Analysis

Second Edition

Mark Tushnet

·HART·
PUBLISHING
OXFORD AND PORTLAND, OREGON
2015

Published in the United Kingdom by Hart Publishing Ltd
16C Worcester Place, Oxford, OX1 2JW
Telephone: +44 (0)1865 517530
Fax: +44 (0)1865 510710
E-mail: mail@hartpub.co.uk
Website: http://www.hartpub.co.uk

Published in North America (US and Canada) by
Hart Publishing
c/o International Specialized Book Services
920 NE 58th Avenue, Suite 300
Portland, OR 97213-3786
USA
Tel: +1 503 287 3093 or toll-free: (1) 800 944 6190
Fax: +1 503 280 8832
E-mail: orders@isbs.com
Website: http://www.isbs.com

First edition, 2008

Mark Tushnet has asserted his right under the Copyright, Designs and Patents Act 1988,
to be identified as the author of this work.

Hart Publishing is an imprint of Bloomsbury Publishing plc.

British Library Cataloguing in Publication Data
Data Available

ISBN: 978-1-84946-604-2

Typeset by Compuscript Ltd, Shannon
Printed and bound in Great Britain by
CPI Group (UK) Ltd, Croydon CR0 4YY

Preface to the Second Edition

The first edition of this work was completed in 2008. Since then there have been significant developments in US constitutional law, flowing largely from the election of Barack Obama to the presidency and from the political responses to that election. The revised edition takes these developments into account, but it is important to emphasize that the *general* structure of the book's presentation remains unchanged—as it should, if, as I believe it did, the original edition accurately described the basic and permanent features of the US constitutional system. In part for that reason, I have not supplemented discussions that remain accurate with references to cases decided since 2008 that confirm or support the discussions. I had valuable research assistance from Michael Qin and Virginia Williamson in preparing the revisions.

Contents

Table of Cases

Table of Legislation

United States

Federal Legislation

Introduction

THE WRITTEN UNITED States Constitution is old, short and difficult to amend. Adopted in 1789 and amended only 27 times since, the Constitution and its amendments do not reach 6,000 words in length. Age, brevity and near-unamendability combine to produce a central but generally overlooked feature of the operative US constitution: Typically offered as a paradigm of a nation with a written constitution, the United States actually operates with a constitution that is more similar to than different from the paradigmatic unwritten constitution of the United Kingdom. Like the UK constitution, the 'efficient' constitution of the United States, to adopt Walter Bagehot's term, can be found in various written forms, but the document called the US Constitution is only one, and not the most important, of them.

The reason for the difference between the canonical and the efficient constitution is clear: the written Constitution's words must somehow be adapted to deal with problems of governance that have arisen since 1789, and the provisions for formal amendment are too cumbersome to serve as the primary mechanism for adaptation. Time produces changes in technology, values and (therefore) the problems people seek to solve through government. One recent case asked the Supreme Court to decide whether the police could install global positioning system (GPS) devices on automobiles, without a warrant, to track the movements of a suspected drug dealer; another asked the Court to decide whether the police could routinely examine the data in the mobile phone of someone they arrested.[1] Whatever the answer—the Court imposed substantial limits on police conduct—it seems clear that the problems of privacy posed by GPS and similar modern technologies are different in kind from the problems of intrusive searches with which the framers were familiar. In nations with more recent constitutions, constitutional

---

[1] See *United States v Jones* 132 S Ct 945 (2012) (the GPS case); *Riley v California*, 134 S Ct 2473 (2014) (the mobile phone case).

provisions address modern problems of privacy directly. The United States must do so in some other way.

Another example comes from the constitutional law of government structure. The modern state grew by expanding the objects of its regulation. This growth made it impossible for legislatures to specify the details of the regulations the nation's people desired. Instead, the national legislature delegated the authority to develop regulations to administrative agencies, and controlled those agencies in part by reviewing how they performed. For example, the national legislature created the Occupational Safety and Health Administration (OSHA) and charged it with responsibility for developing rules designed to reduce the incidence of accidents and injuries at the workplace. But, when OSHA proposed a rule aimed at reducing muscle injuries resulting from repetitive tasks such as typing at a computer, Congress enacted a statute denying OSHA the power to adopt the rule. One tool of review was the 'legislative veto'. In its pristine form, the legislative veto allowed one house of the national legislature to deny legal effect to a regulatory choice made by an administrative agency, if that house concluded that the choice was inconsistent with the public policy the house thought the agency should promote.

After many years of use, the legislative veto succumbed to constitutional challenge. The difficulty was that the agency's regulatory choice, if left unvetoed, would have the force of law. Ordinarily, the legal status quo can be changed only by an action that had the support of both legislative houses and the President. As the Supreme Court saw it, the legislative veto allowed one house to change the legal status quo—understood as the situation prevailing after the agency acted—without getting that agreement.[2] In striking down the legislative veto, Chief Justice Warren Burger wrote for the Supreme Court that '[t]he choices we discern as having been made in the Constitutional Convention impose burdens on governmental processes that often seem clumsy, inefficient, even unworkable'.[3] Yet, any stable government must be workable. If the canonical Constitution makes government unworkable in some important respect, something will be done to repair the defect. The need of the modern state for agencies that could indeed make

---

[2] This analysis overlooked the possibility that the status quo should have been defined as that which existed until the time for all the actions authorized by law—including the legislative veto—had been completed.

[3] *INS v Chadha* 462 US 919 (1983).

regulatory choices subject to supervision by the legislature persisted. With amendment impossible, even after the Supreme Court's decision Congress continued to enact statutes containing provisions authorizing legislative vetoes, although everyone understood that such provisions were unconstitutional. Other tools filled the gap—oversight hearings in which regulators were asked to explain their choices, controls exercised through the agency's budget, closer scrutiny of appointments to the agencies, and many more. These tools were political rather than legal, but were part of the efficient constitution nonetheless. The reason is that the efficient constitution had to accommodate changes in the demand for regulation—had to be 'workable'—even though the canonical Constitution (the 'choices made at the Constitutional Convention') remained unaltered.

These examples illustrate the two mechanisms through which the United States updates its efficient constitution without amending the canonical Constitution: decisions by the Supreme Court 'interpreting' the canonical Constitution, and the ordinary operation of politics mediated through competition between the nation's two major political parties.

More prominent in scholarly writing on constitutional law but probably less important generally, the Supreme Court 'interprets' the Constitution's terms, and in doing so adapts it to contemporary circumstances. Here, the efficient constitution is indeed written, but in hundreds of judicial opinions rather than in a single document. And, notably, the Supreme Court's opinions often make only passing reference to the Constitution's text. Operating in what has been described as a 'common law' manner,[4] the Court takes its own prior decisions as the central texts to be interpreted. A decision rendered today may cite a constitutional provision, but most of the Court's opinion will be devoted to analyzing its previous decisions.[5] These citations can be tracked back until at the

---

[4] D Strauss, 'Common Law Constitutional Interpretation' (1996) 63 *University of Chicago Law Review* 877.

[5] In contrast to practice in some other constitutional courts, the US Supreme Court attempts to render a judgment accompanied by a single opinion the reasoning of which is expressly endorsed by a majority of the Court's justices. After about a decade in which the justices rendered their opinions *seriatim*, Chief Justice John Marshall, who took office in 1801, shifted the Court's practice to one in which the decision was embodied in an 'opinion of the Court'. (Justices can and do author dissenting opinions, and they may in addition concur only in part of a majority's opinion.)

outset of a line of decisions one finds the Constitution's text playing a much larger role. But, for the present-day reader, the Constitution's text has almost disappeared from view.

For all the attention the Supreme Court's decisions attract from the public and in academic writing, another mechanism for updating the Constitution is almost certainly more important. That mechanism is the system of political parties. The Constitution's framers were quite skeptical about the benefits of nationally organized political parties, which they pejoratively called 'factions'. Some of the original Constitution's provisions—most notably, its use of an indirect method of electing the President—make sense only on the assumption that elections would not consist of campaigns organized by political parties on a national basis.[6] The development of such parties transformed the nation's basic structure from one of separation of powers to what has been called separation of parties.[7] Contention between the nation's parties is the structure through which the updating of the nation's governing structure occurs.

Political parties too are almost invisible in the Constitution. In the late twentieth century the Supreme Court invoked the First Amendment's protection of freedom of speech, and a collateral freedom of association, to provide some constitutional footing for political parties. Its decisions dealt with matters on the periphery of the parties' operations, and, notably, assumed that the Constitution allowed legislatures to protect the existing party system, and to some extent encouraged them to do so.[8] The United States has been dominated by a two-party political system for most of its existence. Again notably, the Constitution contains no provisions even encouraging the development of a two-party system. Political scientists agree that electing representatives from single-member districts with only a plurality required for victory pushes strongly in the direction of a two-party system. Elections in the United States take precisely that form, but nothing in the Constitution requires it: A federal *statute* requires that members of the House of Representatives be elected from single-member districts but, as a

---

[6] See ch 1.

[7] D Levinson and R Pildes, 'Separation of Parties, Not Powers' (2006) 119 *Harvard Law Review* 2311.

[8] See ch 2.

matter of *constitutional* law, elections could be held on a proportional basis with voters in each state casting their ballots for party lists. Under the original Constitution, members of the Senate—the upper house of the national legislature, which has a full legislative role—were chosen by state legislatures, again indicating the framers' anticipation that there would not be nationally organized political parties. The Seventeenth Amendment, adopted in 1913, replaced that with direct elections by the voters. Here, each state is a single electoral district, which provides some mild encouragement for the development of a two-party system within each state. The stronger encouragement provided by plurality election is not constitutionally mandated. Nor is there any encouragement in the Constitution for the parties that emerge in one state to be organized on the national level as well. For all the Constitution has to say about it, locally organized political parties could come together in shifting and temporary coalitions in presidential elections.

And yet: one can understand how the US government actually operates—that is, the efficient constitution—only by seeing it as a government fundamentally structured around the existence of two nationally organized political parties. For example, persistent questions in the twentieth century and today arise from the possibilities presented by the existence of divided and unified government. Divided government exists when one or both of the branches of the national legislature are under the effective control of one political party and the presidency is controlled by the other. Divided government means that important legislation advances, in general, only with significant support from both parties and, perhaps more important for constitutional purposes, that legislative oversight of the administration will be reasonably intense. In contrast, a unified government is more like the ones characteristic of a parliamentary system with only a few parties: There truly is a governing party, which can achieve its political goals with relative ease. And the executive administration may be able to have its way without much opposition from the legislature, particularly—as has become increasingly the case in the United States—when the party controlling the government as a whole is committed to a set of core political principles.

The central role of political parties and ordinary partisan contestation in the efficient constitution means that in an important sense nearly all of US constitutionalism is popular constitutionalism. Broadly speaking, constitutionalism is how a nation structures, coordinates and limits public power.[9] The written US Constitution sets up the nation's basic institutions, and in that sense serves constitutionalism's structuring function. Even here, though, politics has its role, because the written Constitution allows the national legislature to create the administrative agencies characteristic of the modern state but otherwise says almost nothing about those agencies. The blanks are filled in by legislative choice as it emerges from ordinary politics. Quotidian politics is also the nation's primary means of coordinating the actions of the nation's basic institutions, through unified or divided government.

The modern revival of interest in popular constitutionalism gives ordinary politics an important role in limiting exercises of public power as well.[10] At first glance this might seem either a conceptual or a political mistake. How can politics effectively limit the exercises of power accomplished through politics? The point of this aspect of constitutionalism, it might be thought, is precisely to place some limits on the ability of the people to use their political power. And, even if somehow a people deeply imbued with constitutional values *might* be able to refrain from abusing their power, how likely is it that they will? Does not US history show, one might ask, that popular constitutionalism is too often racist and fearful of dissent?

Proponents of popular constitutionalism are more optimistic about the people's capacities, somewhat more optimistic in their reading of US history, and more skeptical about the possibility that something other than popular constitutionalism can effectively limit the abuses of political power, than these questions suggest. More important, popular constitutionalism is inevitable, in light of the important place politics has in the efficient constitution. Seen in its best light, popular constitutionalism allows the people to use the ordinary contention between political parties as the means by which they implement and limit the implementation of competing constitutional visions. A president may offer programs and policies animated by a constitutional vision that

---

[9] And, by doing so, provides the mechanisms for structuring, coordinating and limiting private power, through the law of property, tort and contract, and through ordinary regulatory legislation.

[10] The best recent statement is LD Kramer, *The People Themselves: Popular Constitutionalism and Judicial Review* (New York, Oxford University Press, 2004).

he and his party articulate; leaders of the opposing political party may offer modifications or a comprehensive alternative; and the people can choose between them as they cast their ballots in regular elections. The Supreme Court is a participant in this process as well. It too offers a constitutional vision that the people can accept or reject, by electing a president or Senators who will shape and reshape the Court through new appointments and by electing legislators who might use the other tools available to them to induce the Court to change its views and who might press the limits of the Court's constitutional doctrine to and beyond the breaking point.

For all the emphasis the writtenness of the US Constitution has received in constitutional theory and in accounts of US constitutionalism, any description of the US Constitution in context must pay a great deal of attention to ordinary politics. In turn, that implies that any such description must pay much less attention to the Supreme Court and its articulation of constitutional doctrine than is found in most introductory overviews of US constitutional law. These conclusions animate the description of the US Constitution that follows. Other overviews of the US Constitution begin by examining the powers held by the national government, and then turn to government structure and constitutional rights. The emphasis here on the role of politics in US constitutionalism generates a different approach. After a brief description of US constitutional history, we take up the structures of Congress, the national legislative branch and the Presidency, emphasizing the interaction between constitutional language and the politics it produces within each branch and between them. Only with that understanding in hand can we deeply understand the way in which a government nominally of limited powers has become one of plenary power. Deferring discussion of the courts and particularly the Supreme Court flows as well from understanding that politics is at least as important as constitutional language in giving the United States the efficient constitution it has. The Constitution's rights provisions and their judicial enforcement cannot be ignored, of course, but here too our examination will demonstrate the connections between the political and judicial articulations of fundamental rights. The book concludes with an examination of the modes of constitutional change in the United States, where formal constitutional amendments have played a far smaller part than judicial interpretation and political practice.

FURTHER READING

Amar, AR, *America's Constitution: A Biography* (New York, Random House, 2005) (an idiosyncratic work that examines every provision in the Constitution).

Chemerinsky, E, *Constitutional Law: Principles and Policies* (3rd edn Riverwoods, Ill, Aspen Publishers, 2006) (providing an overview of US constitutional doctrine).

Tribe, L, *American Constitutional Law* (2nd edn New York, Foundation Press, 1990) (similar to Chemerinsky, but offering a more complex theoretical account; the first volume of a third edition is available, but Professor Tribe has suspended work on completing that edition).

1

An Overview of the History of the US Constitution

—————

From the Revolution to the Bill of Rights – The Early National Period – The Crisis over Slavery and the Civil War – The Late Nineteenth Century and the Growth of the Modern State – The New Deal Crisis and the New Constitutional Regime – From the Reagan Revolution to the Present – Conclusion

WHEN IN THE late nineteenth century scholars began to write constitutional histories of the United States, they went back to the forest of Germany and Magna Carta to identify the origins of US constitutionalism. For our purposes a more compressed time frame is appropriate. This Chapter surveys constitutional developments from the Revolutionary era through the early twenty-first century, to provide some orientation to the analytical account of US constitutional development that will occupy the remainder of the book. A single short chapter is obviously inadequate to provide more than the barest sense of the course of constitutional development; we will return to some of the episodes noted here in later chapters, which will also provide additional examples that retrospectively fill in some details omitted here.

FROM THE REVOLUTION TO THE BILL OF RIGHTS

The British colonies on the North American continent began to push for independence in the aftermath of the French and Indian Wars of the mid-eighteenth century. By the early 1770s a group of politically active colonists had become increasingly dissatisfied with the imposition on them of regulations adopted by the remote British Parliament in which they had no direct representation. They organized 'committees of correspondence' which began as local groups of independence-minded colonists who coordinated their efforts across colonies but which eventually became quasi-governments parallel to the colonial legislatures under British control.[1]

Meeting in Philadelphia, the colonists declared independence in 1776. Organized as a 'Continental Congress' with representatives from each of the colonies, the rebels began to create something resembling a government for what they hoped would become a new and independent nation. That government was a loose confederation of the former colonies, now denominated 'states'. Near the end of the decade the states decided to regularize their government by entering into a formal confederation. The Articles of Confederation were drafted in 1777 and became effective in 1781, during the Revolutionary War.

Experience under the Articles of Confederation, during the war and after the conflict ended in 1783, was not terribly satisfactory from the point of view of political elites who saw the possibility that the people of the American continent could play a large role in world affairs.[2] The Articles created a legislative body but no chief executive, which made conducting military and foreign affairs particularly cumbersome. Funding the national government's operations—primarily its military ones—proved impossible. The national legislature had no power to impose taxes; all it could do was send requests to the states for contributions, and those 'requisitions' were universally disregarded by states themselves facing fiscal difficulty in the war's aftermath. As members of a confederation, the states saw themselves as fully sovereign, which induced them to engage in economic policies that continental-minded elites thought unwise and damaging to other states. The national government had no power to enforce its international obligations against the states, which threatened to cause diplomatic embarrassment for the new 'nation'.

---

[1] For a good account of how the committees of correspondence functioned as local governments, see RD Brown, *Revolutionary Politics in Massachusetts: The Boston Committee of Correspondence and the Towns, 1772–1774* (New York, WW Norton, 1976).

[2] J Madison, 'Vices of the Political System of the United States' in WT Hutchinson et al, (eds), *Papers of James Madison,* vol 9 (Chicago, University of Chicago Press, 1975).

By 1786 these difficulties led prominent politicians to call a convention in Annapolis, Maryland, to consider amending the Articles—a difficult task, because the Articles, understood as something like a treaty among sovereigns, expressly required that amendments be approved unanimously. When only a few states sent representatives to the convention, it adjourned after asking Congress to convene another convention. Congress responded by resolving to hold another convention in Philadelphia in the next year.

In 1787 enough states did send delegates to what became known as the Constitutional Convention, though some did so reluctantly, and some delegates and even delegations left when they saw the direction the Convention was moving. The Convention's charge was to propose amendments to the Articles of Confederation, but almost from the start the delegates worked on a complete replacement for the Articles. They kept their deliberations secret, which, as Jon Elster has pointed out, allowed them to discuss their problems candidly and to make unprincipled compromises that would be hard to defend when seen as compromises but that could be presented to the public as based on deep principle.[3]

Reflecting what they believed they had learned from their experience as subjects of the British empire, the Convention's members rapidly agreed that the new government they were designing should reflect Montesquieuan principles of separation of powers. Designing a judiciary was not terribly difficult, and—after the delegates toyed with the idea of a multi-member executive—neither was designing the executive branch, to be headed by a president. (Some problems were patched over by the universal recognition that the revered George Washington, who chaired the Convention in a nearly regal manner, would be the first president under the new Constitution.)

The real problem arose in designing the new legislature, which the delegates assumed would be the most important and powerful branch. The main concerns centered on reconciling the recognition that the new legislature would have to have substantial power, to be able to govern in ways that avoided the difficulties that confronted the Confederation, with concern that a powerful national government might reproduce the kind of imperial overreaching that had led to rebellion

---

[3] J Elster, 'Forces and Mechanisms in the Constitution-Making Process' (1995) 45 *Duke Law Journal* 364.

and independence. One way to deal with these concerns was to list the powers the new government would have, but that was not entirely satisfactory because the enumerated powers had to be expansive enough to accommodate all the important things the delegates thought the new government really had to do.

The conflicting concerns were crystallized in two related conflicts. One placed smaller states at odds with larger ones; the other placed states in which slavery was an important economic institution at odds with states where it was not—roughly, the southern states against the northern ones. Smaller states were concerned that they would regularly be outvoted in a legislature in which representation was based on population. Slave states were concerned that a powerful national government might eventually become dominated by opponents of slavery. After long debates, the delegates addressed these problems through several devices. Creating two houses in the national legislature allowed the delegates to base representation in one, the House of Representatives, on population, and to give each state equal representation in the Senate.

Slavery was given some specific guarantees: The national government was barred from prohibiting the interstate trade in slaves for two decades; northern states were placed under an obligation to return slaves who escaped to freedom back to their owners. More important, the apportionment of seats in the House took slavery into account by giving slave states a bonus. It would be based on the free population plus three-fifths of the slave population. And, finally, the president would be chosen through a complex mechanism—not by direct popular election but through an 'electoral college' whose members would be elected in the states, with each state getting a number of electors equal to the number of Representatives it had plus two (justified as taking the state's Senate representation into account, but also giving the small states disproportionate influence in the president's selection, at least for the foreseeable future). These structural devices gave Southerners confidence that they would be able to protect their interests against congressional regulation through the ordinary operation of politics. That confidence was well-placed; until the system broke down in the middle of the nineteenth century, Southerners dominated the presidency and Congress.

Getting the proposed Constitution ratified proved difficult as well. The delegates sought to ease the task by abandoning the pretense that they were simply amending the Articles of Confederation, which would have required unanimous consent from all the states. Instead, they said that the Constitution would take effect when ratified by nine of the existing states. Even so, the campaign for ratification was hard-fought. Opponents of the new Constitution, called the anti-Federalists, raised a flurry of objections.[4] The most important centered on the breadth of power the new government would have. The anti-Federalists were not reassured by the new Constitution's defenders' claims that Congress's powers were actually limited. The anti-Federalists pointed to the final clause in the list of congressional powers, giving Congress the power 'To make all Laws which shall be necessary and proper for carrying into Execution the foregoing Powers'. The anti-Federalists, either out of principle or because it was a good political point, also pointed out that the proposed Constitution did not contain a Bill of Rights.

James Madison and Alexander Hamilton wrote a series of newspaper articles responding to these concerns, as part of the effort to obtain ratification in the crucial state of New York.[5] These articles, later collected as *The Federalist Papers*, are one of the great documents in the Constitution's history, less because of their direct impact on ratification than for the arguments they presented.

Madison articulated the political theory he thought grounded the Constitution in his defense of the separation of powers, which he argued involved balancing the power of one branch against that of the others. He then observed:

> It may be a reflection on human nature, that such devices should be necessary to control the abuses of government. But what is government itself, but the greatest of all reflections on human nature? If men were angels, no government would be necessary.[6]

Human imperfection, or ambition, made government necessary, but also made government a threat to liberty. How could constitutional designers deal with the latter problem? The popular solution, as Madison saw it, was to write down limitations in a constitution. But Madison was skeptical about the ability of 'parchment barriers' to control the impulses of ambitious politicians.[7]

[4] C Kenyon, 'Men of Little Faith' (1955) 12 *William & Mary Quarterly*, 3rd ser 3, is the classic discussion of the anti-federalist objections to the proposed Constitution.
[5] John Jay wrote a few papers in this series, but dropped out of the project rather early.
[6] *The Federalist* no 51.
[7] *The Federalist* no 48.

Madison offered structural arrangements instead. In *The Federalist no. 10* he gave his most extended analysis of the relation between human imperfection and constitutional design. The fundamental problem of government, for Madison, arose from the existence of what he called factions. These were groups of people 'who are united and actuated by some common impulse of passion, or of interest, adverse to the rights of other citizens, or to the permanent and aggregate interests of the community'. Clearly it would be undesirable for factions to control government. But how could factions be controlled? For Madison, the 'causes of faction are ... sown in the nature of man' and it was impossible to eliminate faction without restricting liberty, equally clearly undesirable. Statesmen might transcend faction, but '[e]nlightened statesmen will not always be at the helm'. The trick was to control faction's effects, not its causes. Majority rule could control factions composed of a minority of the public, but that left the problem of a majority faction that would violate minority rights or otherwise fail to pursue the public interest.

For Madison, the solution was the creation of a large republic in which government was conducted by representatives elected by the people. Representation at least allowed for the possibility that the elected representatives would be able

> to refine and enlarge the public views, by passing them through the medium of a chosen body of citizens, whose wisdom may best discern the true interest of their country, and whose patriotism and love of justice will be least likely to sacrifice it to temporary or partial considerations.

Representation alone would not be enough. The representatives themselves might be corrupt, for example. Yet, Madison thought, corruption might occur in individual districts, but coordinating a cabal of corrupt officials elected from different districts would be difficult. He therefore argued that the very size of the new nation, which many at the time thought was a disadvantage, actually was a solution to the problem of faction and corruption. Looking to the people directly, Madison argued that a large republic would be less likely to be controlled by faction than a small one:

> Extend the sphere, and you take in a greater variety of parties and interests; you make it less probable that a majority of the whole will have a common motive to invade the rights of other citizens; or if such a common motive exists, it will be more difficult for all who feel it to discover their own strength, and to act in unison with each other...
>
> The influence of factious leaders may kindle a flame within their particular States, but will be unable to spread a general conflagration through the other

States. A religious sect may degenerate into a political faction in a part of the Confederacy; but the variety of sects dispersed over the entire face of it must secure the national councils against any danger from that source. A rage for paper money, for an abolition of debts, for an equal division of property, or for any other improper or wicked project, will be less apt to pervade the whole body of the Union than a particular member of it; in the same proportion as such a malady is more likely to taint a particular county or district, than an entire State.

In the extent and proper structure of the Union, therefore, we behold a republican remedy for the diseases most incident to republican government.

These basic presuppositions helped Madison and Hamilton explain the new Constitution's details and defend it against the anti-Federalist attack. On the absence of a Bill of Rights, for example, Hamilton noted that the Constitution did contain some protections of individual rights, such as a ban on the adoption of ex post facto laws that imposed criminal penalties on activities lawful when undertaken, but went on to stress that that the enumeration of powers was effectively a bill of rights. Congress was to have the power to do only certain things—important things, no doubt—and it was not given the power to infringe on fundamental rights. This could not alleviate anti-Federalist concerns entirely, of course, because the anti-Federalists worried that Congress would do something plainly within one of the enumerated grants of power that would nonetheless violate fundamental rights. Hamilton devoted a footnote attempting but failing to refute that claim.

Madison addressed the same concern, but emphasized the way in which the new national government's structure would protect against violations of rights. He pointed to federalism and the separation of powers as providing a 'double security' to the people:

> [T]he power surrendered by the people is first divided between two distinct governments, and then the portion allotted to each subdivided among distinct and separate departments.... The different governments will control each other, at the same time that each will be controlled by itself.[8]

The people and their state governments had little to fear from the national government. Even apart from the role that the enumeration of powers played, the people and the state would be able to control the national government. Most policies affecting ordinary people would be

---

[8] *The Federalist* no 51.

set at the state and local level, which would attach the people strongly to their states and less strongly to the national government. 'The operations of the federal government will be most extensive and important in times of war and danger; those of the State governments in times of peace and security.'[9] If the national government did seem to get out of control, the states would be 'alarmed,' and a new rebellion would occur: 'Every government would espouse the common cause. A correspondence would be opened. Plans of resistance would be concerted.'[10]

Madison defended the separation of powers not only as a way of ensuring that government would operate effectively, but also as a way of securing liberty. The reason was that people holding positions in one branch would resist aggrandizement of power by those holding power in other branches.

> [T]he great security against a gradual concentration of the several powers in the same department, consists in giving to those who administer each department the necessary constitutional means and personal motives to resist encroachments of the others.... Ambition must be made to counteract ambition. The interest of the man must be connected with the constitutional rights of the place.[11]

New York did ratify the Constitution, but the fight was close. Realizing that the anti-Federalist focus on the absence of a Bill of Rights was the opposition's most politically effective argument, Federalists around the country fell back. They urged the people to ratify the Constitution in the form it was proposed, and promised that once the new government was in place they would immediately introduce a Bill of Rights to be added to the Constitution as amendments. This strategy succeeded, and the Constitution was ratified.

The effects of the ratification fights lingered. The Virginia legislature refused to elect James Madison to the Senate, despite his prominence at the convention. He stood for a seat in the House of Representatives, but, expecting that his neighbors would readily reward him for his accomplishments, he barely campaigned. Finding himself in an unexpectedly difficult fight for votes with James Monroe, who repeated anti-Federalist concerns about the Constitution, Madison promised to introduce a bill of rights in the first Congress. After his election, Madison compiled all the proposed rights-provisions that had bubbled up

---

[9] *The Federalist* no 45.
[10] *The Federalist* no 46.
[11] *The Federalist* no 51.

during the ratification struggle, added a few of his own, and presented Congress with a list of constitutional amendments. Congress tinkered with the list and with the wording of specific rights, and eventually submitted 12 amendments to the states for ratification. One was predicated on the sensible thought that it would be desirable to members of the House of Representatives to have districts small enough to allow each constituent to truly know who the representative was. This would have increased the size of the House of Representatives as the nation's population increased, and fortunately was not ratified. Another sought to place electoral constraints on the self-interest of national legislators by specifying that salary increases they voted could not take effect until after an election had occurred, allowing opponents to criticize those running for reelection for feathering their own nests. This lingered unratified for two centuries, and eventually became part of the Constitution in 1992.[12] The remaining 10 amendments, ratified in 1791, became the Bill of Rights appended to the original Constitution.

THE EARLY NATIONAL PERIOD

Madison's confidence that the extended republic would prevent the emergence of faction was misplaced. Almost immediately after the Constitution took effect, political parties began to emerge and coordinate their policies across state boundaries, and indeed Madison himself became a leader of the new Jeffersonian–Democratic party. Parties were created for the reasons Madison had identified: People with different interests found it helpful to coordinate political action, sometimes in connection with domestic policies about economic development and, more important in the republic's early years, sometimes in connection with foreign affairs and the nation's relation to the established European powers.

The development of national political parties produced the nation's first constitutional crisis. Political scientists sometimes say that we cannot know whether a nation has a sustainable democratic system until we

---

[12] Although one can readily develop formal arguments against the amendment's constitutionality, on the ground that true amendments can occur only if there is roughly contemporaneous agreement among the requisite number of states, the amendment has not and will not be challenged, and its legal validity now rather clearly rests on its general acceptance.

observe those holding power peacefully relinquishing office when they are defeated in an election.[13] That did not occur in the United States until 1800, and it was not clear until the very end of the crisis that the transfer of power would occur. The crisis began when John Adams, the nation's second president and leader of what was called the Federalist party, responded to severe criticism of his policies by leading Congress to adopt a series of laws restricting the activities of non-citizens and, more important, making it a crime to criticize the president (but not the vice-president, then Thomas Jefferson, a leader of the opposition to Adams's policies). Prosecutions of Jefferson's supporters under the Sedition Act simply heightened political tensions. In the elections of 1800 Jeffersonians seemingly won a sweeping victory. But they almost ran aground because of a flaw in the Constitution's design. Voters cast their ballots not for a candidate for the presidency but for presidential electors, who were then to cast two votes. The framers expected that many electors would vote in turn for local or regional 'favorite son' candidates, and that most elections would be resolved through a second mechanism, the choice by the House of Representatives, voting by states, among the five candidates receiving the most electoral votes. When nationally organized political parties arose, electors cast one vote for the party's presidential candidate and one for its vice-presidential candidate. Thomas Jefferson (running for the presidency) and Aaron Burr (run for the vice-presidency on Jefferson's ticket) received the same number of electoral votes because of a failure of coordination among Jeffersonian politicians.[14]

The Constitution then provided for selection of the president from the two leading candidates by the House of Representatives—but by the *old* House of Representatives, not the newly elected one.[15] The House struggled for weeks over the presidential election, and eventually chose Jefferson over Burr only when a Federalist member of the House concluded that the intrigues by Burr and Federalist leaders were inconsistent with the nation's aspirations to being a democratic republic.

---

[13] For one version, see SP Huntington, *The Third Wave: Democratization in the Late Twentieth Century* (Norman, University of Oklahoma Press, 1991).

[14] The difficulty was resolved by the Twelfth Amendment, which separated the electoral votes for president and vice-president.

[15] For a full account of the events, see B Ackerman, *The Failure of the Founding Fathers: Jefferson, Marshall, and the Rise of Presidential Democracy* (Cambridge, MA, Harvard University Press, 2005).

One issue lingered after the transfer of power in the presidency and Congress. Seeking to secure something in the aftermath of the elections, the departing Federalists created a number of new judgeships and staffed them with Federalists who, the politicians hoped, would protect their party's accomplishments and interests against a legislative assault by the new Congress. Outraged, the Jeffersonians responded by abolishing the newly created positions. The issue came to the Supreme Court in 1803, and the Court, led by the Federalist Chief Justice John Marshall, himself appointed in the last days of the Adams administration, avoided a direct confrontation with Jefferson by acceding to the repeal while almost simultaneously asserting that the courts stood ready to strike down statutes as unconstitutional.[16]

Under Jeffersonian control, and then in the late 1820s and 1830s under control by politicians allied with President Andrew Jackson, Congress was not a strongly nationalistic legislature, and relatively few enduring constitutional questions arose. Jefferson seized the opportunity to purchase the Louisiana Territory and greatly expand the nation's size, even though he believed the purchase to be beyond the power he had under the Constitution.[17] In 1812 Senator Henry Clay, who became a perennial presidential candidate, proposed what he called the 'American system', to promote national economic development by infrastructure investments by the national government and funded from increased tariffs. Jacksonians set their face against these 'internal improvements', as they were called, arguing that the investments were too local and were outside the scope of any power granted to Congress. President Andrew Jackson dealt a death blow to the American system in his veto of a bill aimed at supporting building a road between Maysville and Lexington, Kentucky.

Meanwhile, the Supreme Court under John Marshall did what it could to endorse a nationalist constitutional vision to counter the more state-oriented vision promoted by Jefferson and Jackson. It gave an expansive definition of Congress's power to regulate commerce among

---

[16] *Stuart v Laird* 5 US (1 Cranch) 299 (1803); *Marbury v Madison* 5 US (1 Cranch) 137 (1803). For a more extensive discussion, see ch 4.

[17] For a discussion of the many constitutional issues raised by the Louisiana Purchase, see PS Onuf, '"The Strongest Government on Earth": Jefferson's Republicanism, the Expansion of the Union, and the New Nation's Destiny' in S Levinson and BH Sparrow (eds), *The Louisiana Purchase and American Expansion 1803–1898* (Lanham, MD, Rowman & Littlefield, 2005).

the states,[18] although Congress would not take advantage of that power until late in the century. And, in perhaps the Marshall Court's most important decision, Marshall wrote for a unanimous Court upholding Congress's power to create a national bank.[19] That power had been contested from the very beginning. The issue had been raised during the Constitutional Convention, and the delegates deliberately refrained from giving Congress the power to charter corporations, having in mind the possibility that Congress would charter a national bank. When a bill proposing a national bank was introduced into Congress, Madison gave an eloquent speech explaining why, in his view, creating such a bank was unconstitutional. After the bill's passage, President Washington asked Jefferson and Hamilton for opinions on the bank's constitutionality. The two men disagreed, and Washington accepted Hamilton's nationalist vision in signing the bank bill. Marshall's opinion displayed none of the uncertainties associated with the bank. He deployed a careful reading of the Constitution's text and, importantly, treated the 'necessary and proper clause', about which the anti-Federalists had been so nervous, as expanding rather than limiting Congress's power.

Jacksonians opposed the national bank because they saw it as the instrument of an undemocratic elite pursuing its own selfish interests rather than the public interest. To combat the influence of elites, Jacksonians supported the expansion of the franchise by eliminating property qualifications for voting, and the extension of the franchise by increasing the number and types of officials who were directly elected or appointed by elected officials. At the state level systems of electing judges replaced systems in which judges were appointed by executive officials. The 'spoils system' endorsed the replacement of low-level public officials when one party displaced another. And, though neither movement achieved success during this period, supporters of woman suffrage and the abolition of slavery were able to draw upon the Jacksonian democratizing impulse to explain why their programs were consistent with the nation's deep commitments.

THE CRISIS OVER SLAVERY AND THE CIVIL WAR

The acquisition of the Louisiana Territory was a harbinger of constitutional difficulties to come, not over territorial expansion directly, but

---

[18] *Gibbons v Ogden* 22 US (9 Wheat) 1 (1824).
[19] *McCulloch v Maryland* 17 US (4 Wheat) 316 (1819).

over the preservation of the political balance between slave and free states that assured the South that the national government would always be sympathetic to its claims. That balance was preserved by a tacit agreement to admit new states in pairs, a free Indiana for a slave Mississippi. Maine's application for admission to the union in 1820 forcefully raised the question of that agreement's stability. After a long political battle, Congress adopted the Missouri Compromise, which drew a line across the nation and said that states below the line could have slavery, and those above it could not. This compromise solved the problem of Senate representation, but it could not permanently solve the problem for the House of Representatives and therefore for the presidency. An economically dynamic North attracted immigrants and experienced substantial population increases; a more economically stagnant South did neither. The result was an increasing perception in the South that it could no longer rely on ordinary politics to preserve slavery from congressional attack.[20]

By the 1850s slavery had become central in national politics. Southerners still dominated the national political system even as they feared their displacement, and they maneuvered to obtain greater statutory protection for slavery. The Compromise of 1850 overturned the Missouri Compromise and along the way strengthened the statutes giving slave owners the right to retrieve their escaped slaves from the North. But, given the South's perception of its political prospects, legislation alone was not enough. Slavery needed constitutional protection. And the Supreme Court gave the South what it thought it needed. *Dred Scott v Sandford* (1857) held that Congress did not have the power to prohibit slavery in the territories and—some Northern lawyers thought—hinted that it would be unconstitutional for free states to take the position that slaves voluntarily brought by the owners into a free state were thereby automatically freed.[21]

Aware that the Supreme Court was about to rule in the South's favor, in his inaugural address in 1857 President James Buchanan asked the nation to accept whatever decision the Court made as a permanent resolution of the constitutional controversy over slavery and national power. It did not. After all, the Court had said in effect that the central planks of the new and increasingly strong Republican party were unconstitutional.

---

[20] For a full account, see MA Graber, *Dred Scott and the Problem of Constitutional Evil* (New York, Cambridge University Press, 2006).

[21] *Dred Scott v Sandford* 60 US (19 How) 393 (1857).

Republicans could hardly be expected to go along, and they did not. The nation's party system fractured, with four major candidates running for the presidency in 1860. Coupled with the distribution of electoral votes among the states, the divisions among strong and moderate pro-slavery politicians led to an electoral college victory by the anti-slavery Republican Abraham Lincoln, who received no electoral votes and almost no popular votes in slave states, and under 40 per cent of the popular vote.

And then, as Lincoln later put it, the war came—and along with it, many new constitutional issues, primarily about the scope of the president's power during a rebellion. Acting initially without congressional authorization because the crisis arose while Congress was in recess and intensified before Congress reconvened under Lincoln's call, Lincoln suspended the writ of *habeas corpus*. The aged pro-slavery Chief Justice Roger Taney wrote an opinion condemning Lincoln's action, but he accepted as a regrettable fact that Lincoln was going to get away with the suspension.[22] Later Congress retroactively approved of the suspension. Scholars since then have agreed that only Congress can suspend the writ, but that retroactive authorization may sometimes be constitutionally acceptable. After the war ended, the Supreme Court held that Congress could not suspend the writ in areas where the civil courts remained open and functioning, at least with regard to civilians not themselves under the command of rebel officers.[23]

The Civil War dramatically transformed the written and the efficient Constitution. The Thirteenth Amendment (1865) abolished slavery. The Fifteenth Amendment (1870) guaranteed the right to vote without regard to race. The Fourteenth Amendment (1868) turned out to be the most important. The Bill of Rights protected fundamental rights against violation by the national government. As it turned out, the Fourteenth Amendment protected fundamental rights against violation by state and local governments, although it took nearly a century for that protection to become truly significant in practical terms.

More important in the short run and equally important in the long run, the Civil War experience contributed to a transformation in Americans' understanding of the possibilities for benevolent exercises of national power. Slavery of course had been an institution of state law, and demonstrated to the war's winners that leaving matters to the

---

[22] *Ex p Merryman* 17 F Cas 144 (1862).
[23] *Ex p Milligan* 71 US (4 Wall) 2 (1866).

control of the states did not inevitably favor liberty. The national government's successful conduct of the war, and the effectiveness of the bureaucracies that sprang up to administer the war and its aftermath, demonstrated as well that committing matters to the national government did not inevitably lead to tyranny or inefficiency.[24] The first fruits of that demonstration came during Reconstruction, when national military forces ran governments in the South as an occupying power. By the mid-1870s Reconstruction had become politically discredited, but not because of the inefficiency of the national bureaucracy. White terrorists were simply too numerous to control, and the non-military governments that began to run the states under control of African American politicians and their allies got a reputation, only partly deserved, for corruption. Reconstruction ended with the Compromise of 1877, when a disputed presidential election resulted in an agreement by the incoming Rutherford B Hayes to withdraw troops from the South. But its end did not discredit the newly gained confidence in the ability of the national government to govern effectively.

THE LATE NINETEENTH CENTURY AND THE GROWTH OF THE MODERN STATE

The period from the 1880s through the 1920s, roughly corresponding to what is known as the Progressive era, was one of complex and contradictory constitutional developments. The most important was the growth of administrative capacity in the national government, as bureaucracies grew and began a sustained process of transformation from organizations staffed on the basis of patronage and dominated by political considerations to more modern rationalized bureaucracies. The national government got its first civil service system in 1883, for example.

Some bureaucracies administered public benefit programs such as the system of pensions for veterans of the Civil War. Others regulated businesses. Progressives hoped that bureaucracies, and the government as a whole, would come under the control of trained professionals. Rate-setting agencies, for example, should take their guidance from

---

[24] GM Frederickson, *The Inner Civil War: Northern Intellectuals and the Crisis of the Union* (New York, Harper & Row, 1965).

economists. Progressives pushed for the adoption of specialized courts to deal with juvenile offenders and with family disputes, so that professional social workers could use their expertise to devise appropriate responses to social distress and disorder. Professional judgement, exercised by middle-class public employers, would, Progressives hoped, displace the political decisions made by political appointees influenced by working-class voters.

Courts responded warily to the growth of administrative capacity. They understood that the modern state required modern bureaucracies, but they insisted that those bureaucracies conform to the requirements of the rule of law as interpreted by the courts. Professional discretion had to operate within bounds both procedural and substantive. The courts did not require that Progressive-era agencies follow traditional judicial procedures down to every detail, but they did require conformity to such procedures on many important matters. And, probably more important, agency procedures on all matters were subject to judicial supervision. The new 'fourth branch' of government had always to look over its shoulder to see how the courts were going to respond to its initiatives.

The courts also imposed substantive limitations on Progressive legislation. Agencies could set rates for railroads and other businesses 'affected with a public interest' but the Constitution's protection of property rights meant that the rates could not be 'confiscatory'. Determining whether a rate provided a railroad with adequate compensation for its capital investments might seem an economic and therefore a technical question, but the bar on confiscatory rates converted it into a constitutional and therefore a judicial one.[25]

Rate-regulation was a favored program of Midwestern Populists, mostly farmers, as well as professionally oriented Progressives. Populists continued to press the Jacksonian impulse toward democratization forward. Some Populists favored cross-racial alliances and therefore endorsed the effective enfranchisement of African Americans in the South. Upper-class elites worried about what such alliances might accomplish, and pushed for new measures sharply restricting the ability of African Americans to vote: literacy tests, poll taxes, and more. Southern states adopted these rules, and the number of African American voters dropped dramatically. The democratizing impulse continued to fuel the movement for woman suffrage, which achieved incremental

---

[25] *Smyth v Ames* 169 US 466 (1898).

successes crowned by the adoption of the Nineteenth Amendment in 1920, which said that the right to vote could not be denied 'on account of sex'. Mostly in the nation's west, states adopted forms of direct legislation—the referendum and initiative—that allowed the people to enact constitutional amendments and ordinary laws themselves, without going through what ardent democrats thought were sometimes corrupt legislatures.

By the end of the nineteenth century regulation of business had become widespread, and courts became concerned about some of its manifestations. The doctrines they used developed against a backdrop with two components. Well-established law acknowledged legislative authority to regulate businesses in pursuit of the state's 'police powers', defined as the power to promote health, safety and morals.[26] It also restricted legislative authority to adopt 'class legislation', a term Jacksonians used to describe narrow interest-group legislation.[27]

The Supreme Court established the framework for analyzing regulatory legislation in *Lochner v New York*.[28] New York adopted a comprehensive system for regulating bakeries. Some of the regulations were plainly directed at health and safety, such as a requirement that bakery workers not live where they worked, which would make the workplace unsanitary. The regulations also limited the hours bakers could work up to 60 hours a week. Unionized bakers had pressed the legislature to enact a maximum hours law for years. Large commercial bakers found it relatively easy to organize their workforces to comply with the 60-hour law, but the law placed smaller bakers under real economic pressure, and one of them challenged the law as an unconstitutional deprivation of his liberty and property without due process of law.[29]

---

[26] WJ Novak, *The People's Welfare: Law and Regulation in the Nineteenth Century* (Chapel Hill, University of North Carolina Press, 1996).

[27] H Gillman, *The Constitution Besieged: The Rise and Demise of Lochner Era Police Powers Jurisprudence* (Durham, Duke University Press, 1993).

[28] 198 US 45 (1905).

[29] Both the Fifth Amendment and the Fourteenth Amendment use the term 'due process of law'. The term traces back to Magna Carta, where it appears as *'per legem terrae'* [by the law of the land]. Despite the presence of the word 'process' in the phrase, by the late 19th century it was uncontroversial among lawyers that the Due Process Clauses placed some substantive limitations on government action. The limitation was ordinarily described as a ban on the adoption of 'arbitrary' laws. For a brief history of the idea of substantive due process, see JV Orth, *Due Process of Law: A Brief History* (Lawrence, KS, University Press of Kansas, 2003).

The Supreme Court agreed. According to the Court, and following the Jacksonian rejection of class legislation, the maximum hours law could not survive if it were a 'labor law pure and simple'. By that, the Court meant that the state's police power did not authorize it to shift resources—income—from employers to employees simply because the legislature disagreed with the existing distribution of wealth. This was a reasonably traditional application of the Jacksonian hostility to class legislation.

The Court acknowledged that legislatures could intervene to protect workers who were unable to bargain effectively over wages because they faced coercion from their employers or because they lacked true capacity to enter into contracts. Referring to earlier cases upholding legislative regulation of the contracts of miners and seamen, Justice Rufus Peckham wrote for the Court that those workers did face real constraints, amounting to compulsion, to accept the terms their employers forced on them. Bakers, though, did not. And bakers were as competent as any other worker to gauge their own interests and decide to accept or reject jobs on the terms offered them. A few years later the Court upheld a law limiting the hours women could work in laundries, relying on the idea that women did indeed lack capacity to contract. Then, after women gained the right to vote the Court relied on that and other changes in women's status to strike down a similar law: Women, the Court said, were just as competent as men to negotiate employment contracts.[30]

What of the state's police power with regard to health and safety? Here, *Lochner* was more innovative. The Court engaged in a reasonably close analysis of the evidence available to show that bakeries might be unhealthy places to work. Scrutinizing the evidence, the Court concluded that there was no reason to think that bakers who worked more than 60 hours a week somehow ended up making bread that was unhealthy to consume, nor that such bakers were at greater risk of becoming sick than bakers who worked shorter hours.

Lochner's doctrine placed boundaries around Progressive legislation. Its most enduring legacy was probably the ban on labor laws pure and simple, because that ban impeded the ability of organized labor, an increasingly prominent political actor, to obtain redistributive legislation,

---

[30] *Muller v Oregon* 208 US 412 (1908); *Adkins v Children's Hospital* 261 US 525 (1923).

and directed unions toward strikes and similar forms of economic battles against employers, which state courts regulated quite closely and not favorably to unions.[31] During the so-called *Lochner* era, which lasted until the mid-1930s, the Court mostly upheld police power regulations and invalidated maximum hours and minimum wage laws. Still, *Lochner* showed that there were limits on what governments could do under the heading of exercising their police powers, and operated as a political obstacle when legislators considered how much effort to devote to adopting laws that courts might strike down.

As the *Lochner* era went on, Progressives increasingly railed against the obstructionist courts. They became important voices within the major parties, but always as large minorities that could occasionally build coalitions to get their favored legislation enacted. They did not displace the more conservative factions that continued to control Congress and the presidency, and through them the courts.

THE NEW DEAL CRISIS AND THE NEW
CONSTITUTIONAL REGIME

The New Deal

The Great Depression changed the nation's economy and its politics. Franklin Roosevelt was elected president in 1932 and immediately set about reconstructing the nation's political institutions. A host of laws, not all of them well considered or even well drafted, became the New Deal. What would the Old Court do with them?

Initial indications were encouraging for the New Deal. The Court narrowly upheld a statute enacted in Minnesota that suspended the duty to make timely payments on mortgages, in the face of a quite substantial argument that the drafters of the Constitution's prohibition on law impairing the obligation of contracts wanted to keep states from adopting such mortgage suspension laws in periods of real economic distress.[32] In several closely watched cases the Court also upheld a congressional statute pushed through by Roosevelt allowing people whose

---

[31] WE Forbath, *Law and the Shaping of the American Labor Movement* (Cambridge, MA, Harvard University Press, 1991).

[32] *Home Building and Loan Ass'n v Blaisdell* 290 US 398 (1934).

contracts said they had to use gold to pay what they owed to pay off in paper money instead.[33]

Then the other shoe dropped. The Court struck down a railroad pension plan and the National Industrial Recovery Act (NIRA), the latter being a centerpiece of the New Deal.[34] It invalidated a statute setting wages and hours in the coal industry through an imposed system of collective bargaining, and a statute creating a system of subsidies for farmers who adhered to production quotas.[35] The Court also reaffirmed that maximum hour and minimum wage laws were unconstitutional.[36] In themselves these decisions might not have been so important—the NIRA, widely regarded as a failure, was about to die on its own when the Court found it unconstitutional. But the legal theories the Court adopted seemed to pose a real threat to two of the New Deal's most important initiatives: the Wagner National Labor Relations Act, which established a framework for collective bargaining throughout the economy, and the Social Security Act, which established an income floor for elderly Americans.

After his overwhelming re-election in 1936, Roosevelt proposed to 'pack' the Supreme Court by adding one new justice for each one over the age of 70. The pretense that the plan was aimed at easing burdens on the Court fooled no one, particularly after the justices themselves weighed in with the observation that none of them, young as well as old, believed they were overworked. The plan ran into substantial opposition, mostly from the New Deal's opponents but some from New Deal supporters who believed that the plan was a threat to the rule of law. The plan moved forward in Congress in a closely fought battle, and might have been adopted had not the Senate's majority leader suddenly died from a heart attack.

The Court-packing plan failed, but Roosevelt succeeded. In 1937 the Supreme Court upheld the Wagner Act and the Social Security Act, and overruled the decisions limiting legislative power to set minimum wages.[37] The key votes were cast by Justice Owen Roberts, who had

[33]   *Norman v Baltimore & Ohio R Co* 294 US 240 (1935).

[34]   *Railroad Retirement Board v Alton R Co* 295 US 330 (1935); *ALA Schechter Poultry Corp v United States* 295 US 495 (1935).

[35]   *Carter v Carter Coal Co* 298 US 238 (1936); *United States v Butler* 297 US 1 (1936).

[36]   *Morehead v New York ex rel Tipaldo* 298 US 587 (1936).

[37]   *NLRB v Jones & Laughlin Steel Corp* 301 US 1 (1937); *West Coast Hotel Co v Parrish* 300 US 379 (1937).

previously voted against New Deal and Progressive programs. Roberts's defenders argued that he had good legal reasons for his apparent change in position; the new cases involved different and better-drafted statutes, and the Court had not been asked to overrule the older cases until 1937. Still, the Court's decisions, and Roberts's, were generally described as the 'switch in time that saved nine', that is, that saved the Court from becoming completely discredited and irrelevant to governing. And Roosevelt ended up packing the Court anyway, through the regular process of naming new justices to the Court.

As president, Roosevelt faced a problem within his Democratic party, which was an awkward coalition of Northern urban liberals and Southern conservatives. He managed to hold it together, but he understood that the long-term success of his transformative liberal vision depended on reconstructing the party. The Wagner Act cemented labor unions to the party. Liberal programs drew African Americans away from their traditional affiliation with the party of Abraham Lincoln, particularly as African Americans moving from the rural South to the urban North benefited from New Deal programs. Southern conservative Democrats remained a problem for Roosevelt, and became an even greater problem as the African American component of the New Deal coalition pressed the national government to undermine the southern system of racial segregation. In 1937 and 1938 Roosevelt tried but failed to purge Southern conservatives from the party. He then turned to other methods. His Department of Justice, staffed by committed liberals opposed to segregation, somewhat hesitantly began to side with African Americans as they challenged the electoral arrangements in the South—especially the exclusion of African Americans from the Democratic party primary elections—that perpetuated conservative control.[38]

More important in the long run, Roosevelt's Supreme Court appointments changed the Democratic party coalition. Roosevelt himself was interested only in whether his nominees were liberals on the economic issues at the heart of the New Deal. But, as it happened, the correlation between liberalism on those issues and liberalism on issues such as race relations and civil liberties was reasonably strong, though not perfect. By appointing economic liberals, Roosevelt created a generally liberal Supreme Court. The liberal principles the Court articulated

[38] KJ McMahon, *Reconsidering Roosevelt on Race: How the Presidency Paved the Road to Brown* (Chicago, University of Chicago Press, 2003).

both responded to principles prevalent though not universally shared within the Democratic party coalition and helped reshape the principles around which Democrats coalesced. The Roosevelt Court's liberals had to deal with a problem in constitutional theory. They rejected the Old Court's restrictions on the government's power to regulate the economy, and in doing so argued that courts should defer to the decisions made by democratically elected representatives. But a general theory of judicial deference to the elected branches would not help when the liberals confronted restrictions on civil liberties enthusiastically supported by majorities, sometimes even large majorities. During World War II, for example, Jehovah's Witnesses who refused to salute the flag were widely reviled, harassed and, in cases reaching the Supreme Court, expelled from public schools.[39] In the first expulsion case it confronted, the Court relied on general principles of deference to uphold the expulsions, but within a few years the Court changed its mind. Justice Robert Jackson wrote:

> *If there is any fixed star in our constitutional constellation, it is that no official, high or petty, can prescribe what shall be orthodox in politics, nationalism, religion, or other matters of opinion, or force citizens to confess by word or act their faith therein.*[40]

How could this and similar civil liberties decisions be defended? By identifying defects in the electoral process that eliminated the very grounds for judicial deference. Justice Harlan Fiske Stone provided the account that endured, in a footnote in an opinion upholding a minor economic regulation:

> *It is unnecessary to consider now whether legislation which restricts those political processes which can ordinarily be expected to bring about repeal of undesirable legislation is to be subjected to more exacting judicial scrutiny under the general prohibitions of the Fourteenth Amendment than are most other types of legislation [referring to cases involving restrictions on the right to vote, restraints on publication and on interference with political organizations].*

Nor need we enquire whether similar considerations enter into the review of statutes directed at particular religious, or national, or racial minorities; whether prejudice against discrete and insular minorities may be a special condition, which tends seriously to curtail the operation of those political

---

[39] SF Peters, *Judging Jehovah's Witnesses: Religious Persecution and the Dawn of the Rights Revolution* (Norman, University Press of Kansas, 2000).

[40] *West Virginia Board of Education v Barnette* 319 US 624, 642 (1943).

processes ordinarily to be relied upon to protect minorities, and which may call for a correspondingly more searching judicial inquiry.[41]

Courts could intervene, under this account, when they could identify defects in the processes of democratic representation. Time would show that this account would license judges to engage in reasonably comprehensive supervision of legislative outputs, but for the moment it satisfied the Roosevelt Court's need for a constitutional theory that allowed liberals to strike down the statutes they found troubling while explaining why they did not strike down others.

The nation's involvement in World War II also shaped Roosevelt's legacy to the political order. Prior to the war a strong strand of isolationism ran through the minority Republican party. The war, and the subsequent Cold War with the Soviet Union, weakened Republican isolationists. Republican internationalists cared more about foreign affairs than domestic ones, and were never among the most adamant opponents of the New Deal's domestic programs anyway. They rode to victory with Dwight Eisenhower in 1952, who accepted the basic principles of New Deal constitutionalism in domestic matters.

After the New Deal: The Great Society

World War II and the Cold War were seen as ideological conflicts over freedom. The persistence of segregation by law in the South was an international embarrassment.[42] Invigorated by their experiences during World War II and encouraged by the new ideological climate, African Americans, led by the National Association for the Advancement of Colored People, increased their assaults on segregation, by direct action such as boycotts and by litigation. The latter culminated in the Supreme Court's decision in *Brown v Board of Education* (1954), striking down school segregation and leading to a series of decisions holding all aspects of legally imposed segregation unconstitutional.[43] Under the leadership of Martin Luther King, Jr, the civil rights movement shifted

---

[41] *United States v Carolene Products* 304 US 144, 152 n 4 (1938).

[42] M Dudziak, *Cold War Civil Rights: Race and the Image of American Democracy* (Princeton, Princeton University Press, 2000).

[43] *Brown v Board of Education* 347 US 483 (1954); *Mayor of Baltimore v Dawson* 350 US 877 (1955).

from the courts to the streets. President John F Kennedy's victory probably rested on his appeal to African Americans, although his administration was at best a lukewarm supporter of civil rights initiatives. Demonstrations continued, and after Kennedy's assassination President Lyndon Johnson took the civil rights movement to heart. Congress adopted a series of civil rights acts, even as politically astute Democrats understood that their support for civil rights was generating a political backlash among white Southerners and eventually among working-class whites in the North.

Johnson had begun his career as an employee of one of Roosevelt's New Deal agencies, and he saw himself as Roosevelt's successor. He promoted a 'Great Society' in which the national government would provide a wide range of forms of income support. Under his leadership Congress enacted programs expanding assistance to the poor and created the nation's first large-scale system of payments for medical care of the elderly and the poor. Relying on economic growth to provide the money for these and other programs, Democrats ignored the possibility that their programs would eventually cause serious fiscal problems for the national government. Responding to political pressure from the civil rights movement and its northern supporters, the Democratic party supported important civil rights laws—in 1964, one making it unlawful to discriminate in restaurants, hotels and other public accommodations, and in employment; in 1965, a statute aimed at eliminating racially based restrictions on the right to vote; and in 1968, a law banning racial discrimination in housing sales and rentals. These civil rights acts appealed to important constituencies within the Democratic party, even as they pushed some of the party's long-time supporters in the South towards the Republican party.

The Supreme Court too participated in the Great Society—and in the end contributed to its undermining.[44] Led by Earl Warren, a liberal Republican appointed by Eisenhower in fulfillment of a campaign pledge, the Court upheld Congress's new civil rights statutes. In doing so it re-articulated the expansive theories of national power that animated the New Deal but that had not been at the forefront of constitutional adjudication for a decade or more. Partly in response to the activities of the civil rights movement, partly in response to the

---

[44] LA Powe, Jr, *The Warren Court and American Politics* (Cambridge, MA, Harvard University Press, 2000).

waning of Cold War anxieties, and partly for purely doctrinal reasons, the Warren Court provided strong protection for free expression, even when that expression took forms plainly distasteful to the Court's members and of course to the wider society. And, seeing the criminal justice system as one of the locations where the government dealt regularly and badly with African Americans, the Warren Court embarked on a program to place constitutional limits on commonly accepted police and prosecutorial activities. As crime rates rose, Republicans began to campaign against the Court's decisions, presenting themselves as the party of law and order.

Some of the Warren Court's decisions in traditional areas—racial equality and free expression—implicated sexual autonomy as well. It struck down state bans on interracial marriage, for example, and sharply limited the states' ability to prohibit sexually explicit films and magazines.[45] Personal autonomy gradually emerged as an important theme in the Court's work, culminating in *Roe v Wade* (1973), holding unconstitutional the laws regulating and restricting the availability of abortions in a majority of the nation's states.[46] *Roe* was decided after Warren had been replaced by Chief Justice Warren Burger, appointed by President Richard Nixon, and shows that the 'Warren Court' lasted beyond Warren's tenure.

Roe also helped consolidate a new theorization of constitutional law. The New Deal's constitutional theory rested on ideas of political participation. Defenders of the Warren Court contended that that theory had to rest on a deeper foundation of commitments to individual autonomy, commitments that made political participation meaningful. Then, with those deeper commitments in hand, the theorists could explain the older cases in new ways and, importantly, could explain *Roe* and related cases as well. Ideas of personal autonomy resonated politically as well. The sexual revolution of the 1950s and 1960s and the increasingly widespread use of marijuana led many to believe that government should stay out of important domains of personal life. Democrats responded to that belief, which unfortunately for them sat uncomfortably with their commitments to expansive government regulation of the economy and, more importantly, with many of the more traditionally minded voters who had been at the heart of the New Deal coalition.

---

[45] *Loving v Virginia* 388 US 1 (1967); *Roth v United States* 354 US 476 (1957).
[46] 410 US 113 (1973).

FROM THE REAGAN REVOLUTION TO THE PRESENT

Civil turmoil in the 1960s began to undermine the foundations of the New Deal–Great Society political settlement. The civil rights movement and urban riots began to whittle away at the support working-class whites had given the Roosevelt-inspired Democratic party. The war in Vietnam leached away support from the left of the party. Republicans portrayed the Democratic party, not entirely inaccurately, as merely a coalition of diverse groups who sought their own narrow interests without some core commitments to a larger vision.

Building on modest initiatives by President Dwight Eisenhower to strengthen the Republican party in the South by signaling discomfort with *Brown v Board of Education* and more forceful efforts by Barry Goldwater, the Republican party's presidential candidate in 1964, to deepen Republican support in the South by developing an even broader conservative philosophy of government, President Richard Nixon won a close election in 1968. Nixon understood both that the New Deal-Great Society regime was vulnerable but that it retained significant support in the electorate. He began to implement modestly conservative programs, and appointed four Supreme Court justices who he expected would repudiate the Warren Court. But his initiatives were interrupted by the Watergate scandal, arising from an attempt by employees of the Republican party and the President to burglarize the headquarters of the Democratic party and the subsequent efforts to conceal presidential involvement in the burglary. Congress began the process that would have led to the impeachment and removal of Nixon from office, but before that process reached its conclusion Nixon resigned and left office in disgrace. Nixon's initiatives led congressional Democrats to fear what historian Arthur Schlesinger called an 'imperial presidency',[47] and they reasserted congressional power by limiting the president's power to refuse to spend money Congress appropriated and by attempting to ensure that future presidents would obtain authorization from Congress for substantial military involvements overseas.

The conservative repudiation of the New Deal–Great Society regime was renewed when Ronald Reagan won the presidency in 1980. Reagan was a charismatic conservative, with a broad vision of a government

---

[47] AM Schlesinger, Jr, *The Imperial Presidency* (Boston, Houghton Mifflin Publishing, 1973).

dramatically different in form and scope from the one that preceded him. Reagan Republicanism consisted of a combination of logically independent positions, some of which were in some theoretical tension with others. Social conservatives and the new religious right were part of the Reagan coalition, and to them Reagan Republicanism offered opposition to the Supreme Court's abortion decisions and support for public acknowledgement of the importance of religion in public life and financial assistance to religious institutions, both of which could be accomplished only by transforming the Warren Court's jurisprudence of the religion clauses. Economic conservatives were also part of the Reagan coalition, and to them Reagan Republicanism offered deregulatory initiatives at the national level, limiting the scope of the regulations of business that had proliferated during the later portions of the Great Society regime, and some degree of constitutional protection for property rights.

The Reagan Revolution ran into two difficulties. Transforming constitutional doctrine takes time and a political environment that allows the president to appoint new justices who share the transformative vision. Roosevelt was able to do this because his party controlled the Senate. Except for a brief period, Reagan's did not. Rather than unified government, Reagan had to deal with divided government. When his party did control the Senate, he was able to nominate two strong conservatives, promoting William Rehnquist to Chief Justice and naming Antonin Scalia to fill Rehnquist's seat as Associate Justice. But, after his party lost control of the Senate, Reagan was unable to complete the transformation through the appointment of Robert Bork to the Supreme Court. In the end Reagan had to settle for Anthony Kennedy, a conservative to be sure—Kennedy had worked closely with Reagan when Reagan was governor of California—but not as ideologically committed to the Reagan Revolution as Bork would have been.

Divided government also was the source of Reagan's other difficulty. Democratic control of Congress meant that Reagan could not obtain repeal or substantial amendments to the most important regulatory statutes. Instead, he had to use his power as head of the executive branch. But constitutional and administrative law placed limits on what he could do. In the most notable example, the courts overturned the Reagan administration's effort to relieve the automobile industry of a regulation developed during prior administrations requiring that all cars have automatic mechanisms—automatic seat-belts or airbags—to protect riders in car crashes, finding that Reagan's administrators had failed to provide a good enough explanation for the shift in policy.[48]

Except for a brief period at the outset of President Bill Clinton's first term, divided government persisted through the end of the twentieth century. Partisan divisions intensified, though, leading to Clinton's impeachment in the House and acquittal in the Senate. Divided government and ideological division produced 'gridlock' in the legislative process, meaning that only those policies with substantial support across party lines could be adopted, and initiatives strongly identified with one party were stymied. The result was that new national laws were relatively unambitious in scope, with the exception of budget and tax laws, which could be adopted on strict party votes because of internal legislative rules governing them. Yet, if no large new national initiatives could be undertaken, neither could large-scale repeal of existing laws take place. National policy gradually drifted in a conservative direction, but the major legislation from the New Deal–Great Society era remained in place.

The presidential election in 2000 presented Republicans with an opportunity to consolidate the Reagan Revolution. Democratic presidential candidate Al Gore won the popular vote, but the Supreme Court awarded the presidency to Republican George W Bush, by a five-to-four vote split on partisan lines, in a decision that relied on such an innovative constitutional theory as to make it easy for Democrats to treat the decision as political in the narrowest and most pejorative sense. Still, Gore accepted the Court's decision. Bush took office hoping to complete the Reagan Revolution.

The possibility of doing so increased after the attacks of September 11, 2001, which gave his personal popularity an enormous boost. Believing that post-Watergate developments had seriously weakened the presidency, Bush and his advisers articulated an account of presidential powers under the Constitution, sometimes misleadingly labeled the theory of the unitary presidency, according to which the president had essentially unfettered power to take whatever actions he believed appropriate to defend that nation. Bush implemented programs of surveillance of suspected terrorists outside the United States and some people within the United States who had some contact with those suspects, all without express statutory authorization and sometimes in the face of apparent statutory prohibitions. Some of Bush's initiatives

---

[48] *Motor Vehicles Mfrs Ass'n v State Farm Mutual Ins Co* 463 US 29 (1983).

were endorsed by Congress, but much was done on his own. In several important cases the Supreme Court found that the Constitution did not give the president a 'blank check' to adopt programs in the name of national security.[49]

Bush's political and constitutional position was weakened, perhaps to the point of complete collapse, by a tactical mistake he and his advisers made after September 11. They believed that they could achieve a permanent Republican majority in all the government's branches by winning consistently with the narrowest of margins. The tactic seemed to work in the elections of 2002 and 2004, which gave Republicans majorities in the House and Senate, but the president's decision to go to war with Iraq turned the public against him and his party, and divided government returned after the 2006 elections. By 2008 it appeared that the United States might have united government once again—but this time under Democratic control.

Having lost control of Congress and facing the prospect of losing control of the presidency, Republicans followed the lead John Adams had set two centuries before. They sought to entrench their control in the Supreme Court. After *Bush v Gore*, critics of the decision focused on the possibility that Republican-leaning justices voted for Bush to ensure that a Republican would replace them if they retired. Perhaps concerned that retirement under those circumstances would provoke intense partisan combat over the new nominations, no justice left the Court during Bush's first term. His re-election in 2004 eliminated that problem. Chief Justice William Rehnquist suffered from a severe form of cancer, and Justice Sandra Day O'Connor was concerned about her husband's health. Justice O'Connor announced her retirement in July 2005, and Chief Justice Rehnquist died two months later. Their replacements, Samuel Alito and John Roberts, had been associated for years with strongly conservative legal elements in the Republican party, and their appointments might indeed leave Reagan conservatives controlling the Supreme Court for years after divided government returned or—even more dramatic—Democrats gained control of both Congress and the presidency.

Unified government did return, though only briefly, with the election of Barack Obama and a Democratic majority in both houses of Congress in

---

[49] The phrase 'blank check' comes from *Hamdi v Rumsfeld* 542 US 507 (2004).

2008. Republicans responded by changing some elements in the efficient Constitution, most notably by exploiting the rules of the Senate with the effect of requiring 60 votes to adopt legislation. Partisan polarization intensified, and Democrats lost their 60-vote majority in January 2010. Gridlock returned, though during the brief period of unified government important legislation was adopted, including the first US system of nearly universal health care insurance and an important package of government expenditures aimed at stimulating an economy in severe recession. President Obama continued some of the executive initiatives his predecessors had begun, especially in the area of national security. The inability of Democrats to obtain legislation led the President to rely increasingly heavily on presidential initiatives that could be adopted without congressional approval. These included modifications in environmental regulations and, importantly, several programs suspending the deportation of large groups of noncitizens who had entered the country without authorization. Those initiatives, and the general program of the Democratic Party, intensified Republican opposition.

In 2010 an important faction in the Republican Party emerged. Labeled the Tea Party, the faction pushed the Republican Party as a whole to take increasingly conservative positions. Voter disillusionment with the pace of economic recovery, coupled with major infusions of money into political campaigns, produced a Republican majority in the House of Representatives after the elections of 2010. Joined with the expanded use of the filibuster in the Senate, this led, once again, to gridlock. Conflicts over spending led the United States close to defaulting on its debt obligations in 2011, an outcome averted only by an agreement to cut spending substantially, with Democrats swallowing cuts in spending on their favored domestic programs and Republicans doing the same in connection with military spending. Continuing conflict over spending and national health insurance did produce a government 'shutdown' for two weeks in 2013.

The Tea Party also influenced the Republican Party's selection of a presidential candidate in 2012, by pushing aspirants to the right. That, in turn, impaired the position of Mitt Romney, the nominee in 2012, in the general election, which he lost decisively to President Obama. Still, the Republicans retained a majority in the House of Representatives and, in 2014, expanded that majority while gaining majority control of the Senate as well.

CONCLUSION

The meaning of the US Constitution has varied over the centuries. Supreme Court interpretations of the written Constitution have changed as justices affiliated with political parties and governing regimes replaced justices affiliated with other parties and regimes. Sometimes the Supreme Court has been misaligned with the political forces dominant elsewhere in the system, and when those misalignments persisted too long, constitutional crisis ensued. Eventually, though, the alignments were adjusted and the political order operated smoothly, with the Court articulating and applying the principles animating the public policies advanced in Congress and the presidency.

Looking at the course of constitutional development in the United States as a whole, we see how the efficient Constitution differs from the written one. Much in the efficient Constitution—especially the expansion of national power—occurred without changes in the written Constitution, and received judicial endorsement only belatedly and sometimes grudgingly. And, of course, the courts themselves took on different colorations as the efficient Constitution changed. To understand US constitutional development, then, we must understand US political development first, and the written Constitution only later.

FURTHER READING

Berkin, C, *A Brilliant Solution: Inventing the American Constitution* (New York, Harcourt, 2002) (this work and Collier are recent popular accounts of the Constitutional Convention).

Bowen, CD, *Miracle at Philadelphia: The Story of the Constitutional Convention, May to September 1787* (Boston, Little, Brown & Co, 1986) (a classic popular account).

Collier, C, *Decision in Philadelphia: The Constitutional Convention of 1787* (New York, Ballentine Books, 2007).

Cushman, B, *Rethinking the New Deal Court: The Structure of a Constitutional Revolution* (New York, Oxford University Press, 1998) (both this work and White offer revisionist accounts of the New Deal constitutional revolution).

Forbath, WE, *Law and the Shaping of the American Labor Movement* (Cambridge, MA, Harvard University Press, 1991).

___ 'Politics, State-Building, and the Courts, 1870–1920' in M Grossberg and C Tomlins (eds), *The Cambridge History of Law in America, vol II: The Long Nineteenth Century (1789–1920)* ch19, pp 643–96 (New York, Cambridge University Press, 2008)

Graber, MA, *A New Introduction to American Constitutionalism* (New York, Cambridge University Press, 2013).

Hofstadter, R, *The Idea of a Party System: The Rise of Legitimate Opposition in the United States, 1780–1840* (Berkeley, University of California Press, 1969).

Leuchtenberg, WE, *The Constitution Reborn: The Constitutional Revolution in the Age of Roosevelt* (New York, Oxford University Press, 1995) (this work presents the standard account of the New Deal constitutional revolution).

Rakove, JN, *Original Meanings: Politics and Ideas in the Making of the Constitution* (New York, AA Knopf, 1996) (a prize-winning scholarly account of the Constitution's framing and adoption).

Skowronek, S, *Building a New American State: The Expansion of National Administrative Capacities, 1877–1920* (New York, Cambridge University Press, 1982).

Tushnet, M, *The New Constitutional Order* (Princeton, Princeton University Press, 2003) (analyzing the recent era).

Urofsky, MI and Finkelman, P, *A March of Liberty: A Constitutional History of the United States* (New York, Oxford University Press, 2002) (a good overview of US constitutional history).

White, GE, *The Constitution and the New Deal* (Cambridge, MA, Harvard University Press, 2000).

2

The Constitutional Politics of the Legislative Branch

——◦————

Congress: Its Basic Structure and Roles – The American Party System – Political Parties and the Written Constitution – Conduct of Elections – Legislative Districting and Gerrymandering – Candidate Selection and Gerrymandering – Campaign Financing – Constitutional Politics within Congress – Conclusion

THE UNITED STATES is a federal system. The national government consists of the usual three branches: a legislature, an executive and a judiciary. The governments of sub-national units—the states—mirror this structure.[1] The US Congress, the national legislative branch, consists of two houses: a House of Representatives and a Senate. Members of the House of Representatives, sometimes called, slightly inaccurately, Congressmen and Congresswomen, serve two-year terms, Senators six years. Members of both houses are eligible for re-election indefinitely.

The constitutional role of Congress is shaped by the party system. After a brief introduction to the basic structures of Congress and to its operation, this chapter surveys the way in which the party system has changed since 1789, turning thereafter to legislative districting, candidate recruitment, the financing of campaigns for legislative office and the internal organization of the House and Senate. The important place parties have will become apparent in each section.

---

[1] The legislature of every state save one (Nebraska) is bicameral.

CONGRESS: ITS BASIC STRUCTURE AND ROLES

The United States Congress has two houses. The House of Representatives currently has 435 members, elected from districts within individual states. A census is taken every 10 years to determine the nation's population. That figure is divided by 435 to determine the number of people to be allocated to each territorially defined district. Each state is entitled to at least one representative, and several small states do indeed have only a single representative. The remaining seats are allocated to the remaining states depending on their population. So, for example, if a district should contain 646,000 people, a state with 6.4 million people will get 10 representatives. The guarantee that each state have one representative and the vagaries of arithmetic mean that the division is never precise, and the actual allocation is determined by a complicated formula written into the nation's statute books (and not, notably, into the Constitution).[2] Members of the House of Representatives serve for terms of two years; there is no restriction on their re-election.[3]

The Senate consists of two Senators elected from each state.[4] Each Senator serves a term of six years and, again, there are no limits on re-election. One-third of the Senate is elected every two years. The Constitution's authors believed that longer terms and staggered elections would give Senators the opportunity to take a broader view of public policy than would their counterparts in the House, and would make the Senate a stabilizing force in national policy-making. In recent years, though, rates of re-election in both the House and the Senate have been so high that it is difficult to distinguish between the houses in terms of the *effective* terms of office their members serve.

With one exception, both houses of Congress have the power to initiate legislation on any topic within the nation's powers.[5] The exception is that bills appropriating funds must originate in the House of

---

[2] In 1992 the Supreme Court rejected Montana's challenge to the statutory apportionment formula: *US Dep't of Commerce v Montana* 503 US 442 (1992).

[3] The Supreme Court held it unconstitutional for states to impose term limits on their state's House members: *US Term Limits v Thornton* 514 US 779 (1995).

[4] The 1789 Constitution provided that Senators would be elected by state legislatures. The Seventeenth Amendment, adopted in 1913, replaced that with direct popular election.

[5] On the latter qualification, see ch 5 below.

Representatives. The Senate may amend such bills, and permissible amendments include new appropriations not considered by the House of Representatives. The Origination Clause thus has relatively little effect on appropriations themselves.

Unlike systems of parliamentary government, in the United States there is no *formal* program proposed by the executive government. Every bill must be introduced by a member of the legislature, and the Constitution prohibits members of the legislature from serving simultaneously in the executive branch. Of course, the president has political allies in both houses of Congress, and those allies are happy to introduce legislation drafted by executive officials. Still, the formal power of initiating legislation lies with Congress, as is suggested by the constitutional provision requiring the president 'from time to time give to Congress information of the State of the Union and *recommend* to their Consideration such measures as he shall judge necessary and expedient' (italics added).

Though the president lacks what might be called front-end power to initiate legislation, he or she does have an important power later on. The president must approve of every legislative proposal that has received a majority vote in both the House and the Senate. Here the Constitution's authors understood that they were departing from a strict separation of powers, for they conceptualized the presidential veto power as a legislative one.[6] Congress can override presidential vetoes, but only with supermajorities of two-thirds in each house. Unsurprisingly, most presidential vetoes are sustained—that is, one or both houses are unable to muster the special majorities needed to overcome the veto. Perhaps more important, the threat of a veto shapes legislation as it proceeds through Congress, for members of Congress who hope to make public policy (rather than 'make a statement' to their constituencies) will adapt their proposals to meet the president's demands.[7]

Both houses of Congress conduct much of their legislative work through standing committees, usually identified by the subject matter

[6] Another departure from separation of powers is that the vice-president, an executive official, is formally the presiding officer of the Senate. That role is largely ceremonial, and is almost always delegated to a Senator. The vice-president does have the power to cast the deciding vote when the Senate is evenly divided—a rare but not unknown event.

[7] See CM Cameron, *Veto Bargaining: Presidents and the Politics of Negative Power* (New York, Cambridge University Press, 2000).

of their jurisdiction: the Committee on Agriculture, for example, or the Committee on the Judiciary. Formally, committee members are chosen by party caucuses: the majority party's members meet and vote on who from their party should serve on which committee, and similarly for the minority party. In practice, the party leadership has the controlling hand in placing members on committees. Representatives and Senators will typically express their preferences about committee assignments, and the party leaderships will typically do their best to accommodate those requests. One reason is that members ordinarily bid to serve on committees of particular interest to them and, more important, to their constituents. A Senator from a state with a large number of farmers will seek to serve on the Agriculture Committee, where he or she will be able to shape farm policy in a way that favors constituents. Sometimes, though, party leaders will reject members' bids, in the service of some larger political concerns.

Committee chairs ordinarily have the power to shape their committee agenda, although they will inevitably have to deal with matters presented by the executive branch. Traditionally the committee chair was the member of the majority party who served longest on that committee. In 1994, after becoming the majority party for the first time in decades, Republicans in the House of Representatives imposed term limits on committee chairs. These limits began to bite in 2000 and 2002, and despite the tensions they can cause between party leaders and senior members appear to have become a permanent feature in the House. As with committee membership itself, party leaders sometimes override the seniority tradition in designating committee chairs. For example, after the 2006 elections California representative Jane Harman was slated to become the chair of the House Intelligence Committee, but the Speaker of the House, Nancy Pelosi, believed that Harman had not been sufficiently aggressive in overseeing the activities of the national security community after the attacks of September 11, 2001. Next in line of seniority was Representative Alcee Hastings, a former federal judge who had been impeached and removed from office in 1989, and elected to the House in 1992. Embarrassed at the prospect of Hastings as chair of the Intelligence Committee, Pelosi named the third most senior committee member chair.

Committees hold hearings on legislative proposals and ordinarily are the source of most of the language that eventually works its way into statutes, subject to the qualification that bills drafted in the executive branch are re-worked less substantially than are bills proposed by individual members. Bills approved by committees can be amended on the floor, and in neither house is there a strong sense that modifying a committee proposal is somehow disrespectful of the committee's work or otherwise inappropriate, although of course a proposal endorsed by a committee is more likely to obtain majority support than amendments proposed by those not on the committee.

Another important committee function is oversight of the administration. Committees hold hearings on innumerable subjects, ranging from the use of steroids in professional sports to the performance of executive branch agencies in response to natural disasters such as Hurricane Katrina. Sometimes, as with the steroid-use hearings, the point of the hearings is nominally to consider whether Congress should enact legislation dealing with the problem—but actually to get press and television time for the committee's members.

Legislative oversight hearings are more important, though probably not as important as in other constitutional democracies. Such hearings can be used to expose maladministration of the laws, for example. The degree of oversight varies. A committee with a majority of its members in the same party as the president is much less likely to engage in aggressive oversight of the administration's actions than a committee in a house controlled by the party opposed to the president's. And, in the latter situation, members of the executive administration are unlikely to be terribly responsive to aggressive oversight anyway, characterizing it as mere political theater. Still, the threat of aggressive oversight hearings operates in a way similar to the way the threat of a presidential veto operates. Oversight hearings are costly to executive officials, not merely because they run the risk of adverse public comment but more importantly because preparing for and appearing at them takes time that the officials would prefer to spend doing something they regard as more important. They will therefore shape their behavior so as to reduce the possibility that their actions will come under close oversight by congressional committees, although they can never eliminate the threat of aggressive oversight.

As some of the examples in this section suggest, one can describe the basic functions and operations of Congress in relatively abstract terms, but how Congress actually operates depends importantly on party politics. We therefore turn to that topic.

THE AMERICAN PARTY SYSTEM

Though political parties are not mentioned anywhere in the US Constitution, the party system in the United States has an important role in structuring the exercise of national power and the division of authority between the president and Congress—tasks one might mistakenly attribute to the Constitution's express provisions on national power and on separation of powers. For much of US history the 'national' political parties were coalitions of local parties without much central coordination except during presidential elections. By the end of the twentieth century somewhat more centralized national parties had been created. Chapters five and six show that national power is exercised differently and the separation of powers operates differently under different arrays of party control of government, and under different party systems.

Parties from the Founding Through the Middle of the Twentieth Century

The Constitution's framers knew that politics *might* be conducted through organized political parties operating on a national level, but the Constitution they designed rested in part on the hope that that outcome would not occur. James Madison gave the pejorative label 'factions' to what we now know as political parties. Factions were bad for the polity, Madison believed, because they sought to advance narrow interests rather than the public good. The hope that national parties would not emerge was expressed in the Constitution's provisions for the election of the president. Election was to be indirect. Voters in each state would vote not for a candidate for the presidency, but for electors who, the framers hoped, would deliberate among themselves to choose the best candidate. They would cast two votes, but not (in the original Constitution) for a president and a vice-president separately. Rather, the thought was that electors would end up generating a list of candidates, all of whom would be suitable to serve as president. Even more, the electors were to meet in each state separately, thereby, the framers hoped, making it difficult to coordinate the electors' choices in several states. Under this scheme it was thought unlikely that any candidate would receive a majority of the electors' votes. But, if one candidate did have a majority, he would become president. The vice-president would be the person who received the next largest number of electors' votes. The 'no national parties' assumption here is reasonably clear: If there were several national parties, the president might get a majority of the electors' votes, but the person getting the next largest number might be the presidential candidate from another party.[8]

The design of the Senate and the House of Representatives also was thought to impede the development of national parties. Senators were to be elected indirectly as well, by state legislatures. This, it was thought, would make Senators particularly responsive to local concerns—although their six-year terms were thought as well to give them a chance to develop a national perspective. Only members of the House of Representatives were to be elected directly by the people. Having three different rules for choosing members of the national government created a system whose very complexity might make it difficult to organize a national political party: An organization well suited to organizing a national campaign for the House of Representatives might not be readily adapted to doing the same for Senate elections by the legislatures of states scattered throughout the nation, for example.

In fact national political parties arose relatively quickly after the Constitution went into effect.[9] The framers' generation divided over issues of foreign policy, particularly with respect to the nation's stance

---

[8] The election of 1800 revealed how this scheme could misfire in another way. There were then two national parties. Electors in each state cast their votes for two candidates, assuming that one was for their party's presidential candidate and one for the vice-presidential candidate. Yet, if everyone did so, the winning party's vice-presidential candidate would receive exactly the same number of electoral votes as its presidential candidate. Under the original Constitution, when that occurred the election was to be resolved by the House of Representatives, in which each state's delegation would cast a single vote. An obvious remedy would be to ensure that at least one elector cast his second vote for someone other than the party's vice-presidential candidate but, because the electors met in each state separately, coordinating votes as that remedy would require was difficult. The Federalist party was able to coordinate the votes, but the winning Jeffersonians were not. The election was thrown into the House of Representatives, which after prolonged negotiations eventually chose Jefferson as president. For a good account of the events and their relation to the Constitution's design, see BA Ackerman, *The Failure of the Founding Fathers: Jefferson, Marshall, and the Rise of Presidential Democracy* (Cambridge, Harvard University Press, 2005).

[9] The Twelfth Amendment, adopted in 1804, eliminated the problem parties posed for the original mechanism for selecting the president by directing that electors vote specifically for a president and a vice-president.

in the conflict between revolutionary France and Britain, and over domestic issues, especially with regard to how or whether the national government would encourage economic development. The Constitution, though, meant that political parties were national only in a narrow sense. Parties were organized on the state level. These local parties came together at the national level under the umbrella of a single party label—Federalist or Jeffersonian Democratic–Republican, for example. And they coordinated their choices for president. We might call these 'presidential' parties. But the person chosen as a party's candidate for president had almost no influence on the state or local level. He could not insist that candidates for the House of Representatives running under his party's label agree with him on a broad platform, although the party's brand name generally meant that local candidates would share the presidential party's broad ideology even when they differed with that party's position on some, and sometimes many, specific issues.

National political parties were thus essentially loose federations of local political parties. Political scientists distinguish among the party-as-organization, the party-in-government, and the party-in-the electorate. Broadly speaking, until the late twentieth century what mattered on the local level was the relation between the party-as-organization and the party-in-government. Local political parties took one of two forms. Sometimes they were parties led by local notables, who selected candidates and then solicited votes from an increasingly enlarged electorate, running on platforms consisting of various policy positions. Sometimes they were 'machines', which attracted votes not only by advocating policies but also by providing party supporters with material benefits, such as jobs in the government (increasingly important as the number of such jobs grew) and differential access to other government benefits such as poor relief. In both forms, the party-as-organization exercised substantial control over the party-in-government.

Over the course of the twentieth century, more truly national parties began to become important, although the United States still does not have parties organized as tightly at the national level as is common in other democracies. William McKinley's presidential campaign in 1896, managed by Mark Hanna, is usually described as the first centrally organized presidential campaign. In the 1930s President Franklin D Roosevelt attempted to extend presidential control of the party, by campaigning in 1937 and 1938 against members of his own Democratic party who opposed his New Deal programs. This so-called 'purge' failed when most of Roosevelt's opponents defeated his preferred candidates, but Roosevelt's efforts foreshadowed later developments.

Through most of the twentieth century, the parties in Congress remained loosely organized coalitions. In the 1920s the Republican party held within it political 'progressives' who sought significant reform in domestic policy to benefit workers and the middle class, and conservatives who supported policies aimed at consolidating the power of industrial and financial elites. In the 1950s and 1960s the Democratic party was a coalition of liberal Democrats from cities in the North, and conservative Democrats from the South. Because the parties were coalitions, effective control of Congress rested not always in the party with a nominal majority but sometimes in cross-party groupings assembled out of elements of each party's coalition. These cross-party coalitions could form and re-form over different issues, making 'party government' impossible.

Until the twentieth century local political leaders selected their party's candidates for office, which was what made Roosevelt's intervention in the 1930s so dramatic. The impetus came from the expansion of the franchise.[10] Early in the republic, most states limited eligibility to vote to white male property holders. The property-holding requirements were done away with in the first quarter of the nineteenth century. The Fifteenth Amendment, adopted in 1870, guaranteed the right to vote without regard to race; although African Americans continued to be prevented from voting in the South, they did vote in the North and the West, and became an important voting bloc as African Americans migrated from the South in the aftermath of World War I. After women gained the right to vote in numerous states, especially in the West, in the early twentieth century, the Nineteenth Amendment (1920) guaranteed women everywhere in the nation the right to vote.

The Modern Party System

As the franchise expanded, candidate selection shifted from the backrooms to caucuses and then to conventions. As the party-in-the-electorate became more important as the result of the expansion of

---

[10] See A Keyssar, *The Right to Vote: The Contested History of Democracy in the United States* (New York, Basic Books, 2000).

the franchise and reforms of the political system associated with the Progressive movement of the early twentieth century, caucuses and conventions were themselves displaced by even more open methods of candidate selection—so-called 'primary' elections. These selection methods help identify another important feature of the US party system: membership in a political party is informal and quite fluid. Put another way, there is no formal or legal definition of the party-in-the-electorate. The parties themselves generally impose no requirements for membership, and a person is a 'member' of whatever political party she happens to choose. The Supreme Court has held that parties *can* limit their membership if they want to, for example by requiring that people who wish to participate in party events identify themselves as party members at some point before the caucus. But they can also choose to open themselves up, seeking to attract votes by allowing anyone to affiliate himself with the party at any time. According to the Court, this is an essential characteristic of political parties as associations protected by the First Amendment, and states cannot override a party's decision either to limit participation or to make participation freely available.[11]

Party leaders shifted from designating candidates themselves to choosing candidates in caucuses and conventions because they believed that they could motivate supporters better by giving them an opportunity to participate in candidate selection, while retaining significant control over candidate selection nonetheless, and because the expansion of the franchise produced demands for wider public participation in candidate selection too. Caucuses and conventions were a way of aligning the party-in-the-electorate with the party-as-organization. The next step further weakened the control of the party-as-organization, again in the name of increased public participation that might attach more voters to the party. Starting early in the twentieth century, and becoming nearly universal by its end, candidates were chosen in 'primary' elections. Voters decided which party primary to participate in, and cast their votes to determine who would appear on the final or 'general' election ballot. Local party leaders continued to play an important role in candidate selection, by identifying and supporting their preferred candidates. Sometimes, though, insurgents could nominate

---

[11] *California Democratic Party v Jones* 530 US 567 (2000).

themselves, secure enough support to appear on the ballot, and defeat the leaders' preferred candidate. Where local party organizations were particularly weak, self-nominations of this sort became common. In the middle decades of the twentieth century, self-nomination and candidate selection in primary elections impeded the development of nationally organized political parties that could penetrate to the level of the choice of candidates for the Senate and the House of Representatives.

In the last quarter of the twentieth century, the party system began to change, seemingly permanently, into one in which there were truly national political parties, although still not as strong as those in western European democracies. Mark Hanna had nationalized presidential campaigns. His heirs in the Republican party began to nationalize congressional campaigns, and Democrats followed their lead. The principal reason was probably money. As campaigning for a seat in Congress became more expensive, potential candidates looked for sources of financing. Some particularly wealthy people could still nominate themselves, and the US Senate in particular became something of a 'millionaires' club' (as it had been a century earlier when wealthy men could effectively purchase their seats from state legislators). Other self-nominated candidates could capitalize on their celebrity, but the rest had to spend a lot of time raising money and then spending it on consultants to advise them about what sort of advertising to buy, how to use mail to reach voters, and the like. First the national Republican party and then the national Democratic party offered to help candidates with their campaigns. Support comes in the form of promises of financial support during the campaign, increasing the number of advertisements a candidate can purchase.

This gave the national parties the opportunity to impose some, albeit generally modest, discipline on the candidates they supported. Typically the national parties focus on competitive districts, where both parties have some reasonable chance of winning. They try to identify and support high-quality candidates, with a candidate's quality measured by his or her chances of winning the final election. The national parties would support a candidate who seemed likely to win (or, more precisely, likely to take a seat away from the other party) no matter what policy positions the candidate espoused. Yet, on the margin, the national parties were able to bring somewhat more coherence to their parties-in-Congress by the end of the twentieth century than they had in mid-century. Once again, the party-as-organization became aligned with the party-in-government, but now the latter had significant influence over the former.[12]

POLITICAL PARTIES AND THE WRITTEN CONSTITUTION

The Constitution and Internal Party Organization

Because the text of Constitution does not mention political parties, constitutional regulation of political parties has been indirect and limited.[13] In a series of cases running from the 1920s to 1953, the Supreme Court invoked the Fifteenth Amendment's ban on racial discrimination in voting to invalidate what was known as the 'white primary', that is primary elections conducted in the segregated South by the dominant Democratic party.[14] White primaries were problematic because the Democratic party was so dominant in the South of the period—the region was known as a one-party area—that the person who was chosen in the Democratic party primary was inevitably the winner in the general election.

The Fifteenth Amendment requires action by the government—the Amendment reads 'The right ... to vote shall not be denied ... by any State on account of race'—but the early cases were relatively easy because they involved state laws that barred African Americans from participating in primary elections. Southern states tried to strip government sanction from party-based exclusion of African Americans, but the Court continued to find sufficient state involvement in the machinery of candidate selection to justify invocation of the Fifteenth

---

[12] The rise of the so-called Tea Party faction within the Republican party in the 2010s was less an insurgency against the national party leadership than an example of a relatively common phenomenon in which political entrepreneurs, in this instance a group of strongly conservative and relatively wealthy Republicans, perceive a latent constituency not yet fully mobilized by existing political leaders. See T Skocpol and V Williamson, *The Tea Party and the Remaking of Republican Conservatism* (New York, Oxford University Press, 2013).

[13] For a survey of the issues discussed in this and succeeding sections, S Issacharoff, PS Karlan, and RH Pildes, *The Law of Democracy: Legal Structure of the Political Process* (2nd edn New York, Foundation Press, 2001).

[14] *Nixon v Herndon* 273 US 536 (1927); *Nixon v Condon* 286 US 73 (1932); *Smith v Allwright* 321 US 649 (1944); *Terry v Adams* 345 US 461 (1953).

Amendment. The final white-primary case involved a 'pre-primary' conducted by the Jaybird Association, an all-white political organization in Texas.[15] The organization's members agreed to support the winner in the government-run primary. The Court held that the organization had to allow African Americans to vote in the pre-primary. The ruling is perhaps analytically puzzling. The justices noted that they did not mean to rule out the possibility that a party might be organized along religious lines, yet distinguishing for constitutional purposes between an all-Baptist party and an all-white one is not easy. The decision has been rationalized on the theory that, in the particular location where the Jaybirds operated, the primary—and therefore the pre-primary—was the effective location of ultimate election. As party competition spread, the theoretical problems posed by the white-primary cases disappeared—as indeed did racial discrimination in administering party selection mechanisms.

Political parties are, of course, vehicles for advancing policy positions, and the Supreme Court has therefore unsurprisingly held that political parties are associations protected by the First Amendment, and in particular by the right, read into the Amendment's protection of speech, of political association. Governments have substantial authority to regulate how elections are conducted, as I discuss below, but their power to regulate a political party's internal organization and rules—including, most importantly, rules dealing with party membership and participation in party-based mechanisms for candidate selection—is sharply limited.

As already noted, the Supreme Court has held unconstitutional state laws mandating 'open' primaries in which all voters can participate regardless of their party affiliations. It has also held unconstitutional state laws prohibiting parties from allowing independent voters, that is, those who have not indicated their party affiliation when they registered to vote, to participate in the party's primary.[16] Together these decisions leave it up to parties to decide what form of candidate selection best advances their electoral prospects.

---

[15] *Terry v Adams* 345 US 461 (1953).
[16] *Tashjian v Republican Party* 479 US 208 (1986). For a discussion of registration requirements, see below.

The Supreme Court and the Two-Party System

The decisions just discussed might be taken to suggest that the Constitution requires that states take a 'hands off' approach to party organization. That suggestion would be misleading, however, because the Court has also upheld statutes that in its view protect the integrity of the parties and, perhaps more significantly, the integrity of the two-party system. In the former category are cases upholding state laws barring from the ballot a candidate who had had a registered party affiliation within the year preceding the election in which the person sought to be a candidate.[17] These 'sore loser' statutes were aimed at candidates who ran in a party primary, lost, and then sought to reach the general electorate anyway. The Court later explained its decision as affirming the state's power 'to protect the parties and the party system against the disorganizing effects of independent candidacies launched by unsuccessful putative party nominees'.[18] To the same effect is the Court's decision upholding a state law barring write-in candidacies, that is allowing state officials to disregard votes cast for any candidate whose name does not appear on the printed ballot.[19]

Probably the most dramatic decision endorsing the two-party system is *Timmons v Twin Cities Area New Party*.[20] The New Party hoped to become a viable third party by running 'fusion' candidates. These candidates would appear on the ballot twice: once as New Party candidates and once as candidates for another party (typically, in Minnesota where the case arose, the Democrat–Farmer-Labor party). Fusion candidacies allow third parties to gain a foothold by allowing observers to differentiate between voters' support for a particular candidate and their support for the party the candidate represents. Notably, the New Party did not propose to run a fusion candidate unless the candidate herself agreed. One might have thought that the Court's endorsement of the freedom of parties to choose how to select candidates would imply that the Constitution barred states from prohibiting fusion candidacies. The Court, though, held otherwise, finding specifically that the state

---

[17] *Storer v Brown* 415 US 724 (1974).

[18] *Tashjian v Republican Party* 479 US 208 (1986).

[19] *Burdick v Takushi* 504 US 428 (1992). This decision is obviously related to decisions, discussed below, dealing with state laws regulating who can appear on the general election ballot.

[20] 520 US 351 (1997).

could prohibit fusion candidacies because of a government interest in preserving the two-party system. As Chief Justice Rehnquist put it, 'States … have a strong interest in the stability of their party systems … The Constitution permits [states] to decide that political stability is best served through a healthy two-party system'.

We should not overemphasize the extent to which constitutional doctrine endorses, or allows the government to reinforce, the two-party system, though. Decisions like *Timmons* impede the development of third parties, but, as Chief Justice Rehnquist observed, third parties face 'many hurdles in the American political arena today', and those hurdles are erected by long tradition and elements of constitutional structure that are not touched by judicially announced constitutional doctrine.

CONDUCT OF ELECTIONS

The Constitution locates the power to regulate and conduct elections in the states, subject to a power in Congress to regulate the 'Times, Places, and Manner of holding Elections for Senators and Representatives'. The national government has exercised that power sparingly, but some of its laws, such as that requiring election in single-member districts, are quite important. State regulation of elections is limited by other constitutional provisions, most notably the First Amendment and the provision in the Fourteenth Amendment guaranteeing 'equal protection of the laws' and otherwise only by the requirement that they equate the qualification to vote for members of the House of Representatives to the qualifications they impose on voting for members of the 'most numerous branch of the State Legislature'. The effect is that elections are administered in a highly decentralized way, with state government doing the vast bulk of the work of running elections for national office. A collateral effect is that local political actors have substantial influence on the details of electoral administration. They can structure voting processes with an eye to the partisan benefit flowing from different arrangements, such as allowing voting to begin several weeks before the official voting date (or shortening such 'early voting' periods) or, most mundanely, setting up polling places so that voting lines in some areas are longer than those in others, thereby discouraging voting in the disfavored areas. Reform proposals for greater national intervention in the administration of national elections have made little progress.

Voters

One peculiarity of the US voting system is the existence of registration requirements that are relatively onerous compared to those in other Western democracies. Those who think they may want to vote in an election must register. Registration itself is not terribly difficult. The potential voter must show that she is a US citizen and a resident of the state in which she seeks to register. In addition, a registrant can choose a party affiliation or refrain from doing so, which sometimes has implications for her ability to participate in primary elections.

The Supreme Court has held that voters can be required to register at least 50 days before an election, so that the government can develop accurate voting rolls to determine on election day whether a person who presents himself or herself at the polling booth is indeed qualified to vote.[21] By the turn of the twenty-first century many states had substantially loosened these requirements, allowing voters to register on election day or to cast provisional ballots, to be counted when the voter's qualifications had been verified. Still, voter registration requirements are often cited as one reason for the relatively low rates at which Americans actually vote.[22] In addition, Republicans took advantage of concerns over illegal immigration to tighten registration requirements, enacting laws that placed significant burdens on potential voters to produce sometimes hard-to-come-by documents to establish that they were indeed citizens. Citing the risk of voting fraud as established by evidence about such fraud in the nineteenth century and in the face of strong evidence that fraud at the polling place almost never occurred, in 2008 the Supreme Court upheld an Indiana statute containing the nation's most stringent voter-identification requirements.[23]

Seeing the possibility of gaining partisan advantage by increasing the difficulty of casting ballots, which they assumed would reduce participation by less-motivated, less well-off, and disproportionately Democratic voters, Republican-controlled state legislatures responded with aggressive programs cutting back on prior expansions of voting mechanisms.

[21] *Marston v Lewis* 410 US 679 (1973).
[22] See FF Piven and R Cloward, *Why Americans Still Don't Vote: And Why Politicians Want It That Way* (Boston, Beacon Press, 2000).
[23] *Crawford v Marion County Election Bd* 533 US 181 (2008).

In addition to enacting stringent voter identification requirements, legislatures reduced opportunities for 'early' voting, that is, the possibility of voting before the official election date (for example, on Sundays when voting would not interfere with a person's work responsibilities). These measures might not have the strong partisan effects motivating their enactment, but they probably do reduce participation and perhaps give some small advantages to Republicans.

Parties

Every state guarantees that the candidates of the two major parties will appear on the ballot. The statutes do not say in terms that the candidates of the Democratic and Republican parties will always appear on the ballot. Instead, they say that the candidates of any party that received some substantial support in the immediately preceding election will appear on the ballot. (Occasionally this gives a third party automatic ballot access, but the life span of third parties is so short that ordinarily the third party will appear twice—first when it has a particularly attractive candidate and quite favorable circumstances, and then in the next election—and then lose its automatic access.)

States then specify the conditions under which third parties can appear. Claiming that ballot forms with many candidates confuse voters, they seek to limit access to the ballot to candidates who can demonstrate that they have significant support in the community by presenting petitions signed by a specified number of registered voters. The Supreme Court has analyzed these requirements under the First Amendment and the equal protection clause. The equal protection problem is that these laws impose burdens on third parties that the major parties do not have to satisfy. The Court invalidated what it regarded as significant burdens on a third party's access to the ballot when it confronted a complex set of Ohio rules that required third parties to have what the Court called an elaborate organizational structure, to hold a primary election, and to file petitions no later than nine months preceding an election with signatures of 15 per cent of the number of ballots cast in the preceding election for governor. This, the Court said, gave the two major parties an effective 'monopoly' on ballot access. Later cases upheld access regulations that, in the Court's view, did not 'freeze[] the status quo' because third parties had a realistic opportunity to appear on the ballot.[24] In invalidating a state law requiring that independent candidates for the presidency file nominating petitions early in the election year, the Court articulated its general approach to the problem of ballot access: It would evaluate the burden placed on the third-party candidate in light of the government's interests in avoiding voter confusion and promoting party stability.[25]

Overall the constraints the written Constitution places on the regulation of elections are small, not merely because the Court has said that the government has an interest in promoting the stability of the two-party system but more important because the two-party system emerges out of deeper structures of government and is quite resistant to challenge from third parties.

LEGISLATIVE DISTRICTING AND GERRYMANDERING

Although the national government has the power under the Constitution to regulate the 'Time, Place, and Manner' of elections for national office, it has exercised that power quite parsimoniously. Most regulation of elections occurs through state law. The Supreme Court has imposed a rather strict requirement that each district in the House of Representatives be as nearly as possible equal in population. Taken together with the general rules for apportioning seats in the House, this requirement presents real opportunities for partisan 'gerrymandering', which refers to the practice of drawing district lines with an eye to the likely outcome of an election within that district.

Gerrymandering occurs because most states commit the task of drawing district lines to their legislatures, not to independent experts or bi- or non-partisan commissions.[26] Gerrymandering has deep roots in US history. It received its name from a district whose borders, critics said, resembled a salamander. The district was drawn in Massachusetts

---

[24] *Jenness v Fortson* 403 US 431 (1971). See also *American Party of Texas v White* 415 US 767 (1974) (upholding a state law requiring that minor parties hold a nominating convention and present petitions with signatures totaling 1 per cent of those who voted in the preceding gubernatorial election).

[25] *Anderson v Celebrezze* 460 US 780 (1983).

[26] For an analysis of alternatives to districting by legislatures, see C Elmendorf, 'Election Commissions & Electoral Reform: An Overview' (2006) 5 *Election Law Journal* 425.

in 1812 and signed into law by governor Eldridge Gerry. But gerrymandering became an important legal and constitutional issue only
in the late twentieth century. Questions about the constitutionality of
gerrymandering arose in two settings: gerrymandering on the basis of
the racial composition of the districts drawn, and—more important
here—partisan gerrymandering.

Race-Based Gerrymandering

The Supreme Court addressed a race-based gerrymander in 1960, when
it found unconstitutional a statute that redrew the boundaries of the
city of Tuskegee, Alabama, to ensure that African American voters
would be unable to participate in city elections.[27] Intentionally altering
district boundaries for the purpose of racial exclusion, the Court held,
was unconstitutional. Race-based gerrymandering continued, though
in a dramatically different form, after the Voting Rights Act of 1965, a
national statute, guaranteed minority voters the right to elect representatives of their 'choice'.[28] This was interpreted by the national enforcement agency and the courts to require states to draw district lines in ways
that would ensure that minority voters—usually of African American or
Hispanic origin—would be concentrated enough to guarantee that they
would be able to elect an African American or a Hispanic to represent
them. The Supreme Court eventually held that the Constitution barred
states from drawing district lines when the primary motivation for the
lines chosen was racial rather than partisan.[29] These decisions limited
race-based gerrymandering, but they also implicitly encouraged partisan gerrymandering, that is gerrymandering aimed at achieving some
desired distribution of Representatives between the two major parties.

---

[27] *Gomillion v Lightfoot* 364 US 339 (1960).
[28] The Voting Rights Act also required a subset of states and localitiers to submit
proposed changes in voting rules for 'preclearance' by the Department of Justice,
which would assess the proposed changes with an eye to determining whether
they threatened to reduce minority voting power. The Supreme Court held the
preclearance requirement unconstitutional in *Shelby County v Holder* 133 SCt 2612
(2013). Several jurisdictions previously covered by the requirement moved rapidly
to introduce new voting qualifications that probably would have been blocked by
the Department of Justice.
[29] *Miller v Johnson* 515 US 900 (1995); *Hunt v Cromartie* 532 US 234 (2001).

As the technologies of computing and polling improved, allowing those drawing district lines to make quite accurate predictions about the likely partisan preferences of those who resided in areas defined down to the level of a block of houses, partisan gerrymandering became more effective. Sometimes it takes the form of seeking to ensure that both major parties have their 'fair share' of a state's delegation to the House of Representatives.[30] More often, gerrymandering serves to maximize the probability that incumbents at the time of the apportionment retain their seats by adjusting district lines to move into the district voters who are likely to support the incumbent and move out those likely to oppose him or her. And occasionally gerrymandering is used to give the party controlling the apportionment process as large a share of the state's delegation to Congress as can be done within the constraints set by the 'one person, one vote' rule. In most of its forms, gerrymandering produces some districts of extremely awkward shapes, for example, linking two large areas with a narrow strip running along an important but largely unpopulated transportation corridor to create a district shaped like a bar-bell.

Partisan Gerrymandering

Awkwardly shaped districts trigger close examination, the Court has said, when they result from race-conscious decisions.[31] Not so when they result from partisan gerrymandering. The US Supreme Court has said that, in theory, excessive partisanship in creating districts might be unconstitutional, but it has never found a partisan gerrymander unconstitutional, even when it was quite clear to observers of the political process that partisanship dominated the apportionment process, because the Court's standard is, for all practical purposes, impossible to meet.[32] Indeed, in its most recent decision four justices would have held that partisan gerrymandering presented a 'political question', meaning

---

[30] See, eg, *Gaffney v Cummings* 412 US 735 (1973) (upholding a districting plan aimed at achieving 'political fairness' by making it likely that each major party would win the proportion of congressional seats that matched its statewide share of the vote).

[31] *Shaw v Reno* 509 US 630 (1993).

[32] *Davis v Bandemer* 478 US 109 (1986); *Vieth v Jubilirer* 541 US 267 (2004).

that the courts would not even entertain claims that partisan gerrymandering violated the Constitution. Concurring in the result in the case at hand, Justice Anthony Kennedy said that he would not 'foreclose' all possible challenges to partisan gerrymandering, but even he was unclear on what would be needed to establish a constitutional violation, merely hoping that a workable standard would someday emerge.

The effects of partisan gerrymandering are a matter of some dispute among scholars.[33] Citing statistics showing that incumbents who seek reelection prevail in more than 90 per cent of the contests, political observers believe that gerrymandering entrenches representatives who, they say, can hold office until they decide to retire or run for some other office. The statistics may be misleading, though. They deal only with representatives who seek reelection. Some retire willingly, but others— sometimes tainted by scandal—decide not to run because they believe, and perhaps correctly, that they would lose. Still, we can assume that politicians know something about politics, and engage in partisan gerrymandering because they believe that it benefits them and their parties. The primary benefit does seem to be an increase in the probability that a party will hold on to a seat, even if gerrymandering does not produce strong entrenchment.

Another effect follows from the fact that gerrymandering makes it easy to identify which party's candidate is likely to win in many districts. In those districts the final election loses its meaning. What matters is who gets the opportunity to run as the favored party's candidate. Candidate selection, that is, matters a great deal.

CANDIDATE SELECTION AND GERRYMANDERING

The first important feature of candidate selection in the United States today is that as a general rule potential candidates are self-nominated. In the purest cases, people who believe themselves well-qualified to serve offer themselves as prospective candidates. Neither the national party with which they are affiliated nor any state or local party organization screens these people. As we have seen, candidate selection occurs in

---

[33] For a survey, see TG O'Rourke, 'The Impact of Reapportionment on Congress and State Legislatures' in ME Rush (ed), *Voting Rights and Redistricting in the United States* (Westport, CT, Greenwood Publishing Co, 1998).

a party primary. In a well-gerrymandered district, the primary of the favored political party is for all practical purposes the election in which the district's representative is actually chosen. But voter turnout in US elections is notoriously low, and it is particularly low in primary elections. Those who turn out to vote in a party's primary tend to be those most committed to the party's core political principles. Their votes tend to be cast for equally committed partisans. With strong partisans chosen in districts drawn some to favor one party and some the other, partisan gerrymandering may have a tendency to polarize the House of Representatives. Some have attributed the rise in polarization in Congress, discussed in chapter 3, to partisan gerrymandering. As noted above, though, there is significant disagreement among scholars about that proposition; notably, polarization has occurred in the US Senate as well as in the House, and gerrymandering is impossible for Senate seats, which are chosen on a statewide basis.

These effects, though real, should not be exaggerated. In the past and to some extent still today, there have been local political organizations, pejoratively described as 'machines,' which saw control of government offices not chiefly as a means of advancing well-defined political principles but more as a source of jobs and patronage. These political organizations sometimes put forward a candidate of their own, and sometimes give their endorsement to one of the self-nominated candidates. Their choices are not made on ideological grounds, though. They endorse the candidate who seems more likely to win, and more likely to play along with the machine's interests in patronage. And there is no necessary relationship between that willingness and holding strong ideological positions.

Selection of Senators has many of the characteristics of selection of members of the House of Representatives, with a few important exceptions. Each state is entitled to two Senators, who are elected from the state as a whole and serve six-year terms. The absence of districting means that gerrymandering is impossible. One reason for skepticism about attributing to gerrymandering too much in respect to incumbent entrenchment and political polarization is that entrenchment and polarization seem characteristic of the modern Senate as well as the House. In addition, the smaller number of and longer terms for Senators gives that position more prestige than attaches to a position in the House of Representatives. Attracting high-quality candidates to a Senate race is substantially easier than the same task in the House.

CAMPAIGN FINANCING

Candidates ask supporters to finance their campaigns.[34] National law places some limits on the amounts individuals can contribute to individual campaigns, and bars corporations and labor unions from making direct contributions to political campaigns. These restrictions have been upheld against challenges based on the First Amendment's protection of freedom of speech. The Supreme Court agreed that a contribution of money to a campaign was a form of expression, and, despite a widespread public and academic view that money alone cannot be speech, almost certainly correctly: campaign contributions are the way in which people without the time or talent to speak out on their own advance the candidacies of those who take positions the contributors agree with. But, the Court also held, restrictions on contributions were constitutionally permissible because unlimited contributions created the possibility of corruption, as contributors would condition their continued support on a successful candidate's supporting legislation and policies that offered direct financial benefits to the contributors, and even more, the appearance of corruption, as members of the public who merely voted but did not give large amounts of financial support to candidates believed that contributors exercised undue influence on the candidates' policy positions.[35]

Critics of the Court's decisions make several points. They argue that the Court's doctrine attempts to distinguish between practices that are functionally identical, leading to an extremely complex and unadministrable body of law dealing with a central feature of the political system—a deeply undesirable result. In addition, they point to what has been called the 'hydraulic' nature of campaign finance: 'Money, like water, will always find an outlet.'[36] Yet, if that is so, what is the point of campaign finance regulation? At most, it provides temporary relief

---

[34] A system of public financing for campaign exists in connection with presidential elections, but participation in the system is optional for the candidates. By the early twenty-first century that system had broken down, largely because the amounts provided were thought inadequate, and presidential candidates ordinarily chose to finance their campaigns through fund-raising on their own.

[35] *Buckley v Valeo* 424 US 1 (1976); *McConnell v Federal Election Commission* 540 US 93 (2003).

[36] *McConnell v Federal Election Commission* 540 US, at 224.

from a handful of immediate problems while overlooking some and giving rise to others. And, finally, critics contend that if, as nearly everyone now agrees, the contribution and expenditure of money in political campaigns is in theory indistinguishable from speech—is, indeed, a form of speech—then the general rules of free expression embedded in constitutional doctrine limit the government's power to regulate campaign finance far more sharply than existing statutes do.

The limits placed on campaign contributions can be evaded, or at least stretched, through the creation of organizations affiliated with but nominally independent of the corporations and unions, known as 'political action committees' (PACs). In addition, those who support a candidate because of specific policy positions the candidate advocates can associate in organizations that spend money, without limit, advocating their policy positions, and corporations and labor unions can contribute to these independent advocacy groups. The Supreme Court has upheld statutory requirements that expenditures by these advocacy groups must not be coordinated with campaign expenditures by the candidates themselves,[37] but most political observers believe that this requirement is readily evaded as knowledgeable political operatives for the advocacy groups shape their advertisements without consulting the candidates but in ways that fit well with what the candidates' campaigns are doing. The Supreme Court has held that the First Amendment allows advocacy groups to distribute advertising whose obvious purpose and meaning is candidate support, as long as that advertising does not expressly urge voters to vote for a particular candidate.[38]

Perhaps responding to critics' concerns, and perhaps having the unstated view that restrictions on campaign finance disadvantage Republican candidates more than Democratic ones, the Court moved away from its earlier holdings. It maintained the form of its doctrinal structure, but more recent decisions exhibit great skepticism about the 'anti-corruption' justification for restrictions on contributions. The Court has moved to the position that contributions can be regulated only to avoid traditional bribery, the exchange of a contribution for a

---

[37] *Federal Election Commission v National Conservative Political Action Committee* 470 US 480 (1985).
[38] *Federal Election Commission v Wisconsin Right to Life, Inc* 551 US 449 (2007).

promised vote by the recipient.[39] It also essentially freed 'independent' expenditures from any regulation other than disclosure of the fact of the expenditure and, depending on the source of the expenditure, some disclosure of those contributing to the organization making it. The *Citizens United* decision received great public attention for its holding that corporations could spend money on independent expenditures, but its more important implication, rapidly discerned by specialists, was that expenditures could not be limited in any way.[40]

The national political parties can coordinate expenditures with candidates, subject to some rather high limits on contributions to the national parties. The Supreme Court has not directly addressed the constitutionality of this provision, although it has held that the Constitution protects *uncoordinated* expenditures against regulation.[41] The reason for the statutory ban on coordinating spending between a candidate and the national party is not entirely clear, but appears to be that these restrictions are needed to ensure that the limits on individual contributions to campaigns are not evaded. Political insiders tend to believe that these restrictions are particularly misguided because they interfere with the ability of a national political party to develop a nationally coordinated platform supported by each of the party's candidates everywhere in the nation. As we have seen, though, the modern party system does have parties with reasonably coherent national platforms with which most of each party's candidates agree, so the effects of campaign finance restrictions on the national parties appear to be small.

In general, a campaign can spend any amount it wishes. The cost of campaigns rose dramatically at the end of the twentieth century, with each successive election cycle seeing larger total spending than the preceding one, as candidates placed advertisements on television, hired campaign consultants, spent large amounts of money in efforts to contact voters by mail, and more. Combining limits on individual contributions with no limits on campaign expenditures produces an obvious dynamic: Candidates spend quite large amounts of their time in efforts to raise money to support their campaigns.

---

[39] *McCutcheon v Federal Election Commission* 134 SCt 1434 (2014).
[40] *Citizens United v Federal Election Commission* 558 US 310 (2010).
[41] *Colorado Republican Federal Campaign Committee v Federal Election Committee* 518 US 604 (1996).

The politics of campaign finance legislation is complex. Those who would benefit from unlimited contributions and expenditures—typically, conservatives who believe that they can tap into the wealth of the nation's richest people—oppose nearly all restrictions. Supporters of restrictions have varying motivations. An important one surely is that they believe they can structure the restrictions in ways that make it easier for them to defeat their opponents. After all, incumbents are almost always already better known in their districts than their opponents, and placing a ceiling on what both sides can spend has the effect of making it more difficult for the opponents to become better known. The time-consuming nature of fund-raising, though, offers a better reason than incumbent-protection for restrictions on campaign expenditures. An incumbent who must spend large amounts of time talking with potential contributors cannot spend that time on developing policy expertise. The First Amendment case against limitations on campaign expenditures is strong, though, and it seems unlikely that substantial limits on such expenditures will be adopted.

Lobbying

Lobbying rules and practices are related to campaign finance rules and practices. Even more obviously than campaign contributions, lobbying is a form of political expression protected by the First Amendment. For example, a corporation can hire a lobbyist to work for the enactment of legislation that would put a competitor out of business, without being subject to liability under the antitrust laws.[42] As a result, lobbying is regulated primarily through disclosure of contacts between members of Congress and lobbyists representing clients and interest groups. Public opinion in the United States tends to treat lobbying by business groups as a form of improper influence, while accepting similar activities by self-identified 'public interest' groups. Political insiders, in contrast, tend to see lobbying as a relatively innocuous activity, through which informed representatives convey information to members of Congress on issues about which the members might otherwise have relatively little knowledge.

---

[42] See *Professional Real Estate Investors, Inc v Columbia Pictures Industries, Inc* 508 US 49 (1993).

CONSTITUTIONAL POLITICS WITHIN CONGRESS

Some matters that have been important in other democratic constitutional systems have played a relatively small role in US constitutional law. Election controversies arising out of close elections have occurred with some frequency, but they have been resolved straightforwardly.[43] The Constitution states: 'Each House shall be the Judge of the Elections, Returns, and Qualifications of its own Members.' This has had two effects. There are no significant court decisions dealing with disputed elections, and only one dealing with the Qualifications clause. (There, the Supreme Court held that a member could be excluded only if the House or Senate determined that the member failed to satisfy one of the so-called 'standing' requirements for membership—age, citizenship and state residency.[44] Otherwise the member had to be expelled. The consequential difference between exclusion and expulsion is that the former can be accomplished by ordinary majority vote, whereas the latter requires agreement by two-thirds of the house.) More important, with only a tiny number of exceptions, the winner of a disputed election is the candidate whose party controls a majority of the undisputed seats. Or, put another way, election disputes are not resolved by consideration of the merits of the claims, but rather by purely partisan considerations.

Drawing on the British parliamentary tradition, the Constitution also provides that members of Congress 'shall not be questioned in any other Place' for 'any Speech or Debate'.[45] Here, the relatively few cases are important. Sometimes ordinary citizens sue members of Congress for defamation or similar torts. According to the Supreme Court, the plaintiff's case cannot include evidence of statements made on the floor of the House or Senate or in legislative hearings, but liability could be established by showing that defamatory statements were disseminated to the public, including the legislator's constituents, by means of newsletters and press releases, which were not 'essential' to Congress's

---

[43] For a compilation dealing with the Senate, see AM Butler and W Wolff, *United States Senate Election, Expulsion and Censure Cases, 1793–1990* (Washington, Government Printing Office, 1995).

[44] *Powell v McCormack* 395 US 486 (1969).

[45] For an overview of British and US practice, see JA Chafetz, *Democracy's Privileged Few: Legislative Privilege and Democratic Norms in the British and American Constitutions* (Cambridge, MA, Harvard University Press, 2007).

'deliberative processes'.[46] This holding is predicated on a relatively narrow view of a legislator's duties: As Justice William Brennan contended in a one-sentence dissent, a legislator's duties might well be said to include distribution of the legislator's views to the public. The decision was not controversial, though, and nothing much has come of it.

More important are decisions upholding the ability of the executive branch to prosecute members of Congress for corruption in connection with their official duties. The difficulty, of course, is that often the point of the corruption—be it bribery by someone outside of Congress of a member, or extortion by a member from someone outside— is to obtain legislative action, such as an appropriation benefiting the person outside Congress. One could imagine a system in which corruption would be policed by each house of Congress and by the public through elections. Yet, the pressure to hold those who violate criminal laws against corruption criminally liable is of course large, and prosecutions became if not routine at least not extraordinary in the second half of the twentieth century. The Supreme Court held that the Speech and Debate Clause prevented prosecutors from introducing evidence that the member of Congress actually performed some legislative act, such as making a speech or introducing legislation, as part of a corrupt plan, but that other evidence, such as testimony from the person offering the bribe, might establish that the member had violated the anti-corruption laws.[47]

In other nations, the executive's power to bring charges against legislators has been a powerful tool for bringing legislators under the executive's thumb. Not in the United States. The reason, as we have seen so often, is party politics. The possibility of abuse exists, of course, but is constrained by politics. In the background there is always a concern about the legislator's constituents. A successful prosecution deprives the constituents of the representative they have chosen, and even the pendency of a prosecution interferes with the legislator's ability to serve his or her constituents. Both of these are matters of important theoretical concern, and to some extent practical concern as well. More important, executive officials who supervise the initiation of prosecutions must think about the possibility that the legislator they charge will have allies in Congress with sufficient power to retaliate against the

---

[46] *Hutchinson v Proxmire* 443 US 111 (1979).
[47] *United States v Brewster* 408 US 501 (1972).

administration either directly by holding aggressive 'oversight' hearings in which the administration's actions are questioned, or indirectly by focusing on some matter other than the prosecution: An indicted legislator's friends might be chairs of committees controlling legislation the administration favors, and may interfere with *that* legislation's progress because of their disagreement with the initiation of the prosecution. These political concerns have limited prosecutions of national legislators to cases of almost indisputable corruption in its core sense.

The most significant constitutional provision dealing with Congress's operations is perhaps the simplest and most obvious, the provision giving each house the power to 'determine the Rules of its Proceedings'. Many of the rules adopted are ordinary rules of parliamentary procedure, whose only significant role is to allow each house to conduct its business in an orderly manner. Some, though, have important implications for legislative output. Two examples of many candidates follow, to illustrate how rules affect outcomes, and how politics affects how rules are employed.[48]

The 'Filibuster' in the Senate

The Senate rule allowing 'extended debate', known as a filibuster, is probably the most prominent procedural rule with significant effects.[49] The Senate's rules do not allow a simple majority to terminate debate on any matter. Instead, 60 Senators must vote to terminate debate. When a filibuster occurs, the usual rule that the Senate can act when a majority of its members agree is displaced by one requiring a super-majority for action. That obviously reduces the chance that the action will be taken, which is why filibusters occur: They are tactics used by a minority to block the adoption of legislation that has majority support, but not enough support to overcome the filibuster.

---

[48] For an overview of procedure in the House and Senate, see John V. Sullivan, How Our Laws Are Made, 110th Congress, 1st Sess., Doc. 110-49, available at http://www.gpo.gov/fdsys/pkg/CDOC-110hdoc49/pdf/CDOC-110hdoc49.pdf.

[49] The term derives from a nineteenth century word used to describe an irregular military adventurer, extended metaphorically to describe those who 'hijack' legislative discussions.

Filibusters in the form of truly extended debate—that is, the presence on the floor of the Senate of someone speaking—were never common. True filibusters were physically exhausting. A person or group simply had to hold the floor for a while. When, as inevitably occurred, they observed an absence of a quorum, they could use ordinary parliamentary procedure to call for a quorum count. That gave the filibuster's proponents a chance to take a rest. Even more, the possibility of repeated quorum calls meant that the filibuster's opponents had to be on hand—sometimes sleeping on cots near the Senate's chambers—for the quorum call. All this made a true filibuster hard on the Senators, and deterred them from conducting many filibusters.

In the middle of the twentieth century Southern Senators used the filibuster to block the adoption of civil rights legislation. The political context is important. At the time the Senate's rules required a two-thirds vote, or 67 Senators, to terminate a filibuster. Civil rights legislation might well have had the support of a simple majority in the Senate, consisting of a coalition of liberal Democrats mostly from the North and liberal to moderate Republicans from the Northeast and Midwest. But that coalition, always fragile, was never large enough to stop a filibuster. Liberal Democrats gained a substantial majority in the Senate in the 1960s and, after some struggle, changed the Senate's rules. Their majority was large enough that filibusters would be futile, and the practice disappeared for something more than a decade.

Then the filibuster reappeared, but in a new guise. For reasons that remain obscure, the practice of conducting a true, physical filibuster ended, replaced by a practice in which a Senator announced that he or she intended to engage in extended debate on some proposed action. On receiving that announcement, the Senate's leaders would do a headcount to determine whether there were enough votes to break the filibuster. If the answer was no, the leadership withdrew the proposal from the floor and moved on to another topic. In addition, the increasing polarization of the political parties in the 1990s coupled with the fact that at no point did either party ever have 60 or more Senators meant that the mere announcement of an intention to filibuster inevitably resulted in the proposal's withdrawal.

Special rules applied to budget legislation, but everything else was open to filibuster. Early in the twenty-first century Republicans—who controlled the White House and therefore the judicial nomination process but who lacked the 60 votes to overcome a filibuster in the

Senate—argued that the Constitution barred the Senate from invoking its filibuster rule on judicial nominations. Their arguments were not terribly strong as a matter of law: They argued that there was a tradition of allowing 'up or down' votes on judicial nominations, and that the Constitution's use of the word 'shall' in the nomination clause, which reads, '[The President] ... shall nominate, and by and with the Advice and Consent of the Senate, shall appoint' judges, imposed a duty on the Senate to vote on a proposed nomination. They drew a contrast between this language and the terms used in the following section, which direct the president 'from time to time to give to the Congress Information on the State of the Union, and *recommend* to the Consideration such Measures as he shall judge necessary and expedient'. The controversy flared when the Republican majority leader threatened to use ordinary parliamentary procedures to obtain a ruling from the chair—the (Republican) vice president—that judicial nominations could not be filibustered: a ruling that, if appealed to the Senate as a whole, would be sustained if all Republicans voted to do so. The controversy ebbed when a bipartisan group of Senators, with enough Democrats to ensure that the deal would stick, agreed to allow 'up or down' votes on some but not all of the pending controversial nominations and to vote to break filibusters of future nominations unless there were 'extraordinary' circumstances justifying the filibuster. After 2008, filibusters against judicial and executive nominations, now led by Republicans, persisted and expanded. In 2013 the Senate changed its rules to eliminate the filibuster for such nominations, other than to the Supreme Court, but otherwise the filibuster rules remained in force.

The effect of these developments was straightforward: the Senate could not act on any matter unless there were 60, not 51, votes in favor. And the only proposals that could achieve 60 votes were ones that had significant bipartisan support. In a sense the Senate came to operate as a Grand Coalition, where only those policies supported by parties separated by wide ideological differences could become law. Occasionally a majority party could ram some of its policies through, but only under special circumstances, the most important of which were, first, policies involving the budget, and second, when the minority party was particularly dispirited, as appears to have happened to the Democratic party after their presidential candidate 'lost' the 2000 election as a result of a Supreme Court decision.[50]

---

[50] *Bush v Gore* 531 US 98 (2000).

The House Rules Committee

Each house refers legislative proposals ('bills') to one or more substantive committees for initial consideration. As noted earlier, committees play an important role in shaping and reshaping bills before they receive full consideration from the House or Senate, and determining which committee will have jurisdiction over a bill is an important task of the House and Senate leadership. Committee jurisdiction matters because committee members are chosen in a way that gives each committee its own coloration and substantive tilt. Party leaders assign members to committees but they do so with an eye to maintaining their own leadership positions; that is, they cannot impose their will on recalcitrant members, at least not too frequently or on too many matters important to the members. And sometimes leaders reach their posts by promising key members that the leaders will favor with good committee assignments those who support them in intra-party battles.

Members in turn seek out committee assignments that they believe will benefit them politically. Notoriously, members of committees with jurisdiction over matters affecting agriculture tend to come from states in which farming is an important economic interest, and not from suburbs whose residents have to pay the higher costs for food associated with farm-state subsidy programs. More recently, ideological polarization has made the two committees on the judiciary venues for highly partisan advocates of each party's positions. The appropriations committees are particularly attractive to members, because they are able to channel funds to their own states or districts and, perhaps more important, can do similar favors to other members, thereby giving them a great deal of power within the house. In general, committee members tend to be 'outliers' on their party's spectrum of policy preferences with regard to the issues under the committee's jurisdiction.

Most legislative proposals get no further than submission to a substantive committee. Committees hold hearings and take votes on only a minority of the proposals they receive. The rules generally prohibit floor consideration of proposals that have not received a vote in the substantive committees.[51] There are some devices to get around a

---

[51] Technically, the house can consider on the merits a bill that received a *negative* vote in the substantive committee, but that never happens: Proposals that fail to receive a favorable committee vote are dead.

recalcitrant or overworked committee. Sometimes, but not always, subject to an ordinary but quite generous requirement of germaneness, proposals can be offered as amendments to legislation that *has* reached the floor,[52] although a member who attempts to do so must be sure that committee members and party leaders will not be offended by the attempt to go around the committee. Even less common, each house as a whole has the power to 'discharge' a bill from a committee that has failed to act, by simple majority vote. Again, this power is rarely used because of norms of reciprocity: Every member knows that at some point he or she will find it politically convenient to be able to tell constituents that the member would have liked to vote on a proposal, but unfortunately the member did not have the opportunity to do so because the committee bottled the proposal up.

Bills that survive committee consideration then go to the floor of the House or Senate. Senate consideration takes place under ordinary rules of parliamentary procedure, including, as we have seen, extended debate.[53] Amendments can be offered by any Senator, subject to a loose requirement that the amendment must be germane to the bill. On important measures, though, and precisely to avoid the kind of political contention that would produce a filibuster, party leaders on both sides of the aisle—that is, the leaders of both parties—reach an informal agreement about how much debate will occur, which amendments may be offered, and the like. These agreements are not enforced through rulings on parliamentary procedure, but rather by each side's awareness that similar issues will recur and that cooperation now will make cooperation later easier.

The situation is different in the House. After a bill receives a favorable vote from a substantive committee, it is directed to the Rules Committee.[54] There it receives a formal 'rule' governing the length of

---

[52] Relatedly, proposals can be added to appropriations bills as 'riders', typically either to direct an expenditure or to specify that appropriated funds may not be used to some specified activity. Germaneness rules are tighter with respect to these riders.

[53] The final stage in the process of appropriating funds by the national government is ordinarily a 'reconciliation' vote aimed at bringing expenditures and taxes into alignment (or at least at bringing the gap between expenditures and taxes into the open). Debate in the Senate on a reconciliation bill is limited to 20 hours. Although that particular limit is often disregarded, filibusters are impossible on reconciliation bills.

[54] Less important bills may bypass the Rules Committee by being placed on a 'calendar' for the consideration of such proposals, typically by unanimous consent.

consideration and, more important, the number and nature of amendments that can be offered on the floor. The rule might specify which amendments will be in order and how much time will be devoted to debating them. Or, more interesting, the rule can be 'closed', that is can require that the House vote on the committee-approved bill without amendment. The House itself must then approve the rule under which it will consider the proposal, but the committee's proposed rule almost never fails. The chair of the Rules Committee is obviously an important member of the House leadership. In the past some committee chairs were almost as powerful as the Speaker of the House, who is the majority party's leader. Today, largely as a result of the House's polarization, the Rules Committee chair works closely with but is clearly subordinate to the Speaker.

These procedures shape the legislative policy that Congress ultimately adopts.[55] All of them result from discretionary choices by the House and Senate, not mandatory ones imposed by the Constitution. But the discretion and the way it is exercised is dominated by ordinary politics.

CONCLUSION

The written Constitution creates the legislative branch, and sets out a few boundary markers on how Congress operates. Yet, one who reads only the written Constitution will know little about Congress. The efficient constitution gives Congress much more definition. Political parties, unmentioned in the written constitution, are the tools that define Congress.

---

[55] Proposals that have passed the House and Senate in different forms must be sent to a 'conference' committee, which produces a single proposal on which each house votes. The leadership in each house chooses the members of the conference committee and, because the policy preferences of the conference committee's members can have decisive effects, the power to appoint members is a significant one.

FURTHER READING

Chambers, WN and Burnham, WD, *American Party Systems: Stages of Political Development* (New York, Oxford University Press, 1975) (providing an overview of the development of the party system).

Oleszek, WJ, *Congressional Procedures and the Policy Process* (7th edn Washington, CQ Press, 2007) (an overview of congressional processes).

Sinclair, B, *Unorthodox Lawmaking: New Legislative Processes in the US Congress* (3rd edn Washington, CQ Press, 2007) (describes the contemporary processes of congressional lawmaking).

3

The Constitutional Politics of the Executive Branch

————◆————

The President as Party Leader – The President's Role in Legislation – The Unitary Executive and the Modern Administrative State – The Unitary Executive in Foreign Affairs – Conclusion

T HE CONSTITUTION'S FRAMERS believed that Congress would be the predominant institution in the national government. The president, they believed, would serve primarily as an executive or manager of the programs Congress adopted. This expectation is captured in the fact that Congress is the subject of the Constitution's first Article, consisting of 10 sections and about 2,250 words, the president the subject of Article II, with four sections and 1,000 words. Popular terminology reflects this expectation as well: Americans use the term 'the government' to mean Congress in the first instance and the combination of Congress and the executive branch secondarily, and use the term 'the administration' where people accustomed to parliamentary government would use the term 'the government'.

The president was not to be a mere figurehead, though. In the checks-and-balances system the Constitution created, the president was given a source of political authority—and power—different from the sources of authority and power for the houses of Congress. The president was also given some power to influence legislation directly, by recommending that Congress adopt laws and, more important, by vetoing laws Congress adopted. (Yet, indicating the assumption that Congress was the primary actor in the constitutional system, the president's veto power was limited, not substantively but procedurally, by the ability of Congress to make its laws effective despite the president's disapproval, if they could muster a two-thirds majority in both houses to override the veto.) These political and constitutional resources, the framers believed, would create a government that had enough power to accomplish the nation's purposes but not so powerful as to engage in imprudent ventures or threaten the rights of the nation's citizens.

It did not work out quite as the framers expected. Rather rapidly the president came to dominate the US political system. In part that was because the president, as the only political figure chosen, albeit indirectly, by the nation's entire electorate, could claim to speak for the nation as a whole, in contrast to Senators and members of the House of Representatives, who could speak only for their states and districts. More important, though, presidents became leaders of national political parties. As we have seen, the nation's constitutional structures ended up encouraging the development of such parties. And, once political parties were in place, the written Constitution in turn encouraged the president to serve as a party's leader: the national parties needed some mechanism to coordinate their actions across state lines, particularly on the important task of selecting a president, and the presidency itself became that mechanism.

The written Constitution still limits the president's power. The president can be removed from office by impeachment, which requires a majority vote in the House of Representatives and a two-thirds vote in the Senate. The latter margin is so substantial that no president has ever been removed from office by impeachment, although Richard Nixon resigned when his removal by the Senate seemed certain. Notably, Nixon left office when, and largely because, he had lost substantial support from his own party. In contrast, William Clinton was impeached—that is, charges were made against him—by a majority of the Republican-controlled House of Representatives, but was not convicted in the Senate, even though Republicans also controlled the Senate, because he retained nearly unanimous support from his Democratic colleagues in Congress.

The meaningful limitation on presidential power contained in the written Constitution is the term limitation: presidents can serve no more than two terms. It is often asserted that George Washington's refusal to run for a third term established a tradition that lasted until Franklin D Roosevelt ran for a third term in 1940, but that is somewhat overstated. Several presidents contemplated running for a third term before Roosevelt did, but refrained from doing so because they surveyed the political landscape and found it unfavorable entirely apart from the two-term 'tradition'. Nonetheless, Republicans pushed for a formal constitutional amendment limiting the president to two terms, which was adopted in 1951. This limitation ensures that a re-elected president will be a 'lame duck', that is someone who cannot use the full power of the presidency, including threats about future retaliation against opponents, in seeking to advance his or her programs.

Questions of presidential power are basically questions about the relative power of the president and Congress. The questions' resolution occurs through the interaction of the written Constitution and politics, with the latter playing the larger role. In defending their exercises of power against challenges from Congress, presidents claim to speak for the nation as a whole.[1] The political system weakens the basis for that claim. The reason is the way the system of indirect election through the electoral college has worked out. By custom and state law in all but two states, all of a state's electoral votes are cast for the person who receives a majority (or, in elections with serious third-party candidates, a plurality) of the votes cast in the state's presidential election. In addition, in every election only a handful of states are truly 'in play', as political insiders put it. That is, well before the date of the election well-informed politicians are quite confident in their judgments about which candidate will receive a majority of the votes in a large number of states. The 'winner take all' allocation of electoral votes in those states makes the election essentially uncontested, with the candidates devoting all their efforts to the 'battleground' states where each has a realistic prospect of gaining a majority of the votes. Once the election is over, the president—who ignored a large number of states during the campaign—may be said to speak for citizens in the uncontested states and the battleground states he or she won, but not as easily for voters in the states the candidate ignored. And, on the other side of the struggle between president and Congress, members of Congress with 'sure' seats, whose reelection is a near certainty, can take a broad view on a large number of issues as long as they satisfy their constituents on a small number of issues that are particularly important to the constituency.

The efficient constitution makes the president the nation's dominant political actor, but not one whose dominance is assured. There remain checks and balances, but they too result from how the party system operates.

---

[1] JK Tulis, *The Rhetorical Presidency* (Princeton, Princeton University Press, 1987).

THE PRESIDENT AS PARTY LEADER

The Constitution's Text

Like the written Constitution's description of Congress's powers, its description of presidential powers does not correspond well to the president's powers under the efficient constitution. Article II gives the president two—or, controversially, three—broad powers, and a series of relatively narrow ones. The first broad power is that the president is to be the Commander in Chief of the nation's armed forces. Traditionally this has been understood to give the president power to make not merely tactical choices about the conduct of military operations but also the primary decisions about the deployment of US military force, subject to check by Congress, largely through the power of Congress to provide or refuse to provide funds for the president's initiatives.

President George W Bush made extremely expansive claims about the scope of his power as commander in chief in connection with the 'war on terror'. Because, in his view, that war had no well-defined battlefields, the president's power as commander in chief, even if limited to tactical choices regarding the conduct of the war on terror, authorized him to engage in activities within the nation's borders, such as surveillance of those whose activities might help identify terrorists and arrests and indefinite detention of those the president designated as 'enemy combatants'. These claims in turn were met with substantial resistance, academic and political, and the extent to which they will settle into the efficient constitution remains unclear. Part of the reaction has been an argument that the commander-in-chief clause actually is not a power-conferring clause but is instead no more than a statement that hierarchical control of the armed forces rests in the president and cannot be shifted elsewhere.[2]

The president is also given a duty to 'take Care that the Laws be faithfully executed'. An important interpretive question arises here. The president has the duty to ensure that the laws enacted by Congress are enforced, though—as a controversy over a presidential policy adopted

---

[2] Although President Barack Obama continued and to some degree expanded some of the existing surveillance programs, he retreated from the expansive claims of inherent executive power made by his predecessor, and relied far more heavily on the argument that the programs were authorized by congressional legislation.

after the 2014 elections to defer the removal from the United States of a large group of those present without authorization showed—the president also has some discretion in setting priorities for enforcing the law. What, though, of laws the president believes to be unconstitutional? The supremacy clause of Article VI states that '[t]his Constitution, and the Laws of the United States which shall be made in Pursuance thereof … shall be the supreme Law of the Land'. The words 'in pursuance thereof' might have been read to mean the laws adopted by the methods laid out in the Constitution are supreme law, but early on an alternative interpretation took hold. According to that interpretation, laws are made 'in pursuance of' the Constitution only to the extent that they are consistent with the Constitution's *substantive* provisions. The Constitution thereby became supreme over laws enacted by Congress.

As we will see, nearly everyone today agrees that the courts have the power and indeed the duty to set aside congressional legislation that, in their view, is inconsistent with the Constitution. Can the president similarly disregard unconstitutional laws? Advocates of a strong presidency say yes: The duty to take care that the laws be enforced encompasses *all* the laws, including the Constitution. Against that seemingly obvious proposition are two points, one textual-structural and one more general. The president already has the power to obstruct the adoption of laws he or she thinks unconstitutional, through the power to veto legislation. Giving the president a power to refuse to enforce unconstitutional laws allows the president to refuse to enforce laws he or she refrained from vetoing, and indeed a power to refrain from enforcing laws enacted after a veto was overridden. This seems inconsistent with the structure of the veto power.[3] Further, a presidential power to disregard enacted statutes in the name of the Constitution is in real tension with the checks-and-balances theory when the president refuses to comply with a statute that the president believes to be an unconstitutional restriction on presidential power: Congress sought to check the president's power by enacting a statute, perhaps demonstrating the strength of its view

---

[3] One might respond to this concern by noting the possibility that the president is dealing with a statute signed by a president who did not share the current president's views on constitutionality, or who was otherwise constrained to sign the statute. Yet, noting this possibility transforms the problem from one about presidential power broadly understood into a temporal one, about which president's constitutional views—the present one's or the earlier one's—should prevail.

that some check was needed by overriding a veto, and yet the check is rendered ineffective by the president's disregard of the statute.

These difficulties have been resolved by politics rather than constitutional law. Presidents know that refusals to enforce laws, even on constitutional grounds, will annoy members of Congress. They therefore tend to be extremely cautious in their actual behavior even if, as sometimes occurs, they assert quite extensive authority to disregard unconstitutional laws. One instructive example comes from the administration of Bill Clinton. A rider attached to a general appropriations bill purported to require that the president discharge from military service any service member who had HIV/AIDS. Military officials strongly opposed this provision as a matter of policy, and some in the administration believed that it was unconstitutionally discriminatory. The president found himself constrained to sign the bill because it appropriated essential funds for military operations. But, rather than refuse to discharge HIV-positive service members, the administration took the position that in any litigation against the policy brought by such a person it would present the arguments for the policy's unconstitutionality to the courts, and let them resolve the question. The administration also worked to get the requirement repealed, which occurred before the administration actually took steps against any service member.[4] Similarly, although President George W Bush's administration consistently asserted that it had the power to disregard unconstitutional congressional restrictions on presidential power, it rarely acted in a manner predicated on that assertion. Instead, it argued that the statutes, fairly read, did not apply to the action in question. More recently, President Barack Obama's administration applied the Defense of Marriage Act, restricting the federal benefits available to same-sex couples whose marriages were recognized under state law, but refused to defend its constitutionality; some observers believed that doing both was internally inconsistent, but the Supreme Court's decision finding the statute unconstitutional defused any continuing controversy over the administration's position.

The third expansive power is said to arise from the first words of Article II: 'The executive Power shall be vested in a President of the United States of America.' This might be read as a simple statement that the United States shall have a single rather than a plural executive.

---

[4] The episode is described in DE Johnsen, 'Presidential Non-Enforcement of Constitutionally Objectionable Statutes' (2000) 63 *Law & Contemporary Problems* 7.

Advocates of a more expansive view contrast this sentence with the first sentence of Article I: 'All legislative Powers herein granted shall be vested in a Congress of the United States...' They argue that the contrast demonstrates that the president has all the powers associated in 1789 with the term 'executive power', whereas Congress does not, being limited to those legislative powers later granted. On this view, the question then becomes, What were the powers of an executive in 1789? Answering that question is complicated by the fact that the Constitution's framers were working from models of executive power in Great Britain and in the colonies and states prior to 1789. They believed that the new representative government they were creating rendered obsolete some aspects of the governmental structures that preceded them, even as other aspects remained vibrant. Which components of pre-existing 'executive' power were to be retained, which rejected? Typically, proponents of the view that the vesting clause confers substantial power focus on the executive's power to conduct foreign affairs. But, as before, one can acknowledge the existence of a generic power to conduct foreign affairs and still hold that Congress has substantial power to regulate the president's actions.[5]

Proponents of the view that the 'executive power' is extensive in itself have some difficulty with the fact that Article II also describes some rather discrete presidential powers: the power to 'grant Reprieves and Pardons for Offenses against the United States, except in cases of Impeachment' and the power to 'require the Opinion, in Writing, of the principal Officer in each of the Executive Departments, upon any Subject relating to the Duties of their respective Offices', for example. They reconcile these provisions with their broader views in two ways. First, they say, these provisions when carefully read actually are restrictions on a broad executive power: The president can pardon only those convicted of offenses against the United States and not offenses against the states, and the president cannot require opinions on matters outside a cabinet member's jurisdiction. These readings are, it can fairly be said, implausible. More plausibly, proponents of extensive presidential power treat these provisions as redundant, describing powers already encompassed by the general term 'executive power'. The difficulty here is a

---

[5] See SD Prakash and MD Ramsey, 'The Executive Power over Foreign Affairs' (2001) 111 *Yale Law Journal* 231.

small one: Redundancy in a constitution is sometimes defensible, but usually when the failure to mention something specific might mislead people into thinking that a general term did not cover the specific issue. It is hard to see why a constitution's drafters would insert the 'opinions in writing' clause out of an abundance of caution, as lawyers sometimes put it, to ensure that people would not think that the president lacked such a power.

The President and the Party System

All these questions deal with interpreting the written Constitution. They are nice interpretive questions, with 'nice' used in the older sense of 'subtle'. They are also generally irrelevant to the efficient Constitution. The reason is, once again, that the efficient Constitution is structured around the party system. A president who leads an ideologically unified party that controls both houses of Congress can exercise power extremely expansively, without fear—and without concern for the strength of the arguments drawn from the written Constitution. A president facing a Congress controlled by the other major party must be more cautious no matter how strong his or her legal advisers believe their constitutional case to be. And, of course, there are intermediate cases. Two intermediate categories are especially important.

—   When congressional parties are loose coalitions, a nominally united or divided government might actually be divided or united on specific issues. Consider a president whose party controls Congress but is a coalition. The minority party in Congress might be able to pull one or more factions within that coalition into its camp if the president overreaches on a matter of particular concern to that faction. A president facing a Congress controlled by an opposition coalition might similarly be able to sustain his or her position by attracting support from some in the opposition.

—   'Control' of Congress depends on congressional and constitutional rules. As we saw in chapter two, a party truly controls the Senate only if it has a filibuster-proof majority, that is, has more than 60 members who are willing to hold together when a filibuster is threatened. Notably, numbers alone will not do. The 60 Senators must *agree* as well. Strong, ideologically organized parties rather than coalitional ones seem almost a necessity for party control of the Senate. Such parties began to emerge in the late twentieth century, but neither major party attained the requisite 60-vote majority in the Senate. Even more, a determined president can succeed by vetoing legislation that attempts to control presidential power. As a result, divided government actually requires that there be a veto-proof majority—two-thirds in opposition to the president in both the House of Representatives and the Senate. For all practical purposes, this is impossible under modern circumstances. Of course a president who uses the veto to block legislation is going to fail when he or she proposes an affirmative agenda of public policy. The veto strategy can be pursued by a president who does not care about getting new laws enacted, whether because he or she accepts defeat or believes that existing law can be used (creatively, perhaps) to accomplish the desired goals. But even the latter is politically risky, as the president's opponents will accuse the president, and perhaps not unreasonably, of distorting and even disregarding existing law to put in place policies that he or she could not push through Congress. Here too, though, the opposition lacking a veto-proof majority will find it hard to displace the president's policies.

The written Constitution is not irrelevant to the efficient one, of course, wholly apart from the fact that the written Constitution creates the governmental structures within which party-political contention occurs. Constitutional arguments are resources in political contention. The fact that a president can make a credible argument in favor of the claim that Congress has unconstitutionally attempted to limit presidential power is itself a political resource. And, perhaps more important, when a president's constitutional arguments seem strained, his or her political position might be weakened. Yet, we should not overemphasize the political effects of constitutional arguments. The written Constitution is sufficiently open to interpretation that credible arguments can be made either way in nearly every interesting or politically important case. It is unclear whether such arguments actually sway anyone. For the most part they reinforce positions already held on policy grounds: A person who believes that Congress has unwisely hobbled the president is likely to find the arguments that the statute is unconstitutional more persuasive than the arguments in favor of the statute's constitutionality, and vice versa. Perhaps there are a few people on the margin who shift from supporting the president to supporting Congress once they hear the arguments, and perhaps this possibility itself has political effects on politicians who might worry that there are just enough of them to affect the outcomes of elections. But, in the main, these effects are quite likely to be small.

The President and 'Political Time'

The written Constitution's provisions only indirectly define the president's powers. Whether a president leads a unified government or must deal with divided government matters more. In addition, the president must choose what sort of role to play. Here a concept and typology developed by political scientist Stephen Skowronek are quite useful in understanding the president's actual place in the US constitutional system.[6] The concept is 'political time'. The political calendar runs in chronological time. The United States holds a presidential election every four years, with a successful candidate able to run for reelection only once. Senators face the voters every six years, members of the House of Representatives every two years, with no limits on reelection.

Political time differs from chronological time. The term describes the way in which each president relates to his or her predecessors and anticipates successors. Skowronek's typology has four types of presidents, distinguished along two dimensions. He begins with the observation that the United States has experienced a series of constitutional 'regimes'. These regimes are distinguished by their ideological commitments and their institutional innovations. So, for example, the New Deal constitutional regime was committed to a form of pluralist liberalism, discussed in chapter seven below, and operated through administrative agencies that developed close ties to interest group constituencies and their representatives in Congress. According to Skowronek, constitutional regimes are sometimes 'resilient', sometimes 'vulnerable'. Presidential candidates can be affiliated with or opposed to the prevailing constitutional regime.

These two categories with their divisions then describe four types of president. Consider first a presidential candidate affiliated with a resilient constitutional regime. If elected, that candidate will simply

---

[6] S Skowronek, *The Politics Presidents Make: Leadership from John Adams to George Bush* (Cambridge, MA, Harvard University Press, 1993).

pursue the regime's commitments. Yet, most presidents, unsurprisingly, try to leave their own mark on public policy. So, according to Skowronek, these presidents pursue a 'politics of articulation', in which they offer policy and institutional innovations that they offer as extensions of existing commitments. They face two difficulties, though. First, of course, their innovations may fail, and may help convert a resilient regime into a vulnerable one. In addition, they almost inevitably face resistance from those who came to office under their predecessors and who believe that the existing commitments and institutions are working well and need no tinkering. This resistance contributes to the gradual erosion of a regime's resilience even if the president does nothing in particular to weaken the regime. We might see George W Bush as a recent exemplar in this category.

A president who opposes the commitments of a resilient regime faces real difficulties. Such a president must be resigned to working within a system dedicated to policies and institutions with which he or she disagrees. The president's policies may involve modest tinkering around the edges of existing ones. Alternatively, the president might strike out in entirely new directions, offering innovative policies that do not take on the regime's existing commitments but that hold out some promise that the president will do something to establish his or her historical reputation—and that might lay the groundwork for a transition to another regime, though almost certainly after the president has left office. Skowronek calls these options a 'politics of preemption'. The primary modern example of a preemptive president is Dwight Eisenhower, who induced a Republican party that had previously opposed the New Deal's social welfare programs and internationalist agenda to accept those innovations. Bill Clinton also pursued a politics of pre-emption: Working within the framework established by Ronald Reagan's presidency, and facing a hostile Congress, Clinton sought to present his elimination of 'welfare as we know it' as a Democratic initiative. Skowronek used his typology to support his speculation, in 1993, that Clinton faced a real possibility of impeachment because Reagan's Republican heirs would resent and seek to overcome Clinton's effort to appropriate Reaganite political themes.

Presidents committed to the principles of vulnerable regimes tend to be regarded as failures or tragic figures. They are seen, during their presidencies and after, as trying their best to shore up a set of institutions that no longer seem worth defending, and yet contribute nothing to the transformation of those institutions into something better. Here the primary modern example is Jimmy Carter, who proved unable to extend the New Deal's commitments into the 1980s.

Finally, there are transformative presidencies. They occur when a president comes to office opposed to the principles and institutions of a vulnerable regime. Like Ronald Reagan, they can seize the chance political time offers them. In a 'politics of reconstruction', they can tear down vulnerable institutions in the name of new principles, while building upon institutional strengths created by prior presidents. Skowronek notes, though, that chronological time may have come to conflict with political time. In his view, each regime leaves behind a residue of ideas and institutions, which are not completely eliminated in the politics of reconstruction. In particular, institutions tend not to be destroyed and replaced, but to persist with new ones layered on to them. This institutional residue generates resistance—increasing over chronological time as the residue thickens—to transformation. With a president limited to eight years in office, Skowronek suggests, the chance that a politics of reconstruction will succeed diminishes as time passes.

Skowronek's arguments cast an interesting light on the presidency of Barack Obama. He entered office, one might think, with the potential for becoming a transformative president after the exhaustion of the ideas and policy agenda of the Reagan revolution during the George W Bush administration. Yet, except for a brief period during the first years of his presidency, he had to deal with divided government, at first as a result of the aggressive use by Senate Republicans of the filibuster rule, then, coupled with that, by Republican control of the House of Representatives, and, finally, by a Congress both houses of which were controlled by Republicans. In addition, the political parties became more ideologically homogeneous, Republicans more so than Democrats, and moved further from the ideological center, again Republicans more than Democrats. The debt crisis of 2011 and the government shutdown were only the most dramatic illustrations of hyperpolarization's effects; general gridlock, a low level of legislative action, and increasingly muscular exercises of the president's power as chief executive were more pervasive effects. Tensions over the latter produced their own effects, with the House of Representatives voting to sue the president for his executive actions—and further threats of shutting down the government and impeaching the president.

At this writing it is premature to rule out the possibility that in retrospect President Obama will be seen as a transformative president, but the stretching out of political time to extend through two presidential terms suggests that no president can be transformational in the way Skowronek describes. Rather, a transformational presidency may now be one that is begun by one president and completed by a successor, no longer simply an affiliated president, in Skowronek's terms, but a participant in the transformation.

As with all political-science constructs, Skowronek's washes away many details. It nonetheless provides real illumination of the political dimensions of the US constitutional system.

THE PRESIDENT'S ROLE IN LEGISLATION

The national government's version of separation of powers differs from the classical one in several ways. The 1780 Massachusetts Constitution stated the classic conception:

> In the government of this commonwealth, the legislative department shall never exercise the executive and judicial powers, or either of them; the executive shall never exercise the legislative and judicial powers, or either of them; the judicial shall never exercise the legislative and executive powers, or either of them; to the end it may be a government of laws, and not of men.[7]

The US Constitution departs from this conception of separated powers in several ways. The Senate must confirm presidential nominees and ratify treaties negotiated by the president. And, notably, the president participates in the legislative process.

A minor provision in the Constitution, authorizing the president to recommend that Congress consider 'such Measures as he shall deem necessary and expedient' has taken on a large role. Today the president plays the dominant role in developing legislative proposals, and laws that are solely the work of members of Congress are rare. Of course, the president will consult with members of Congress as the executive branch works on developing a legislative program, if for no other reason than to ensure that the 'president's' proposal has sufficient support in Congress, and members of Congress will seek out officials in the executive branch to endorse proposals the members themselves

---

[7] Massachusetts Constitution, art XXX (1780).

generate, for essentially the same reason. As in parliamentary systems like that in the United Kingdom, though, the executive branch has a large measure of control over the legislative agenda.

The Presidential Veto Power

The president's control over legislation is enhanced by another departure from classical separation of powers. The president has a suspensive veto, which can be overridden only by a two-thirds vote in both houses of Congress. Some of the Constitution's framers believed that the veto was essential to preserve the constitutional system, and should be exercised only for constitutional reasons—when a bill that was adopted by both houses trenched on the president's constitutional prerogatives, for example, or otherwise violated the Constitution. That position was rejected early on, with President George Washington vetoing a few bills on policy grounds. Policy-based vetoes were probably in the minority through the nineteenth century, but today neither the president nor Congress finds it unusual that a veto be based only on the president's objection to the bill's wisdom as a matter of public policy.

As we have seen in chapter two, modern divided governments almost never are divided enough to make a veto-override possible, except perhaps at the very end of a repudiated presidency.[8] When the president actually vetoes legislation, his or her opponents can make the case to the public that the president is an obstructionist responsible for creating gridlock in the national policy-making process. But, coupled with the filibuster's use by the president's allies in the Senate, the veto threat makes it possible for a president in divided government to shift the blame to Congress, which appears unable to get anything to the president's desk.

Presidential Signing Statements

The president has another tool to shape legislation—the signing statement.[9] Since early in the nation's history, and with increasing

---

[8] For a discussion of how veto threats can shape legislation, see ch 2.

[9] For a critical overview of the use of signing statements, see Report of the American Bar Association Task Force on Presidential Signing Statements and the Separation of Powers Doctrine, available at <http://www.abanet.org/media/docs/signstatereport.pdf>.

frequency as divided government took hold near the end of the twentieth century, presidents would refrain from vetoing legislation but would instead sign the bill into law, and simultaneously issue a statement specifying the way the president would direct executive officials to implement it. A typical signing statement would assert that certain provisions would be unconstitutional were they interpreted to impose specific limitations on the president's powers, and that the president would therefore interpret those provisions in a way consistent with his interpretation of the Constitution. Where a statute clearly—or even not so clearly—gives the administration discretion in implementing a statute, signing statements can be entirely unexceptionable and indeed desirable, because they bring out into the open the administration's enforcement choices, which otherwise might be concealed in discrete and difficult to identify decisions as the statute is actually implemented.

Signing statements are more problematic when the statute purports to impose limits on the president's discretion, for example by directing that he or she make certain reports or appoint officials whose credentials match a list Congress has specified. A signing statement asserting that the provision if interpreted as mandatory, as on its face it appears to be, would be unconstitutional and that the president will therefore interpret it to be merely advisory or suggestive seems to be the functional equivalent of a 'single provision' veto.

Presidential signing statements proliferated for two reasons. The first is divided government, which creates more opportunities than unified government for disagreements between Congress and the president on legislation. Divided government alone, though, is not enough, because the president has the veto power. Signing statements substitute for the veto when the provisions to which the president objects are bundled together with provisions he or she finds acceptable, in a package that for all practical purposes must be signed. The proliferation of these bundled laws is the second reason for the increased use of signing statements. Typically these packages are large-scale appropriations bills, funding a wide range of essential government operations. The consultation requirement mentioned above, for example, was part of the 'Emergency Supplemental Appropriations Act for Defense, the Global War on Terror, and Hurricane Recovery' in 2006. Signing statements are convenient for the president in connection with such statutes, but it is not clear that they are truly essential given the president's veto power.

The president could have vetoed the appropriations bill, returned it to Congress, and placed public pressure on Congress to enact the bill without the objectionable provisions.[10]

These problematic signing statements have not led to a constitutional confrontation even though they clearly annoy members of Congress. The reason is that a president who believes it unconstitutional to limit his or her discretion sharply can exercise discretion in a manner compatible with—though in the president's view not constitutionally mandated by—the statute. An example is provided by the aftermath of Hurricane Katrina. The federal agency charged with dealing with natural disasters performed incredibly badly. Its ineffectiveness was attributed by observers to the inexperience of the person heading the agency, who had no experience in emergency management and whose primary credentials for the job were his strong political ties to President George W Bush. A statute enacted after Katrina reorganized the agency, and specified that the agency head had to have significant emergency management experience.[11] President Bush signed the legislation, with an accompanying signing statement asserting that Congress could not constitutionally limit his discretion to choose an agency head: 'The executive branch shall construe s 503(c)(2) in a manner consistent with the Appointments Clause of the Constitution.' As a matter of constitutional interpretation this was quite frivolous, because

---

[10] The Supreme Court held unconstitutional one mechanism to enhance the president's veto-power in connection with these bundled appropriations bills. Congress enacted a statute authorizing the president to sign an appropriations bill and then, within a few days, veto specific appropriations contained in the bill (but not the kinds of substantive provisions to which signing statements have been directed). The Court held that this line-item veto was unconstitutional, because it gave the president the effective power to amend a statute already in force. As the dissents in the case pointed out, this was a quite formal point: one might have said that the appropriations statute was not in force until the time for exercising the line-item veto expired. Probably more important was that the very name seemed inconsistent with the way the veto-power was defined in the written Constitution: *Clinton v New York* 547 US 417 (1998).

[11] 'The Administrator shall be appointed from among individuals who have— (A) a demonstrated ability in and knowledge of emergency management and homeland security; and (B) not less than 5 years of executive leadership and management experience in the public or private sector.': 6 USC § 503(c)(2), as amended by Department of Homeland Security Appropriations Act 2007.

the statute did not, as the president said it did, 'rule[] out a large portion of those persons best qualified by experience and knowledge to fill the office'.[12] Yet there is no way to generate a judicial ruling on President Bush's assertions. When it came time to name a new agency head, though, President Bush did in fact nominate someone with the kind of experience Congress sought. More generally, in many settings the president will be willing to exercise discretion in a way compatible with a statutory provision that the president asserts is unconstitutional because it is mandatory. The signing statements in these settings are theoretical statements about presidential power, not real-world exercises of power. One can imagine a setting in which a president would be unwilling to exercise discretion in such a manner, and would therefore be willing to confront Congress directly. They have not yet occurred, though.

Some signing statements are even more problematic. The best justification for signing statements is that they bring into the open presidential interpretations that will affect how statutes are actually implemented. Some signing statements are so general that they fail to illuminate the administration's actual choices, as when a signing statement asserts no more than that the president will direct that the statue be implemented in a manner 'consistent with the constitutional authority of the President' or similar formulations.

Although President Obama occasionally used signing statements, he did so less often than President Bush, and rarely used the most problematic forms invoking controversial positions on the scope of presidential power without elaboration. Signing statements represent a modern version of the veto power, adapted to deal with the contours of the world of modern politics, and the president's and Congress's adaptations of the original constitutional design to deal with contemporary problems of governance. Bundled appropriations bills are only one indication of changes in the practice of governance. The rise of the administrative state is an even more important indication.

---

[12] Statement on Signing the Department of Homeland Security Appropriations Act 2007, 4 October 2006, available at <http://www.presidency.ucsb.edu/ws/index.php?pid=23960>.

THE UNITARY EXECUTIVE AND THE MODERN
ADMINISTRATIVE STATE

Seeking to ensure both vigor in and political accountability for the enforcement of the laws Congress enacted, the Constitution's framers deliberately choose to have a single president at the head of the executive branch, rejecting suggestions for a plural executive. The president 'shall take Care that the Laws be faithfully executed, and shall Commission all the Officers of the United States.' The connection between the 'take care' clause and the provision on commissioning officers may be accidental, but it is suggestive nonetheless. The president also has the power to appoint the 'Officers of the United States', although Congress has the power to 'vest the Appointment of such inferior Officers, as they think proper, in the President alone, in the Courts of Law, or in the Heads of Departments'. Taken together, these provisions strongly suggest that the president was to be the head of the administration, and responsible for its actions, and that the framers understood that a single person could not possibly execute the laws personally. There would have to be subordinate ('inferior') officers, and it would frequently make sense to staff the government's bureaucracies by allowing lower-level officials to hire and fire those on the front line of administration—subject, of course, to the president's ultimate control and therefore responsibility.

The President, the Cabinet and the Executive Bureaucracy

Today the 'Heads of Departments' are called members of the president's Cabinet. They are nominated by the president and must be confirmed by the Senate, which has a strong though not invariable tradition of deferring to the president's choice of those he or she wishes to serve. At present there are 15 Cabinet members, but that number is a bit misleading. In practice there are major Cabinet departments—the Departments of State, Treasury, Defense and Justice—and minor ones, such as the Departments of Veterans Affairs and Housing and Urban Development. From time to time, as political circumstances and personal ties dictate, heads of one or two minor departments may become members of what is sometimes called the 'inner Cabinet' of major department heads.[13]

The president selects Cabinet members primarily to satisfy political pressures, among which of course are pressures to have important departments administered competently. In modern times presidents have sought to make the Cabinet 'look like America', as President Clinton put it: Some degree of demographic representation seems required. Some departments are constituency oriented in an obvious sense, such as the Departments of Agriculture and Veterans Affairs. The heads of those departments are chosen to satisfy the relevant constituencies and the interest groups that speak for them. Finally, sometimes presidents have given cabinet positions to figures with their own political support within the president's party, independent of the president's. This allowed the president both to assert some control over and gain some support from potential rivals. The tradition of reserving one or two Cabinet positions for important politicians has waned recently, though it did not disappear, as President Obama's appointment of Hillary Clinton as Secretary of State showed. The tradition may have weakened because increasing presidential domination of the political parties has meant that presidents once elected rarely face rivals from within their party.

Another more recent mode of presidential control over Cabinet departments has been what Elena Kagan calls 'presidential administration'.[14] The bureaucracy within the office of the presidency ('the White House staff') grew substantially in the later years of the twentieth century, giving that office the power to oversee the actions of Cabinet departments and bring them into line with White House policy if they began to stray. Faced with gridlock in Congress, President Obama used presidential administration to advance his policy agenda in ways that might contribute to strengthening the Democratic party coalition, as with environmental regulations and suspension of removal of persons

---

[13] In addition, by statute several other officials have Cabinet 'rank', which basically means that they too must be nominated by the president and confirmed by the Senate: the White House Chief of Staff, the United States Trade Representative, and the administrator of the Environmental Protection Agency, among a few others.

[14] E Kagan, 'Presidential Administration' (2001) 114 *Harvard Law Review* 2245.

present in the United States without authorization. Importantly, he was able to use presidential administration for these purposes because his predecessors, some with quite different policy agendas, had created the institutional framework within which presidential administration operated.

Cabinet members are the heads of the bureaucracies of the executive branch. Lower-level bureaucrats are civil servants, who carry out most of the day-to-day administration of the law. Through much of the nineteenth-century low-level national officials—the predecessors of today's bureaucrats—though formally appointed by the president were actually the products of a system of political patronage, in which the president's local political allies doled out jobs to their own supporters. Characterized by its opponents as a 'spoils' system—in which the victors in an election gained the spoils of victory, control of federal jobs—this system actually fit well with the idea that the president headed a unified national executive branch.

Prodded into action by reform agitation that crystallized after a man whose mental illness took the form of an obsession about having lost out on a patronage job assassinated President James Garfield, Congress enacted the Civil Service or Pendleton Act in 1883. The Act created a Civil Service Commission, now known as the Office of Personnel Management, charged with identifying candidates for a wide range of low-level federal jobs based solely on merit. Later revisions of the civil service system made the federal administration a modern bureaucracy.

Presidential control was preserved in two ways. Policy-making officials in every executive bureaucracy remained subject to direct presidential appointment and control, 'excepted from' the civil service system, in the law's terms. There are relatively few civil servants who work at the highest levels of the policy-making process—no 'Permanent Secretaries' to cabinet members of the sort that exist in the United Kingdom.

In addition, presidential control is nominally preserved by the possibility of removing civil servants from their positions for 'cause' but actually removing a federal employee is quite difficult; complex procedures must be followed, and a careful record identifying the 'cause' for the removal must be compiled. As a matter of tradition if not law, it is impossible to remove a civil servant from his or her position solely because the civil servant is not an enthusiastic supporter of a president's policy agenda, or even because the civil servant is obstructing the implementation of that agenda by using the ordinary tools a bureaucrat has—delay, insistence on documentation, and the like. The effect of civil service rules, then, is to make it difficult for a reconstructive president to shift the bureaucracy's direction. Because the president is reconstructive, the bureaucrats already in place are likely to disagree with the president's policies. And because of civil service rules, the president cannot easily replace those bureaucrats. In the last decades of the twentieth century presidential administrations invented a technique called 'burrowing', in which relatively low-level officials who received political rather than civil service appointments took over civil-service jobs by passing the required examinations and being selected through a 'merit' process in which they clearly had an edge.

The President and the Administration of Policy by 'Independent' Agencies

As the nation and its government grew, the president's responsibility for administration necessarily became attenuated. Innovations in administration created additional difficulties. In 1887 Congress created the Interstate Commerce Commission, the first of a number of so-called 'independent' administrative agencies. These agencies, which include the Federal Trade Commission and the National Labor Relations Board, are independent because their members are appointed for fixed terms that extend beyond a four-year presidential term. At least early in a president's tenure, the actions these agencies take cannot fairly be taken as responsive to presidential control. Independent agencies are thus in some tension with placing the duty to enforce the laws on the president at the peak of the hierarchy of government.

The tension between the idea that the executive branch was 'unitary'—that is, united under the president's ultimate control—and the modern administrative state first came to the Supreme Court in two important cases decided in 1926 and 1935. *Myers v United States* provoked massive opinions from a sharply divided Supreme Court.[15] The facts of the case were quite minor. In 1920 President Woodrow Wilson dismissed a local postmaster, basically because the postmaster, a patronage appointee in the first place, had gotten involved in disputes with other local politicians. The postmaster argued that the removal violated a

---

[15] 272 US 52 (1926).

federal statute that allowed a president to remove a postmaster during his four-year term only with the Senate's advice and consent. The president responded that this limitation on the president's power to remove federal officials was unconstitutional.

Trivial in itself, the dispute raised basic constitutional issues; President Andrew Johnson had been impeached, though not convicted by the Senate, for violating a similar statutory provision when he removed Edwin Stanton as Secretary of War without securing agreement from the Senate. When the *Myers* case reached the Supreme Court, the Chief Justice was William Howard Taft, a former president who used the case as an opportunity to define broadly the president's power as head of a unitary executive branch.[16] Taft's opinion examined in detail an extensive congressional debate in 1789 over whether the Senate, which clearly had to consent to appointments, also had to consent to removals. The 'Decision of 1789', as it came to be known, was that the president could remove Senate-confirmed officials at will, because, according to Taft, the president was politically accountable for every action taken by low-level federal officials, and therefore had to have the power to ensure that they did what the president wanted, which in turn required that the president be able to threaten officials with removal if they disagreed with the president's positions.

Taft's position would have clearly made the president the head of a unitary executive branch. Applied to postmasters, the theory of the unitary executive did no more than convert the positions from patronage posts held at the sufferance of Senators and their local allies to patronage posts held at the sufferance of the president. Applied more broadly, as Taft's language suggested, the theory threatened to impede the operation of the modern administrative state. Bureaucracies in the modern state are not merely 'transmission belts', administering clear policy defined by Congress in its laws. Instead, Congress delegates authority to bureaucracies, allowing them to make policy within broad guidelines Congress sets. Twice during the New Deal, but never before or since, the Supreme Court held that Congress had delegated 'too

---

[16] Ironically, as President Taft had regularly complied with the statute he found unconstitutional as Chief Justice. He removed many postmasters during his time as president, but obtained the consent of the Senate for each removal. See JL Entin, 'The Case of the Pompous Postmaster: The Story of *Myers v United States*' available at <http://ssrn.com/abstract=845026>.

much' lawmaking authority to agencies.[17] All the Constitution requires, the Court asserts, is that Congress specify some 'intelligible principle' to guide the agency as it develops rules and policies in more detail. The Court's most recent non-delegation decision held that Congress provided such a principle when it directed the Environmental Protection Agency to set air pollution standards that, with 'an adequate margin of safety, are requisite to protect the public health'.[18] If this is an 'intelligible principle', anything is.

Still, Congress retains a continuing interest in exactly what the bureaucracies do, that is in the policies the bureaucrats make. Giving the president unfettered power to remove policy-making bureaucrats has the effect, in the modern state, of transferring some degree of supervisory power from Congress to the president. Modern statutes address this concern in two ways. Historically, Congress used independent agencies such as the Interstate Commerce Commission, created in 1887, and the Federal Trade Commission, created in 1914. These agencies are sometimes said to form a fourth branch of government, because they are law-making and law-enforcing bodies located in none of the three other branches. From the congressional point of view, independent agencies are something of a compromise. Unable to enact detailed legislation itself on all the matters the independent agencies deal with, but unwilling to delegate complete control over law-making to officials directly controlled by the president, Congress settled on independent agencies headed by commissioners who serve fixed terms and cannot be removed by the president simply because the commissioners are not carrying out the president's policies.

Myers clearly suggested that independent agencies were unconstitutional. The Supreme Court unanimously rejected that suggestion, though, after Franklin Roosevelt dismissed William E Humphrey, a conservative member of the Federal Trade Commission, in 1935.[19] In the Court's eyes, because the FTC was not merely an administrator of well-defined policy (as postmasters were) but had important roles in making policy and enforcing it through case-specific decisions, the general principles of separation of powers were not violated by giving its

[17] *Panama Refining Co v Ryan* 293 US 388 (1935); *ALA Schechter Poultry Corp v United States* 295 US 495 (1935).

[18] *Whitman v American Trucking Associations, Inc* 531 US 457 (2001).

[19] *Humphrey's Executor v United States* 295 US 602 (1935).

commissioners, hybrids of law-makers, law-enforcers, and law-appliers, independence from presidential control. The Court revisited the issue, in a slightly different doctrinal setting, when it upheld the constitutionality of a statute authorizing the appointment of independent counsels to investigate alleged wrongdoing by high-level executive officials. The investigations clearly could be threatened should the president have the power to control their direction by threatening to fire the investigator. To protect against that, the statute said that the counsel would be named by a special panel of judges, and, more important, that the counsel, once appointed, could be removed only under quite narrow circumstances. Adopting what scholars have called a 'functional' view of separation of powers, the Court concluded that the statute did not disrupt the balance of power between the president and Congress to a degree sufficient to find the statute unconstitutional.[20]

Congress allowed the independent counsel statute to lapse after the unpleasant experience of Independent Counsel Kenneth Starr's investigation of Bill Clinton. Conservatives who regained power with Ronald Reagan's election in 1980 sought to define Reagan's reconstructive presidency, and displace the prior New Deal regime, by reviving the unitary-executive theory. They were prominent supporters of challenges to the independent counsel statue, for example. As a matter of constitutional law, whether we are concerned with the interpretation of the written Constitution or the operation of the efficient one, the theory of the unitary executive has not prevailed.[21]

The Struggle Between the President and Congress Over Administrative Agencies

Congress no longer creates independent agencies in the mold of the Federal Trade Commission. It specifies that officials who have clear

---

[20] *Morrison v Olson* 487 US 654 (1988). For the language of 'functionalism', see P Strauss, 'Formal and Functional Approaches to Separation-of-Powers Questions: A Foolish Inconsistency?' (1972) 72 *Cornell Law Review* 488.

[21] *Free Enterprise Fund v Public Company Accounting Oversight Board*, 130 SCt 3138 (2010), provided some modest support for a weak unitary executive theory in holding unconstitutional a statute creating two levels of independence from presidential removal rather than one. The Securities and Exchange Commission, an independent agency whose members, the Court assumed, are not removable at will, appointed the Board, and could not itself remove Board members at will.

and substantial policy-making authority delegated to them serve at the pleasure of the president, removable at will. Important modern administrative agencies such as those responsible for environmental protection and workplace safety and health are not independent agencies but rather are located within the executive branch, subject to the president's control. Yet, if Congress is to retain some control over the actual implementation of the authority it has delegated to executive officials, it needs some substitute for direct control over personnel.

The substitutes have been formal and informal, with the latter being far more important—another indication of the difference between the written and the efficient Constitution. Indeed, the Supreme Court held unconstitutional one quite effective method of congressional oversight of the executive branch's use of the authority delegated to it, and yet Congress quickly came up with nearly perfect substitutes for the method the Court ruled out of bounds.

Suppose Congress delegates law-making authority to an administrative agency. How can it ensure that the agency is exercising that power in a way of which Congress approves? An obvious mechanism is this: Congress observes what the agency does, and—if it disapproves of the action—directs that the agency rescind it. More formally, the agency has to report to Congress, or to a committee, what it has done, and the committee, one house of Congress, or both houses pass a resolution disapproving the action. This mechanism is known as the legislative veto.

The Supreme Court struck the legislative veto down, in a case where its use was particularly unsympathetic.[22] Reporting to a congressional committee as required, the Department of Justice identified a number of aliens who it had determined were eligible for deportation but for whom deportation would cause an 'extreme hardship' and who therefore would not be deported. One of them was Jagdish Chadha, who had been born in Kenya of Indian parents; neither Kenya nor India regarded him as a citizen, and he came to the United States with a British passport but with no real connections to Britain. Disagreeing with some of the applications of the 'extreme hardship' standard, the committee introduced a resolution to deny effect to the suspension of deportation of those aliens. The House of Representatives adopted the resolution, with the effect of directing that the Department of Justice

---

[22] *Immigration and Naturalization Service v Chadha* 462 US 919 (1983).

carry through with their deportation. The Senate did not consider the resolution nor, of course, was it presented to the president for his signature. Chadha challenged the constitutionality of the legislative veto. Although one justice found the procedure objectionable because its focus on individuals made it seem like an adjudication by a legislative chamber, the Court majority offered a broader challenge to any form of legislative veto. The difficulty, according to the Court, was that legislative vetoes were 'Article I legislative act[s]' that could not be legally effective without agreement from the Senate and signature by the president. According to Chief Justice Warren Burger's majority opinion, legislative acts have 'the purpose and effect of altering the legal rights, duties and relations of persons ... outside the legislative branch.'

The legislative veto here altered Chadha's legal rights—he would be deported rather than remain in the United States—and the duties of the Attorney-General, who would have to deport Chadha contrary to his determination of 'extreme hardship'.

On the facts, perhaps the legislative veto here seems unfair to the alien. Yet, the Court's analysis is hardly invulnerable. Its concern was that Congress was improperly altering Chadha's legal rights when it exercised a legislative veto. But one could have as easily said that Chadha had no right to the agency's outcome until the time for exercising the legislative veto had passed. And the legislative-veto process provided an effective way for Congress to supervise the way in which the Department of Justice was administering its delegated authority to suspend deportation for 'extreme hardship'. The Court responded:

> The choices we discern as having been made in the Constitutional Convention can impose burdens on governmental processes that often seem clumsy, inefficient, even unworkable ... With all the obvious flaws of delay, untidiness, and potential for abuse, we have not yet found a better way to preserve freedom than by making the exercise of power subject to the carefully crafted restraints spelled out in the Constitution.

Exactly how those restraints were 'spelled out' is unclear: The only provisions of the written Constitution the Court cited were the Presentment Clause, which requires that all bills that have passed both the House and Senate be presented to the president for signature, and a parallel clause saying that 'Every Order, Resolution, or Vote to which the Concurrence of the Senate and the House of Representatives may be necessary ... shall be presented to the President'. The Court underlined 'shall be' when it quoted this provision, but typographical emphasis cannot overcome the problem that the very issue in the case was whether the House's veto *was* a vote that required the Senate's concurrence.

Even on the Court's own terms, of course, alternative mechanisms for legislative control can be easily devised. The most obvious is to shift from exercising the legislative veto after the agency has acted to delaying the effective date of the agency's action until after Congress has had a chance to disapprove the action: The agency reports to Congress what it *proposes* to do, and Congress indicates its disapproval. Because the agency has not acted, the disapproval violates no one's vested legal rights.

That might seem too formalistic to overcome the Court's concern that the legislative veto allows Congress to do something significant without getting both houses to agree and getting the president to sign legislation, although devising a solid constitutional argument against this 'deferred implementation' veto is quite difficult. Another technique allows the agency's action to take effect, but places legislation that would change the result on a 'fast track' for consideration. This is not quite as good a substitute, because to deny effect to the agency's action Congress must have enough votes to overcome the possibility of a presidential veto.

We can understand 'fast track' legislation and the like as efforts to work around the impediments the written constitution, as interpreted by the Supreme Court, places in the way of the efficient constitution. With the development of an efficient constitution for divided and strongly polarized government, such workarounds may become increasingly difficult to implement. An example is the practice of 'recess appointments' made by presidents unable to secure confirmation of their nominees in a polarized Senate. Taking advantage of a constitutional provision written when Congress met relatively infrequently, presidents increased the number of appointments they made during brief congressional recesses. Congress responded by refusing to declare a formal recess, instead suspending its sessions for periods of three days or so. The Supreme Court held that appointments made during those three-day periods were not authorized by the Constitution, though were Congress to suspend its sessions for ten days, the president could make recess appointments.[23] The three-day recesses may be

---

[23] *National Labor Relations Board v Noel Canning* 134 SCt 2550 (2014).

understood as Congress's effort to work around the president's use of the recess appointment power, but the Supreme Court's decision may make it difficult for the president to devise a workaround for the new congressional practice.

The formal mechanisms Congress uses to supervise the operation of the executive branch are less important than informal ones. Congress clearly has oversight powers, and an agency that adopts a regulation—or implements delegated authority—of which Congress disapproves may find itself in political trouble. Congress may deny it funds to implement the regulation. The agency's general budget request might run into trouble. The agency head may be called before a congressional committee, or before a number of committees, to explain and defend the action. Appearing at these hearings is a burden on the agency head, disrupting the agency's daily work. Agencies would prefer to avoid any of these forms of congressional oversight. One way to do so is to refrain from adopting the regulation, or to work informally with members of Congress in shaping it. Functionally, members of Congress have enough political weapons in their hands that the elimination of the formal mechanism of the legislative veto has little effect. Indeed, Congress continues to include provisions for legislative vetoes in the statutes it enacts. The *Chadha* decision means that everyone knows that Congress cannot lawfully exercise such a veto, and it has never tried. Yet, the insertion of the legislative-veto provisions in the legislation signals to the executive branch that Congress will be particularly alert in exercising oversight with respect to the subject matter the provisions identify. A prudent agency head will take the existence of the provisions as a signal to take care in exercising delegated authority.

Informal interactions between agencies and members of Congress weaken the president's ability to control agencies that are nominally within a hierarchically organized executive branch in which everyone reports upward ending at the president. During the 1960s and 1970s, and continuing in a somewhat weaker form through the end of the twentieth century, these informal contacts were bolstered by another feature of US politics that further weakened presidential control over the executive bureaucracy. Representatives of private interests—'lobbyists'—and, later, representatives of non-governmental organizations who presented themselves as speaking for the public interest play an important role in the development and administration of the law. Disparaged because they are said to channel campaign contributions to legislators to 'buy' votes for the interests they represent, as noted in chapter two lobbyists are more important when, and because, they provide information to members of Congress about policy issues and, importantly, about how executive agencies are exercising the delegated authorities they already have. Lobbyists deal with agencies on a routine basis and know what they are doing, probably in more detail than even members of the president's staff. The effect was to create what was called an 'iron triangle' consisting of members of Congress, bureaucrats and lobbyists. The iron triangle, it was said, was able to resist efforts by the president to direct agency policy: Bureaucrats whose favored programs were threatened by presidential initiatives could call on the lobbyists with whom they dealt, who would then contact influential members of Congress, who would tell the administration to withdraw its initiatives.

The iron triangle was probably never as impenetrable as this description suggests. It resulted from the long resilience of the New Deal regime, and weakened as that regime became vulnerable. The reconstructive presidency of Ronald Reagan attempted to transform the iron triangle, and to some extent succeeded over a two-decade period extending beyond Reagan's presidency and even beyond that of his immediate successor in re-creating an iron triangle of lobbyists, bureaucrats and the presidency. The older iron triangle retained some strength as the residue of the New Deal regime, and as the Reagan Revolution itself became vulnerable, the two competing iron triangles staggered on.

The Struggle Between the President and Congress Over the Budget

The national budget process is both complex and simple: complex because it, unlike other forms of legislation, appears to be regulated by legislation setting out procedures for dealing with budget issues, and simple, because that framework legislation has essentially no effect, making the budget process no different from the processes for enacting any other statutes.

The framework legislation requires that the president submit a budget each year, and that Congress appropriate money by the end of each fiscal year. The president does indeed submit a budget, but the president's proposals are regularly described as 'dead on arrival'. Rather than using the president's proposals as the basis for developing appropriations legislation, Congress typically uses the prior year's budget as its guideline. Then individual members seek support for projects they are particularly interested in, and a fair amount of bargaining among members occurs. In the end, there is a budget, developed unsystematically and, notably, without any real effort to match expenditures with revenues.

Presidents regularly criticize Congress for disregarding their budget submissions and for adding unnecessary expenditures of primary local benefit, referring to such provisions as 'pork', excess fat on the president's lean budget. Members of Congress respond that the projects do indeed serve important public purposes that they, closer than the president to their communities, understand better. Recently presidents have criticized members of Congress as well for 'earmarks' in the budget. Here is how earmarks work: Congress creates some general program, for example for funding scientific research, and appropriates a specified amount to be awarded by an executive branch agency based on the agency's evaluation of the merits of proposals submitted to it. An earmark designates a specific project, for example for research at the University of Northern Iowa into conversion of corn into ethanol, to receive funding without going through the agency's evaluation process. Presidents criticize earmarks for increasing government expenditures, but it is unclear exactly why they do. The real effect of earmarks is to transfer the power to identify projects for funding from the executive branch agency to Congress itself. Earmarking is thus part of the struggle between Congress and the president over substantive policy, not over the size of the budget. The constitutional politics of the budget are no different from the constitutional politics of other matters.

Conclusion

Even as the iron triangles lost their tight grip on the way in which executive bureaucracies worked in the late twentieth century, presidents continued to face obstacles caused by the accumulated residue of prior regimes, as Skowronek observed. The efficient Constitution, then, enables a president to be reconstructive only by determined action sustained over nearly the entire course of a two-term presidency and perhaps beyond. Yet, near the end of the second term, the president is a lame duck, and may find it increasingly difficult to continue the project of transforming the bureaucracy, and a successor 'affiliated' president faces his or her own difficulties in struggling to extend the reconstructive president's gains while making an independent mark on policy. Presidents who assert that they are the head of a unitary executive branch are right only when political forces are arrayed particularly favorably to them, which is increasingly rare.

THE UNITARY EXECUTIVE IN FOREIGN AFFAIRS

Advocates of expansive presidential power argue that the president's powers in foreign affairs are even more extensive than in domestic affairs. The Constitution designates the president as commander-in-chief of the armed forces. Although some contend that this provision simply prevents Congress from naming a favored military officer commander-in-chief, most scholars agree that the commander-in-chief power has substantive content, giving the president authority to make military decisions even in the face of congressional disapproval. As we have seen, advocates of presidential power point to a difference between the language of the so-called vesting clauses in Article I, dealing with congressional power, and Article II. The difference, it is argued, assumes that the executive power has some substantive content independent of anything else in Article II. And the primary candidate for that content is some sort of special authority in connection with foreign affairs. Finally, advocates of strong presidential powers in foreign affairs argue that the 'take Care' clause has special resonance in that setting. They argue that the president's duty to 'take Care that the Laws be faithfully executed' includes a duty to preserve the nation, even if doing so requires that the president take actions that are otherwise unauthorized or even unconstitutional.[24] As Abraham Lincoln put it in a related context, 'Are all the laws, but one, to go unexecuted, and the government itself to go to pieces, lest that one be violated?'.[25]

---

[24] MS Paulsen, 'The Constitution of Necessity' (2004) 79 *Notre Dame L Rev* 1257.
[25] Abraham Lincoln, Message to Congress, 4 July 1861. Lincoln was referring to his suspension of the writ of habeas corpus pending Congress's convening after Southern armed forces attacked a national military post at Fort Sumter, South Carolina. Lincoln contended that his suspension of the writ was not unconstitutional under the circumstances, but added the quoted line as a back-up position.

For much of the period after World War II, presidential assertions of expansive authority in foreign affairs were relatively uncontroversial. Political elites, including congressional leaders, joined in a national security consensus that the exigencies of the US confrontation with the Soviet Union required that the president be given a largely free hand to develop and implement national security policy. That consensus began to dissolve as the American involvement in Vietnam stretched out. At first individual members of Congress began to challenge the president's assertions of expansive power, and eventually Congress enacted laws—over the president's veto—seemingly imposing real limits on the president's power. The end of the Cold War damped down conflicts between the president and Congress, but they were revived in heightened form after the September 11 attacks by al-Qaeda on US territory. President George W Bush argued that his authority in foreign affairs authorized him to develop surveillance programs that some regarded as unconstitutionally intrusive on privacy, and other quite expansive assertions of presidential authority. As the United States seemed to become mired in a war in Iraq, the constitutional conflicts between president and Congress escalated. Politics mattered here: President Bush was able to implement his programs without serious obstruction when Congress was controlled by his Republican party, but ran into difficulty—which he usually overcame—when congressional control reverted to Democrats after the elections in 2006.

The Basics of Constitutional Doctrine: The *Steel Seizure* Case

Justice Robert Jackson's opinion in *Youngstown Sheet & Tube Co v Sawyer* (also known as the *Steel Seizure* case) provides the framework for thinking about presidential power in foreign affairs (even though, taking the administration at its word, the justices considered the case itself to involve only domestic affairs). After World War II the United States experienced the usual economic difficulties associated with the transition from war to peace. Prices for consumer goods had been frozen during the war, and labor unions had tempered their wage demands. When the war ended, pent-up demand for consumer goods needed to be satisfied, as did union demands for wage increases. The combination raised the possibility of severe inflation. Over several years, unions and employers gradually worked out accommodations that entailed modest increases in wages and similarly modest increases in prices. By 1950 the steel industry and its workers had reached an agreement of this sort. The government, though, imposed a freeze on price and wage increases. The steel unions threatened a strike. To pacify them, President Harry Truman appointed a commission to examine whether the wage increases the unions had negotiated were justified. The commission's report said that the wage increases were justified, but the steel companies were unwilling to raise wages while prices were still frozen. The unions again threatened a strike. Concerned that interrupting steel production would rather quickly cause difficulties in procuring weapons and equipment for the armed forces then engaged in the Korean War, President Truman issued an Executive Order directing that the Secretary of Commerce take control of the steel companies. The effect would have been to allow the government to order wage increases without the steel companies' permission. The president claimed that the Constitution supported his action through its grant of the executive power to the president and through its designation of the president as 'commander in chief'.

The Supreme Court rejected President Truman's claims.[26] According to Justice Hugo Black's majority opinion, the commander-in-chief power might support such actions in a 'theater of war' but that 'expanding concept' could not extend 'to tak[ing] possession of private property in order to keep labor disputes from stopping production'. Nor did any statutes authorize the seizures. Two statutes did give the president power to seize manufacturing plants if various conditions were satisfied, but the administration refused to take the steps that would have satisfied those conditions, largely for political reasons.

Justice Jackson's concurring opinion made those statutory provisions central to his analysis of presidential power. He identified three 'practical situations' in which questions of presidential power might arise, of which two are important here. First, Justice Jackson said, there were cases in which the president acted 'pursuant to an express or implied authorization' from Congress. In such cases 'his authority is at its maximum, for it includes all that he possesses in his own right plus all that Congress can delegate'. In contrast were the cases, of which *Youngstown* was an example, in which the president acted in a manner 'incompatible

---

[26] *Youngstown Sheet & Tube Co v Sawyer* 343 US 579 (1952).

with the expressed or implied will of Congress'. There, Justice Jackson said, the president's power was 'at its lowest ebb, for then he can rely only upon his own constitutional powers minus any constitutional powers of Congress over the matter'.

Justice Jackson's approach initially shifts attention from the Constitution to the statute books, as the president and his or her critics look for statutory authorization or prohibition. When a president's assertion of power has become contentious, the search in the statute books has a common structure in which the contending sides try to figure out what old statutes mean in a new situation. The statutes need not be all that old; they simply have to have been adopted when there was no disagreement between Congress and the president about what the right answer was to the questions then on the table.[27]

'Contemporary imponderables' matter even when the Court searches for statutory authorization. *Dames & Moore v Reagan* involved a challenge to the constitutionality of the agreement to settle claims by US corporations against Iran as part of the deal negotiated to release hostages held by Iran.[28] Upholding the agreement, the Court struggled to find authorizations in a number of statutes read in light of historical practice, but almost certainly more important were the facts that a popular president supported the deal and that the political consequences of overturning the deal would have been substantial and probably bad for the United States.

Another example of how Jackson's categories work in practice is the controversy, starting around 2005 and extending to the present, over the legality of a program adopted by the George W Bush administration to engage in surveillance of communications between non-US citizens who it believed were connected to al-Qaeda and recipients in the United States. As a general matter, similar forms of surveillance were regulated by provisions in the Foreign Intelligence Surveillance Act (FISA), adopted in 1978 and periodically amended thereafter, including in the aftermath of the September 11 attacks on the World Trade Center. Some aspects of the Bush administration's surveillance program were inconsistent with FISA's requirements. The map provided by Justice Jackson made the first question raised in the controversy whether any

---

[27] The possibility that a statute was enacted by overriding a presidential veto is discussed below.

[28] 453 US 654 (1981).

statute authorized or prohibited those aspects of the program. Critics of the program said that FISA probably expressly and certainly implicitly prohibited surveillance programs that did not comply with its requirements. The administration responded that the statute authorizing the president to use military force against those responsible for the September 11 attacks should be interpreted to authorize the president to use all techniques ordinarily used by military commanders to determine an enemy's plans, including surveillance on the battlefield. And, in the circumstances presented by al-Qaeda's manner of operations, 'battlefield' surveillance could occur anywhere a person associated with al-Qaeda was found.

In addition, the administration contended that, even if FISA purported to prohibit the surveillance program, the president had power as commander-in-chief to determine the tactics to be used against al-Qaeda, and surveillance was a tactic. True, Justice Jackson's framework implied that the president's power to implement such a program would be at its 'lowest ebb' but that metaphor does not imply that there is no residual presidential power when Congress purports to prohibit presidential action.[29]

Of course there is much more statutory, constitutional, and doctrinal detail to the arguments about the surveillance program. Once we have seen the structure of the argument, though, we can move immediately to an analysis of how the arguments are resolved. The answer here, as we have seen elsewhere, is that the arguments are resolved by politics, which itself has a structure. In foreign affairs the president has the advantage of being able to move first and quickly. Those characteristics were among those the framers thought important: The president would have confidential information readily available, and as a single decision-maker would be able to select a course of action more quickly than the multimember Congress. And, once the president moves, he or she enjoys, at least for a while, what political scientists have called a 'rally-round-the-flag' effect.[30] Politically astute presidents may take advantage

---

[29] In general President Obama scaled back claims that his actions against terrorism were founded in important part on a president's duty to defend the nation against 'sudden attacks', and relied heavily on existing statutory authorities. The constitutional duty to defend the nation continued to play a back-up role in some arguments for Obama's administration policies, though.

[30] See, eg, MJ Hetherington and M Nelson, 'Anatomy of a Rally Effect: George W Bush and the War on Terrorism' (Jan 2003) *PS: Political Science & Politics* 37 (describing the effect and providing references to the political science literature).

of the moment to propose to Congress wide-ranging legislation authorizing a great deal, not merely to ensure that presidential actions fall into Justice Jackson's first category but for the more important political reason of making more difficult opposition in the future from those who signed on at the outset. Yet, at these same early moments presidents may not know exactly what they will want to do and, again more important, may not want to attract immediate political opposition if their plans are described openly. As a result, statutes enacted early will often do no more than provide the basis for arguing that Congress has implicitly authorized the president's actions. If the president's actions become unpopular opponents will be able to argue that the statute's ambiguous language is actually a prohibition, not an authorization.

The longer the time span between the statute's adoption and the occurrence of opposition, the less helpful are the statutory arguments and the more the purely constitutional arguments come into focus, although it is worth observing that *all* the legal questions associated with the government's actions after the September 11 attacks proceeded no farther than the statutory step as of early 2008. When the Constitution itself comes into play, politics matters: The key determinants of whether the president will be able to execute controversial policies effectively are, first, how strong the political opposition is; second, how strongly the president's allies in Congress—that is, the members of the president's party—support the president; and third, how effective the president's allies are in deploying the legislative tools they have available to them to block the president's opponents from doing anything substantial to limit the president's power. President Truman lost the *Steel Seizure* case, one might say, because he was a deeply unpopular president at the time, without much support even from his own Democratic party. President George W Bush was more successful in the last years of his presidency, despite his personal unpopularity and the public distaste for the war in Iraq, because the Republican party in Congress was united in supporting him and had enough votes in the Senate and House to stop congressional Democrats from taking effective action against the president's programs.

The Power to Declare War

We come, finally, to what has often—and oddly—been the primary focus of discussions of the power of the president and Congress in foreign affairs: the power to place the nation at war. The Constitution's language is clear: Article I gives Congress the power 'to declare War'. Initially the language was 'make War' but delegates at the Constitutional Convention were concerned that such language would disable the nation from acting promptly against what one speaker called 'sudden attacks'. The shift in language has had unfortunate consequences. Some critics of presidential power are dismayed that it is linguistically possible to read 'declare War' to mean 'create the legal state of affairs known in international law as "war"' without implying anything about the president's unilateral power to deploy military force. Other critics are dismayed that the United States has regularly gotten involved in large-scale military conflicts even though Congress has not adopted something formally labeled a declaration of war.[31] The latter point is largely irrelevant. The 'declare War' clause does not require that Congress adopt a document using the magic words 'declare war'. All it does require is congressional action that has the effect of committing US armed forces to armed conflict. And, for political reasons, presidents rarely if ever deploy military forces in a way that amounts to creating a state of war without getting *some* sort of congressional authorization in advance— although if military operations go badly, members of Congress will say that they did not intend to authorize quite what the president has done.

Congress attempted to regulate the process by which the United States got involved in major military operations in response to the experience of the Vietnam War. Over President Richard Nixon's veto, Congress adopted the War Powers Resolution in 1973.[32] The Resolution requires that the president submit a report to Congress within two days of the introduction of US armed forces into hostilities, and that the use of armed forces shall end after 60 days unless Congress authorizes the continuing use of force in some statute other than an appropriations act to support the military operations. Presidents have regularly asserted that the Resolution unconstitutionally limits their power as commander-in-chief, and just as regularly have submitted the reports referred to in the Resolution, albeit ordinarily with the grudging formulation that they are doing so 'consistent with' the Resolution but not because they are required to do so. And Congress has ordinarily taken actions that

---

[31] Recent controversies involve US involvement in operations in support of rebels against Muammar Qaddafi in Libya and against the so-called Islamic State in the Levant (ISIL), although the Obama administration sought to keep the involvement at a level below 'large scale.'

[32] 50 USC §§ 1541–48.

are, again, 'consistent with' the Resolution's requirement for continuing authorization. Further, since 1973 Congress has adopted express authorizations for the use of military force—twice in respect to actions against Iraq, once in respect to those responsible for the September 11 attacks—more regularly than in the decades before 1973. For all the attention the 'declare War' clause attracts in the literature on the Constitution, it is no longer a provision that makes a difference in real controversies, because the political accommodation expressed in the War Powers Resolution and the express authorizations for the use of military force seem to have eliminated any real political controversy, and therefore any real constitutional one.

Some Generalizations about the Constitutional Politics of Executive Power in Foreign Affairs

Suppose we consider the political constitution along two dimensions, one involving the structure of the party system and the other whether the national government is under unified or divided party control.[33] The classical version of separation of powers, in which ambition counters ambition, will arise when we have divided government with ideologically unified parties. Not the interests of the man but the interests of the party will be conjoined to the interests of the place, as a president and his or her supporters in Congress seek to advance presidential prerogatives against the resistance of a unified competing party in Congress.[34] Contests will be resolved by the balance of political forces, with each side deploying the weapons available to it in political contention: internal legislative rules to obstruct or structure the progress of a proposal through Congress, congressional oversight hearings, the rhetorical resources of the presidency, and the like.

---

[33] As argued above, divided government can occur even when the government is nominally unified, if the minority party in Congress is able to use procedural devices, such as the filibuster in the United States Senate, that have the effect of imposing supermajority requirements (where the required supermajority is larger than the actual one).

[34] Even if the competition is only for the moment, with the party controlling Congress hoping to take over the presidency in the next election. That is, one can expect a party that strongly defends presidential prerogatives when it controls the presidency but not Congress to abandon that position if their opponents win the presidency and they take over Congress.

The situation is not dramatically different with divided government and parties that are coalitions. Added to the mix will be efforts by the supporters of presidential or congressional prerogative to peel away some members of the party controlling the presidency or Congress. This will be possible to the extent that the issues that divide and unite coalitions include either issues about congressional and presidential power as such,[35] or about the specific policy issue that divides the president and the party controlling Congress.[36] Again, the contest will be resolved politically, although we can expect the president to prevail somewhat more often here than in the prior scenario because the party controlling Congress will have to expend more political resources to bring enough members of the president's party to their side than they have to do when they are ideologically unified in opposition to the president. The president's prospects improve further when there is unified government with parties that are coalitions, although presidential success is not guaranteed. The reason is that there is some chance that the minority party may be able to pull away enough members of the president's (coalitional) party for them to prevail on specific issues.[37] The final category is unified government with ideologically organized parties.[38] Here the president gets what he asks for.

The discussion so far has been rather skeletal. What follows attempts to show how some flesh might be put on the bones of the account.

[35] In this configuration, we might describe a 'presidential party' consisting of political officials in the executive branch and some members of Congress, and a 'congressional party' consisting almost entirely of members of Congress, although perhaps with some allies in the executive branch. See JM Burns, *The Deadlock of Democracy: Four-Party Politics in America* (Englewood Cliffs, NJ, Prentice-Hall, 1963) 241–64. For completeness, I should mention also the possibility that some of those who work in the executive bureaucracy might act as members of the congressional party or even the opposition party (for example, by leaking information for political purposes).

[36] That is, it does not matter much whether, for example, a Congress controlled by Democrats opposes presidential power as such or a Republican president's policies about military tribunals, as long as some Republicans in Congress care about either congressional power or oppose the president's policies on the merits.

[37] In the most general terms, this describes the development of national domestic policy during the presidency of John F Kennedy and the first years of the presidency of William J Clinton, when Democrats also controlled Congress but were unable to enact the full presidential agenda because the minority Republicans obtained enough votes from Democrats to block presidential initiatives.

[38] Or, perhaps, unified government with the majority party being ideologically coherent and the minority being a coalitional party (or closer to being one than to being ideologically coherent).

First, the 'rally-round-the-flag' effect increases support for the president in all party configurations. That is, it may push the political system toward unified government. This effect dissipates, though, and a formally divided government might seem more unified for a while, then revert to its prior divided state.

Second, assume that we are in one of the configurations of power in which some degree of congressional ambition seeks to counter presidential ambition. How might the politics of that confrontation play itself out? Some suggest that the president has a systematic advantage over Congress.[39] The executive branch is nominally unified under the president, and so can develop a single position, whereas Congress has many members who seek to advance both a general view and more parochial interests. The president has readier access to relevant information than Congress does, and can keep the information secret even from Congress.[40] Finally, the president can act quickly, whereas Congress takes time to deliberate and enact legislation.

One might wonder, though, about whether these characteristics give the president much of an advantage over Congress, except in the very short run. It is easy to exaggerate the unity within the executive: it is part of the folk-lore of Washington, for example, that the Department of State and the Department of Defense are regularly at odds over the proper response to external threats. Leaks from within the executive bureaucracy are common, and not always at the behest of the president. Specialized committees and their professional staff members can over time acquire expertise and information equivalent to, or exceeding, that of the president's political appointees and employees in the executive bureaucracy. Congress can organize itself to engage in real-time oversight of executive operations, and at least has attempted to do so by

---

[39] See, eg, E Posner and A Vermeule, *Terror in the Balance: Security, Liberty, and the Courts* 47(New York, Oxford University Press, 2007) (including among the 'institutional disadvantages' of Congress 'lack of information about what is happening' and 'inability to act quickly and with one voice'); *ibid* at 170 ('congressional deliberation is slow and unsuited for emergencies. Congress has trouble keeping secrets and is always vulnerable to obstructionism at the behest of members of Congress who place the interests of their constituents ahead of those of the nation as a whole').

[40] *See United States v Curtiss-Wright Corp* 299 US 304, 320 (1936) (in foreign affairs, the president 'has his confidential sources of information').

requiring that the president notify a select group of congressional leaders of some operations.[41]

Focusing on oversight rather than legislation brings an additional consideration into view. Congress and the president interact regularly, and on a large range of issues. Repeat players, including the president, have to keep the entire playing field in mind. A president who capitalizes on a momentary advantage with respect to a particular emergency-related issue might find himself facing retaliation, not over emergency-related issues, but over nominations to unrelated executive positions or over some purely domestic program.

None of this is to say that claims about the president's advantages in emergencies are entirely mistaken, but only that one can easily overstate them and, in particular, overestimate the extent to which temporary advantages translate into permanent ones. The political configurations—unified versus divided government, the types of political parties we have—are more important in structuring presidential and congressional power in foreign affairs than the differences between the institutional characteristics of the executive branch and Congress.

CONCLUSION

Justice Jackson's *Youngstown* opinion described a second category, where the president acted 'in the absence of a congressional grant or denial of authority'. There the president could rely on the office's inherent powers in what Jackson called a 'twilight zone' in which the actual distribution of power between president and Congress was uncertain. In that zone, Jackson continued: 'any actual test of power is likely to depend on the imperatives of events and contemporary imponderables

---

[41] National Security Act of 1957, 50 USC § 413(a)(1), provides that '[t]he President shall ensure that the congressional intelligence committees are kept fully and currently informed of the intelligence activities of the United States,' and § 413(b)(1) provides, 'the Director of Central Intelligence ... shall keep the congressional intelligence committees fully and currently informed of all covert actions...' The latter provision has come to be understood as allowing disclosure only to the so-called 'gang of Eight', the party leaders and chairs and ranking members of the House and Senate Intelligence Committees. See S Shane, 'Report Questions Legality of Briefings on Surveillance' *New York Times* (New York 19 January 2006 at p A19) (describing the controversy over whether disclosure of a surveillance program to the 'Gang of Eight' was consistent with this National Security Act).

rather than on abstract theories of law'. This is plainly unsatisfactory as a legal test courts could apply in the twilight zone. But it is decidedly helpful in illuminating how contests of power are actually resolved. We can take Jackson's mention of 'the imperatives of events and contemporary imponderables' to refer to politics. And indeed politics actually resolves contests of power even when Congress has authorized presidential action (although such contests are unlikely to arise when today's Congress authorized the action at issue) and when it has purported to prohibit presidential action.

We can see a single pattern in every area of executive authority. The written Constitution makes arguments about strong, even exclusive, presidential power available to presidents who want to exercise such power. Sometimes the arguments prevail, but not because they are commanded by the text or any other sources of constitutional interpretation. The written Constitution provides a structure within which politicians affiliated with major political parties struggle to dominate. Sometimes presidents prevail in those struggles, sometimes Congress does. The key determinants appear to be whether the government is divided or unified, where in political time a president finds himself or herself, and—crucially—the relative political talents of presidents and their adversaries. The written Constitution tells us almost nothing about these elements of the efficient constitution.

FURTHER READING

Balkin, JM and Levinson, S, 'The Processes of Constitutional Change: From Partisan Entrenchment to the National Surveillance State' (2006) 75 *Fordham Law Review* 489 (describing the possibility that recent developments in presidential power will persist).

Barron, DJ and Lederman, MS, 'The Commander-in-Chief at the Lowest Ebb' (parts I and II) (2008) 121 *Harvard L Rev* 689, 941 (a two-part article reviewing the constitutional history and practice of congressional regulation of the president's powers in conducting military operations).

Posner, EA and Vermeule, A, *The Executive Unbound: After the Madisonian Republic* (New York, Oxford University Press, 2011).

Pozen, DE, 'The Leaky Leviathan: Why the Government Condemns and Condones Unlawful Disclosures of Information' (2013) 127 *Harvard Law Review* 512.

Tushnet, M, 'The Political Constitution of Emergency Powers: Some Lessons from *Hamdan*' (2007) 91 *Minnesota L Rev* 1451 (describes various arrays of political power and their implications in emergency situations).

Wildavsky, AB and Caiden, N, *The New Politics of the Budgetary Process* (4th edn New York, Longman, 2001).

4

The Constitutional Politics of the Judicial Branch

Judicial Selection – Judicial Review and Judicial Supremacy – Political Constraints on the Jurisdiction of the Federal Courts – Doctrinal Constraints on the Jurisdiction of the Federal Courts – Standing – Conclusion

THE US SUPREME Court is at the top of a hierarchically organized, though somewhat complex, judicial system. There are two sub-systems of courts: one in the states and the other for the national government.[1] The courts in the national judicial system are usually called the federal courts. State courts and the lower-level federal courts have trial-level courts and appellate courts.[2] Most American courts are generalist courts, with jurisdiction over claims of any sort.[3]

---

[1] The written Constitution requires that there be a Supreme Court, and gives Congress discretion to create lower-level national courts. Congress created lower-level courts in the First Judiciary Act, enacted in 1789. The jurisdiction of those courts has varied over the centuries, but the details of lower-court jurisdiction need not be explored here except when specific changes in that jurisdiction illuminate more general questions about how the national courts fit into the constitutional system as a whole.

[2] Most states have intermediate appellate courts and a supreme court. The names of these courts vary. For example, New York's trial courts are called 'supreme courts' and its highest court is the Court of Appeals. Massachusetts's highest court is the Supreme Judicial Court.

[3] There are some specialized courts in both sub-systems. Many states have specialized trial-level family courts, with appeals to the generalist appellate courts. Some state courts authorize only a specialized court to hear claims against the

The US Supreme Court, on which this chapter focuses, has discretionary authority to hear appeals from decisions on matters of national law—statutory as well as constitutional—by the appellate courts in the national court system and by the highest state court authorized to decide the question of national law. Usually, but not always, that court is the state's supreme court: in one notable case the US Supreme Court heard an appeal from a decision by the Police Court of the city of Louisville, Kentucky, which had imposed a small fine on the defendant, because under state law there were no appeals from such courts when small fines were imposed.[4]

In the terms used by students of comparative constitutional law, the United States has a decentralized system of constitutional review, because (subject only to scattered statutory restrictions) every court in the country has the authority to decide a constitutional question, and the US Supreme Court is a generalist constitutional court, because it has authority to determine the meaning of national law—statutory or constitutional.[5] Yet, unlike some other constitutional courts, the US Supreme Court has essentially complete discretion to determine which cases it will decide on the merits.[6] This allows the Court to engage in

government. The national court system includes specialized trial-level courts for claims against the national government, a specialized court for tax matters, and a court of appeals with exclusive authority to decide patent cases; the latter court has jurisdiction over some other types of cases as well.

[4] *Thompson v City of Louisville* 362 US 199 (1960).

[5] As a result, there is no controversy in the United States over the practice of construing a national statute to avoid holding it unconstitutional, even if the construction is somewhat strained. There is somewhat more controversy over the practice of construing a national statute to avoid deciding a difficult constitutional question, although the practice is reasonably well settled. The concern is that this latter practice allows the courts to create a 'shadow' constitutional rule—one that influences statutory interpretation even though it might not be adopted as a constitutional interpretation were the question directly presented. Importantly, in cases coming from the state courts the national courts have no authority to construe state statutes to avoid holding them unconstitutional; they must take the state statute to mean what the state courts said it meant, and decide only whether, given that interpretation, the statute is constitutional or not.

[6] The Court operates with a 'rule of four', meaning that four justices—one short of a majority—can set a case for consideration on the merits. For a discussion of how the discretion to choose cases for decision is exercised, see HW Perry, *Deciding to Decide: Agenda Setting in the United States Supreme Court* (Cambridge, MA, Harvard University Press, 1991).

explicit or implicit political calculations about what it should do: it may decide to avoid taking a case because the justices, or enough of them, fear that resolving the case on the merits would be too politically controversial; or it may decide to decide a case on the merits precisely because the justices, or enough of them, believe that doing so would resolve an important political controversy—and in doing so might enhance the Court's own power.

As political scientist Martin Shapiro observed, courts are components of a nation's political system,[7] and the most interesting questions about the US courts is how they mesh with the other components of the political system. This chapter examines the political dimensions of the judicial branch by discussing two main topics—judicial selection and the limits, political and constitutional, on the national courts' power to decide constitutional questions.

JUDICIAL SELECTION

Typically, in both the state and the national systems judges are chosen from the practicing bar. They usually have some experience in the private practice of law, and many have been prosecutors for the government or have served as government lawyers in other capacities. That commonality aside, the processes for selecting judges differ dramatically between the state systems and the national system.

State Courts

The vast majority of judges in the state systems are elected. Jacksonians in the 1820s and 1830s advocated judicial elections as a way of democratizing the government and displacing established elites. By the early twentieth century advocates of 'good government' were dismayed by what they saw as the partisan corruption of what should have been a politically neutral judicial process. They proposed a system of merit selection, in which leaders of the bar and the judiciary would serve on a commission, along with a few non-lawyer members, to develop a list of

---

[7] M Shapiro, *Courts: A Comparative and Political Analysis* (Chicago, University of Chicago Press, 1981).

possible judges, which was then submitted to the governor who would choose someone on the list. This plan has been adopted in a few states, but selection by means of ordinary elections remains the prevailing system. The details of judicial elections vary. In some states judges are initially appointed by the state's governor, then face a 'retention' election in which voters are asked whether the judge should continue to serve. Some judicial elections are formally non-partisan; in other states the elections are ordinary partisan contests, with each major party nominating a preferred candidate. In the late twentieth century judicial elections came to resemble ordinary partisan elections even more closely. State courts revised the law of liability for accidental injury to favor plaintiffs, partly because voters tended to see themselves more as plaintiffs suing large corporations than as consumers facing higher prices because of more expansive liability rules, and partly because trial lawyers representing plaintiffs gave substantial contributions to judges campaigning for election or re-election. Corporate interests responded by making equally large contributions to candidates who, they hoped, would be more business-friendly once elected, and the costs of judicial elections escalated enormously. By the first decade of the twenty-first century, no one was surprised, though some were dismayed, that in a few judicial elections the total campaign costs for both sides exceeded $10 million.

The US Supreme Court too treated judicial elections as ordinary elections, applying the First Amendment's protection of free expression to attempts to limit campaign promises by judges no differently from the Amendment's application to elections for legislators. *Minnesota Republican Party v White* involved that state's judicial code of ethics, which was interpreted to prohibit judicial candidates from announcing their position on issues that might come before them if they were elected.[8] A candidate for a position on the state supreme court challenged this 'announce' provision on the ground that it restricted his ability to develop a campaign platform, which he believed should consist precisely of an announcement to the electorate of his positions on important issues of legal policy and interpretation.

The Supreme Court agreed, with the Court's conservatives upholding the First Amendment challenge and its liberals voting to reject it. According to Justice Antonin Scalia, prohibiting a candidate from announcing his or her position on legal questions—even those likely to

---

[8]   536 US 765 (2002).

come before the court after the candidate's election—denied the candidate the ability to make 'relevant' information available to the electorate. And denying candidates that ability did not serve strong interests in impartiality in any useful sense, he continued. The ban extended well beyond a prohibition on announcing what the candidate would do in a particular pending case; candidates necessarily brought to their positions views they had developed throughout their lives and merely announcing what those views were would not make the candidates less impartial in any useful sense; and there was no reason to think that, having stated a position on a legal question, a candidate once elected would be less open-minded than if he or she held the position but had not announced it. Justice Scalia observed accurately that those who supported the ban on announcing positions were attempting to structure judicial elections so that they were not like ordinary elections. The case exposed the tension between good-government reformers' interest in judicial selection based on merit and the very fact of judicial elections: The 'announce' provision was an awkward attempt to convert judicial elections into a merit-based selection system.

Federal Courts

Selection of federal judges (again, those in the national court system) is different. The written Constitution provides that the president 'shall nominate, and by and with the Advice and Consent of the Senate, shall appoint' judges for the federal courts. The Senate has never exercised its power to 'advise' the president on judicial appointments in any formal way, although informal advice is common. The president, then, takes the initiative in presenting the Senate with nominees for the federal courts, and the Senate's role is simply to vote 'yes' or 'no' on the appointment.

The way the executive branch handles the nomination process varies depending on the president's political interest in judicial appointments. The task of evaluating potential nominees is divided between the Department of Justice and the executive office of the president—that is, the White House and specifically the office of the president's counsel. This produces a natural division of labor: the Department of Justice tends to concentrate its attention on nominees' qualifications, including the nominees' judicial philosophy, while the White House tends to focus on the political dimensions of the appointment. Yet, if a president believes that there is political value to be gained from appointing judges with identifiable judicial philosophies, the two offices may find coordination easy. For the past several decades, this has been especially true of Republican presidents, who have campaigned against 'judicial activism' and who believed that conservative legal activists were an important political constituency.

One non-governmental organization has played an important role in the judicial selection process as well. The American Bar Association is the nation's peak organization of lawyers. Membership in the ABA is voluntary but quite widespread. Starting in the mid-twentieth century, presidents gave the ABA a formal role in the nomination process, by asking the Association to provide the administration with an evaluation of potential nominees' qualifications before the president forwarded a nomination to the Senate. By the late twentieth century Republican presidents had become troubled by the ABA's role, largely because they perceived—correctly—that the ABA's membership was becoming increasingly liberal and believed—only somewhat less accurately— that the evaluations the ABA provided were overly influenced by its members' political views and were no longer purely merit based. President George W Bush removed the ABA from its formal role in the judicial selection process, treating the ABA as it would any other non-governmental organization that took an interest in judicial nominations. Perhaps unsurprisingly, President Barack Obama restored the ABA's formal role in the process.

The president's choice is sometimes constrained by long-standing political norms, whose force varies depending on the level of judge in question. Appointments to the federal trial courts are basically patronage appointments. Federal trial-level judges, called 'district judges', are appointed to districts consisting of a single state or, more often, part of a single state. That gives local Senators a particularly strong political interest in influencing the nominations. Nominees are usually local lawyers who have been active in the president's party and who are associates of party leaders in the state.[9] In a state with one or two Senators from the president's party, those Senators typically come up with a list of lawyers whose appointment they would support, and the president

---

[9] Here I describe the general practice, from which there are of course occasional deviations, including a rare selection based entirely on merit.

chooses from that list. Some Senators imbued with good-government values appoint a committee to screen potential nominees and present the Senator with a more merit-based list, which the Senator will then evaluate and perhaps revise before sending it on to the president. Even here, though, it seems clear that the appointments have some degree of patronage about them. Similar practices occur when there are no Senators from the president's party in a state; local party leaders—the governor, for example, or other party activists—will come up with the list of candidates for appointment. Only in truly extraordinary cases will a president reject every name on the list sent by the Senators or party leaders, because the political costs of doing so are quite high.

The selection process for federal appellate courts, known as the circuit courts of appeal, is roughly similar, although the president faces somewhat weaker constraints in those appointments. The circuit courts hear appeals from district courts in several states, so no single Senator or pair of Senators has the same relation to circuit court nominations as occurs with trial-level nominations. Still, there are longstanding traditions that informally allocate a fixed number of appeals court judges to states within the circuits. When a 'California' judge retires or dies, the usual expectation is that the replacement will be from California as well.

The federal appeals court that sits in the District of Columbia is sometimes described as the nation's second most important federal court, after the Supreme Court. Its importance arises from the conjuncture of two facts—one legal and one political. The District of Columbia court of appeals is the preferred jurisdiction for review of major national administrative initiatives, including most notably in the twenty-first century those involving environmental law, consumer rights and workplace safety and health. The District of Columbia court of appeals determines whether the executive's initiatives are consistent with underlying statutory law, including whether administrative agencies have failed to do what the underlying statutes require. The administrative law rulings of the DC circuit court can have a major impact on the shape of national policy. In addition, the District of Columbia has no Senators whose political interests need to be satisfied in the judicial selection process. The White House thus has an almost completely free hand in nominations to that DC circuit court. One result is that that court has become something of a 'farm team' for the Supreme Court: In 2014, four Supreme Court justices had served on the DC circuit before their appointments to the Supreme Court.

The Supreme Court

Selection of federal district and appellate judges is a political process. So is selection of Supreme Court justices. The contours of the politics of Supreme Court nominations have varied over US history. Merit has only rarely played the dominant role; the nomination of the progressive Benjamin Cardozo by the conservative Republican president Herbert Hoover in 1932 is often described as the only appointment based solely on merit in the twentieth century. And, although in 2014 eight members on the Supreme Court had been promoted from a federal appeals court, prior judicial service, whether on the federal courts or on state courts, has not been a prerequisite to appointment to the Supreme Court. Most Supreme Court justices did have some prior judicial service, but for many it was not an important qualification for appointment. Hugo L Black had served briefly as a municipal court judge in Alabama in 1911–12, but he abandoned the courts for electoral politics and was serving as a Senator when Franklin Roosevelt appointed him to the Supreme Court in 1937. Earl Warren, arguably the greatest chief justice in the twentieth century, never served as a judge before he was appointed to the Supreme Court; he had been a crusading prosecutor in California before he was elected that state's governor, the post he held when he was nominated for the Chief Justiceship in 1954.

For the first century of the Supreme Court's history, the justices were required to 'ride circuit', that is, to preside over trials and hearings around the country. To ease the burden of travel somewhat, a tradition arose of having one justice from each of the nation's circuits, and when a new circuit was created so was a new position on the Supreme Court. Circuit riding ended, but the tradition of seeking justices from each of the nation's regions persisted into the middle of the twentieth century, finally disappearing around 1970. Other traditions of representation have also waxed and waned. The appointment of Louis Brandeis in 1916 led to the sense among Court-watchers that there ought to be a 'Jewish' seat on the Court, and indeed there has been since then. The appointment of Thurgood Marshall in 1967 had the same effect in connection with race, and Marshall's successor was another African American, Clarence Thomas. During his campaign for the presidency Ronald Reagan promised to appoint a woman to the Court, and did so at the first opportunity, naming Sandra Day O'Connor as the first woman justice. Sonia Sotomayor, nominated by President Barack Obama, is the first Hispanic American named to the Court. Demographic representation is thus something of a tradition in Supreme Court appointments, but not a universal one: The appointments of John Roberts and Samuel Alito by President George W Bush gave the Court five Catholic justices, which was noted but not thought truly noteworthy. The appointment of Elena Kagan to the Supreme Court led to some comments about the fact that the Court then had no Protestant members, but to even more comments about the fact that all of the justices had received their legal education in the nation's most elite law schools.

Geographic and demographic representation has mattered in the past primarily for political reasons. Presidents have made Supreme Court appointments with an eye to the political benefits they could gain. Probably the clearest example is President Dwight D Eisenhower's nomination of William Brennan in 1956. Eisenhower, a moderate to conservative Republican, nominated Brennan, who he believed to be a moderate Democrat, because Eisenhower, running for re-election, wanted to strengthen his appeal to urban, Northeastern Catholic and Democratic voters, and could do so by nominating Brennan, a Northeastern Catholic Democrat from New Jersey who fitted the bill.

The politics associated with Supreme Court nominations typically mirrors the way politics is being conducted elsewhere. For long periods of US history, Supreme Court nominations were patronage appointments. A president would reward a political supporter or seek to secure continuing loyalty by nominating him or his preferred candidate. Some nominations were a different kind of patronage—appointments of the president's personal friends and advisers. Demographic and geographic representation in nominations was the form that interest-group politics took in the appointment process.

All these versions of politics continue to play a role. In 2008, for example, there was widespread agreement that the next Supreme Court nomination should probably go to a person of Hispanic origin, and if possible a woman, because the Hispanic electorate had become important politically and because Justice O'Connor's departure left 'only' one woman on the Court. But, in the last decades of the twentieth century another form of appointment politics became increasingly important. Political scientist David Alistair Yalof calls the new process 'criterion-driven'.[10] Anticipating a Supreme Court vacancy, the White House and the Department of Justice develop criteria that they will seek to satisfy

[10] DA Yalof, *Pursuit of Justice: Presidential Politics and the Selection of Supreme Court Nominees* (Chicago, University of Chicago Press, 1999).

when the possibility of a nomination materializes. Some of these criteria have been representational, as when President Richard Nixon looked for a Southerner to appoint to the Court. More important, though, have been two other criteria. The first is age. Presidents, particularly reconstructive ones, sometimes see the Supreme Court as one vehicle for preserving their legacy. To do so, though, they incline to appointing relatively young justices, who will maintain the president's perspective for what the president anticipates will be a long tenure.[11]

Even more important has been an increase in attention to the criterion of judicial philosophy or ideology, particularly on the part of Republican presidents. Their concern has been that dismantling the New Deal's constitutional legacy and constructing a new conservative constitutional order, tasks that they pursued in the executive branch and in Congress, also required dismantling the Warren Court and reconstructing it in a new image. Reconstruction, that is, required attention to what potential nominees would do if appointed to the Supreme Court. Not surprisingly, then, nominations by Republicans since the 1960s have been more criterion-driven than nominations by Democrats. That criterion-driven appointments matter was dramatically shown in 2006–07, the first year in which new justices John Roberts and Samuel Alito served on the Court. They joined holdover conservative justices in sharply revising constitutional law in three areas—abortion, campaign finance, and affirmative action—where Justice O'Connor had cast the deciding vote with the Court's more liberal members.[12]

The role of judicial philosophy in nominations has had another effect. Some criteria (age and gender, for example) are easily determined. Judicial philosophy is not. Those who compile lists of potential nominees who fit the desired criterion of judicial philosophy need evidence about candidates' judicial philosophy. Potential nominees can

---

[11] The average length of tenure of Supreme Court justices has risen from roughly 15 years in the years up to 1970 to roughly 26 years more recently, not primarily because nominees have been younger at the time of their appointment but because of the extension of the average life span. For documentation, see SG Calabresi and JT Lindgren, 'Term Limits for the Supreme Court: Life Tenure Reconsidered' (2006) 29 *Harvard J of L and Public Policy* 770.

[12] *Gonzales v Carhart* 550 US 124 (2007) (limiting *Stenberg v Carhart* 530 US 914 (2000); *FEC v Wisconsin Right to Life, Inc* 551 US 449 (2007) (restricting *McConnell v FEC* 540 US 93 (2003)); *Parents Involved in Community Schools v Seattle School Dist No 1* 551 US 701 (2007) (restricting *Grutter v Bollinger* 539 US 306 (2003)).

say what their philosophy would be once appointed, but judges actually display their philosophy in their work. Because credible evidence of judicial philosophy is more readily available from the records of sitting judges than from statements by potential nominees who are not judges, the more important judicial philosophy is as a criterion for appointment, the more likely it is that the pool of potential nominees will be rich with those already sitting as judges.[13] This in turn has had a feedback effect on federal appellate judges. Some appear to have attempted to position themselves to become Supreme Court nominees, by giving speeches and writing opinions that, they believe, will bring them to the attention of the list-makers. Before they become nominees, they are candidates for nomination. Given how rare Supreme Court vacancies are, and how complex are the politics of judicial nominations, 'running' for a Supreme Court nomination is basically irrational. Still, some candidacies, notably those of John Roberts and Samuel Alito, have succeeded, leading other judges to hold on to the hope that their own candidacies would succeed as well.

With judicial philosophy an important criterion for selection, a nominee's opponents will scour the record for examples of rulings said to show that the nominee's judicial philosophy is unacceptable, even though the rulings were arguably compelled by Supreme Court precedent with which the lower court judge could not reasonably disagree. Again there are feedback effects. An ambitious judge might soften the hard edges of his or her true philosophy, for example, or sprinkle an occasional decision going counter to the judge's seeming philosophy among the rest, to show that the judge is not 'rigid.'

Not all nominations go through, and some confirmations are hard-fought. In the nineteenth century, patronage nominations sometimes ran aground on intra-party factional fights, when the president sought to reward one faction and thereby irritated another. As we have seen in the preceding chapters, party unity and ideological coherence increased in the late twentieth century, and today a president whose party also controls the Senate will almost certainly be able to place his or her nominees on the Supreme Court. The modern version of the problem of factional division occurs under divided government. Since the middle of the twentieth century, controversial nominations have foundered in

---

[13] Some Senators will also be concerned about judicial philosophy when they are asked to confirm a nomination.

a president's second term, when the opposition party sees some hope of taking over the presidency and gaining control of the nomination process, and when the president and the Senate are controlled by different parties. President Lyndon Johnson's nomination of Abe Fortas to succeed Earl Warren as Chief Justice failed because it was made in 1968, when Johnson had already announced that he would not run for re-election and was politically weakened by the War in Vietnam; Republicans anticipated winning the presidential election that fall, and blocked Fortas's nomination. Robert Bork's nomination failed in 1987 because President Ronald Reagan was in his second term, was weakened by the Iran-contra scandal, and faced a Senate controlled by Democrats. Clarence Thomas's nomination in 1991 was controversial, but he was narrowly confirmed; it may be significant that the nomination occurred during President George HW Bush's first and as it turned out only term.

JUDICIAL REVIEW AND JUDICIAL SUPREMACY

Supreme Court appointments are politically important because of the Court's power of judicial (that is, constitutional) review—the power to determine that statutes enacted by Congress and state legislatures are inconsistent with the Constitution and therefore have no legal effect. The written Constitution makes no direct provision for judicial review, but at the time the Constitution was adopted nearly all knowledgeable participants in the process assumed that the courts did have that power.

Establishing Judicial Review

The Supreme Court simply confirmed the prevailing understanding in its 1803 decision in *Marbury v Madison*.[14] The Court was faced with a political dilemma. Federalists had lost the elections of 1800. In the last weeks of their control of Congress and the presidency, they created a number of new positions for federal judges, hoping to use the courts to defend whatever Federalist programs they could. Outgoing President John Adams nominated his Secretary of State John Marshall for the vacant position of Chief Justice, and the Federalist Senate quickly

---

[14]   5 US (1 Cranch) 137 (1803).

confirmed him.[15] The incoming Jeffersonians were outraged at the power grab embodied in the new judgeships. In a constitutionally questionable move, they abolished some of the newly created judgeships, and—to freeze the status quo ante—enacted a statute directing that the Supreme Court suspend its next session. As Chief Justice, Marshall knew how explosive it would have been to confront the Jeffersonians on so central a matter. But he found a vehicle to attack them from the side.

As it happened, some of the new judges had not received their commissions—the documents showing that the Senate had indeed confirmed them—before Adams left office. John Marshall continued to serve as Secretary of State through the end of the Adams administration, and the commissions were sitting on his desk, undelivered, when Jefferson took office. Unsurprisingly, Jefferson decided not to deliver the commissions. William Marbury, who thought he was going to become a justice of the peace in the District of Columbia, sued James Madison, the new Secretary of State, seeking an order from the Supreme Court directing Madison to deliver the commission.

John Marshall's opinion for the Supreme Court denied Marbury the order he sought, thereby avoiding a direct confrontation with Jefferson. Marshall did use the occasion to chastise Jefferson and Madison for violating Marbury's right to the commission, which infuriated Jefferson. But, Marshall wrote, the problem was that Marbury sought a remedy from a court that was not authorized to give it. Stretching the language of the applicable statute, Marshall agreed that Congress had enacted a statute that *purported* to give the Court the power to issue the writ Marbury sought. But then, stretching the language of the Constitution, Marshall held that Article III's definition of the jurisdiction of the Supreme Court barred Congress from doing so. And, the Court said, it could disregard Congress's unconstitutional directive because that was what judicial review meant.

American law students spend days puzzling over the details of *Marbury v Madison*, which are themselves not terribly interesting or even important. The important question was whether Congress could abolish the newly created judgeships. And on that the Supreme Court

---

[15] Adams had offered the position to others, who declined, so although the offer to Marshall came at the last minute, the vacancy itself was not created in the aftermath of the Federalist defeat.

simply avoided facing up to the constitutional question. A case decided within a week of *Marbury* indirectly presented it, and the Court offhandedly upheld what Congress had done.[16]

Departmentalism

Marshall's arguments in favor of judicial review mix some weak ones with some strong ones. His strongest argument posited a congressional enactment that—unlike the one actually before the Court—plainly violated the unequivocal terms of the Constitution. Surely, Marshall said, the very idea of a constitution as a law superior to ordinary statutes, expressed in the Supremacy Clause, implied that the courts had to invalidate such a statute. True enough, but the real problem for judicial review arises when Congress enacts a statute that, on one reasonable interpretation of the Constitution—Congress's interpretation—is perfectly constitutional, and that, on another reasonable interpretation—the Court's—is unconstitutional. Neither the Supremacy Clause nor the idea of a constitution superior to ordinary law, nor anything else Marshall invoked, tells us which reasonable view ought to prevail, and there are reasons grounded in democratic theory for thinking that Congress's should.

When *Marbury* was decided, it might have been taken to exemplify relatively narrow views of judicial review, which have sometimes been called 'departmentalist'. Departmentalism comes in two versions. The narrower holds that the president and the courts have the power to ignore statutes that, in their view, unconstitutionally interfere with their duties or powers. Almost all of the exercises of judicial review prior to 1789 involved statutes that at least arguably intruded on the courts' ability to carry out their functions as they understood them, and *Marbury* itself could have been treated as a departmentalist case in this sense. This narrow idea of departmentalism disappeared soon after 1803, though.

A broader idea of departmentalism retained its hold until some time in the twentieth century, and still has occasional defenders. The broader departmentalist view is that each branch has the right to interpret the Constitution independently, when constitutional questions come before

[16] *Stuart v Laird* 5 US (1 Cranch) 299 (1803).

it. So, for example, suppose the Supreme Court upholds a statute against constitutional challenge. A departmentalist of this sort would say that the president could pardon people convicted of violating the statute because he or she concluded that the statute was unconstitutional, no matter what the Court said. President Thomas Jefferson took exactly that position when he pardoned those convicted of violating the Sedition Act, which he concluded violated constitutional limitations on congressional power. Similarly, President Andrew Jackson vetoed the recharter of the Bank of the United States in 1832, because—notwithstanding the Supreme Court's decision in *McCulloch v Maryland* that Congress had the power to create the Bank—in Jackson's view Congress had no such power.

The intuition behind this version of departmentalism is that the branch that in some sense comes last in line is entitled to arrive at and act on its own judgment of constitutionality. Sometimes difficult analytic questions might be posed about who comes last in line. One can imagine a constitutional system in which a president's decision to pardon a criminal was subject to judicial review, for example. Such difficulties aside, nearly everything the Supreme Court has done can be fit into this version of departmentalism, because Congress and the president have found it useful to rely on the courts to administer the law and have been willing to accept the occasional declaration of unconstitutionality as one of the costs of doing so.

The second version of departmentalism accepts as normatively acceptable decisions by government officials other than judges about the Constitution's meaning, even when those decisions are inconsistent with what the courts have said—at least until the officials seek some assistance from the courts, which then become last in line and are able to make their judgments stick. President Abraham Lincoln's first inaugural address provided a classic exposition. A severe critic of the Court's decision in the *Dred Scott* case, Lincoln nonetheless agreed that the Court's decisions were 'binding … upon the parties to a suit, as to the object of that suit'. He also agreed that the Court's decisions should be given 'very high respect and consideration in parallel cases' and even that some 'erroneous' decisions ought to be followed until they were overruled. But, he continued:

> [T]he candid citizen must confess that if the policy of the government, upon vital questions affecting the whole people, is to be irrevocably fixed by decisions of the Supreme Court, the instant they are made, in ordinary litigation between parties in personal actions, the people will have ceased

to be their own rulers, having to that extent practically resigned the government into the hands of that eminent tribunal.

Judicial Supremacy

By the middle of the twentieth century departmentalism had been displaced by the view that the courts' interpretations always had normative priority. The system, that is, became one of judicial supremacy. We can date the consolidation of judicial supremacy rather precisely. Southern states resisted the Supreme Court's decision holding that public school segregation was unconstitutional. In 1957 and 1958, a crisis over desegregation occurred in Little Rock, Arkansas. Orval Faubus, the state's governor, intervened in the local school board's decision-making and directed that the schools remain segregated. Facing what it believed to be the prospect of serious violence if the schools tried to operate on a desegregated basis, a federal court suspended the desegregation order it had previously made. Governor Faubus contended that, at least until he and the school board were subject to a final order from the Supreme Court (which they were not, at the time), they had the right to act on their view that the Court's desegregation decision was a mistaken interpretation of the Constitution.

The Supreme Court unanimously reversed. Relying on *Marbury*'s statement that '[i]t is emphatically the province and duty of the judicial department to say what the law is', the Court wrote that '[t]his decision declared the basic principle that the federal judiciary is supreme in the exposition of the law of the Constitution'. According to the Court, it 'follows' that the Court's constitutional interpretation in the original desegregation cases 'is the supreme law of the land' and had 'binding effect'. The key point here is that the Court's interpretations of the Constitution become supreme and binding on other officials. Those officials can express disagreement with what the Court has said the constitution means, but as long as the Court's interpretation stands they must act in a manner consistent with what the Court has said.

In its broadest scope, judicial supremacy raises real questions about the propriety of Jefferson's pardons and Jackson's bank veto. Yet, when in 1987 Edwin Meese, Attorney General during the Reagan administration, asserted the president's power to interpret the Constitution independently—in the older departmentalist tradition—he ran into a buzz-saw of criticism for undermining the Supreme Court's role in the US constitutional system.[17]

Occasional voices could be heard expressing respectable disagreement with judicial supremacy, but at least in the short to middle run what the courts said the Constitution meant *was* what the Constitution meant. As Lincoln suggested, in some versions of democratic theory this poses a problem, because the people are unable to have their way even when the policies they favor are supported by decent constitutional reasoning, albeit reasoning the courts find unpersuasive.

Perhaps more important, judicial supremacy is sometimes a problem for politicians as well. Sometimes they might be happy to fob difficult policy questions off on to the courts in the guise of constitutional questions.[18] There are some political advantages in doing so. Politicians can then disclaim responsibility for their inability to achieve goals some of their constituents want. They can also 'run against the courts', winning support from those who disagree with the courts but not necessarily losing support from those who agree with the courts and understand that, under a system of judicial supremacy, there is nothing politicians can do in the short run to change the courts' rulings. Judicial supremacy's advantages to politicians are sometimes offset, though, by the political importance of the programs the courts stop them from implementing. This gives politicians an interest in having available some mechanisms for bringing the courts back into line. The Constitution provides those mechanisms, thereby striking a balance between judicial independence and supremacy in the short to middle run and coordination of the courts with the political branches in the long run.

POLITICAL CONSTRAINTS ON THE JURISDICTION OF THE FEDERAL COURTS

Whether and how the courts are coordinated with the political branches are descriptive and normative questions. Two of the most famous observations about the Supreme Court capture these two dimensions of the coordination question.

---

[17] For Meese's speech and some responses, see Symposium, 'Perspectives on the Authoritativeness of Supreme Court Decisions' (1987) 61 *Tulane L Rev* 979.

[18] MA Graber, 'The Nonmajoritarian Difficulty: Legislative Deference to the Judiciary' (1993) 7 *Studies in American Political Development* 35.

— Political scientist Robert Dahl wrote in 1957: 'the policy views dominant on the Court are never for long out of line with the policy views dominant among the lawmaking majorities of the United States'.[19] Dahl's insight has been confirmed, though in qualified form, since then. The Warren Court, notable for its 'activism' and therefore seemingly at odds with legislative majorities, actually worked hand-in-glove with the dominant New Deal/Great Society Democratic majority in Congress. As law professor Lucas A Powe shows, the Warren Court's decisions disciplined the US South in the service of a national majority and brought aberrant outliers into line with national policy preferences.[20] When a vulnerable political regime succumbs to a reconstructive president, there will be transitional difficulties, as occurred during the New Deal when the Supreme Court, still controlled by justices appointed in the prior era, resisted President Roosevelt's initiatives. Eventually, though, the Court came into line as justices resigned and were replaced by Roosevelt appointees. Of course, 'transitions' may take a long time, and confrontations may therefore persist. Indeed, if a transition takes long enough, the reconstructive energy may wane, the new regime may become vulnerable, and the recalcitrant justices may prevail.

— Law professor Alexander Bickel gave the label 'countermajoritarian difficulty' in 1962 to the normative problem of coordination.[21] Judicial review inevitably displaced decisions by elected representatives. How could that be justified in a democracy? Bickel overstated the problem. In separation-of-powers disputes, the courts intervene on behalf of one branch against the other, but the intervention is not obviously countermajoritarian because the winning side—the one the Court agrees with—has some democratic warrant. Similarly, when the Court acts during periods of divided government, its action may reject the position taken by one branch but accept that taken by the other. And, as Dahl pointed out, in periods of unified government the Court rarely acts against the unified will of the political branches. Still, some countermajoritarian problems can arise,

[19] RA Dahl, 'Decision-Making in a Democracy: The Supreme Court as a National Policy-Maker' (1957) 6 *Journal of Public Law* 279, 285.

[20] LA Powe, *The Warren Court and American Politics* (Cambridge, MA, Harvard University Press, 2001).

[21] AM Bickel, *The Least Dangerous Branch: The Supreme Court at the Bar of Politics* (Indianapolis, Bobbs-Merrill, 1962) 16.

and coordination between the courts and the political branches reduces, though it does not eliminate, the difficulty. Once reduced in scope, the countermajoritarian difficulty may be less difficult—less a problem for a theory of democratic constitutionalism—than it appeared to Bickel.

The written Constitution contains several mechanisms for coordination, but only one—making judicial nominations a political process—has had any real effects.

Impeachment

Federal judges serve during 'good Behaviour' and can be removed from office by impeachment for 'Treason, Bribery, or other high Crimes and Misdemeanors'. This combination has been taken to establish that judges have tenure for life unless they are removed by impeachment.[22]

The transition from Federalist rule to Jeffersonian rule in 1800–01 provided the first and, as it turned out, the last opportunity to test whether impeachment could be used to coordinate the judiciary with the political branches. Jeffersonians had won decisive victories in the presidential and congressional elections, leaving Federalists controlling only the judiciary. Supreme Court justice Samuel Chase was a highly partisan Federalist judge, whose conduct of trials of prominent Jeffersonians was at least heavy handed and possibly a serious interference with the defendants' ability to present legally available defenses (although the claim that they had such defenses was itself controversial). In 1804 Jeffersonians began impeachment proceedings against Justice Chase, hoping that success would allow them to begin a more thorough cleansing of the Federalist judiciary. The Jeffersonian controlled Senate refused to convict Chase, largely because of extraneous political concerns (by the time of the impeachment trial, the prosecutor representing the House had turned against Jefferson on another issue, and alienated some of Jefferson's supporters in the Senate). The failure of the Chase

---

[22] Occasionally scholars have suggested that judges can be removed from office by some sort of judicial process when they are physically or mentally disabled, the thought being that a judicial process does not pose the threat to judicial independence that a political one, even limited to removal for disability, would, but the strong consensus is that the only mode of removal is impeachment.

impeachment proceeding has been taken to establish a convention—or to create an interpretation of the 'good Behaviour' requirement—that impeachment cannot be used to remove a federal judge simply because of disagreement with the judge's rulings.[23] Impeachment has since been used to remove federal judges who committed crimes (or declared their allegiance to the Confederacy during the Civil War).[24]

Manipulation of the Size of the Court

Removing judges is one way to change the Court's composition. Changing the Court's size is another. It too has been used to coordinate the Court with the political branches, although it no longer seems to be an available option. During the Civil War Congress created a 10th circuit court and added a justice to the Supreme Court. President Lincoln appointed California supreme court justice Stephen Field to the newly created position, in part to ensure that there would be a Unionist Democrat on the Court. After Lincoln's assassination and replacement by Andrew Johnson, who was at odds with the Republican majorities in Congress, Congress reduced the size of the Supreme Court to deny Johnson the ability to appoint replacements for two justices who died while in office. When Ulysses S Grant became president, Congress authorized a new position on the Court, re-establishing its size at nine.

In 1937 President Roosevelt reacted to Court decisions threatening important New Deal programs by proposing to expand the Supreme Court. His 'Court-packing plan', as it came to be called, would have authorized the president to appoint an additional justice for every justice above the age of 70. Roosevelt tried to present this as an effort to relieve an aging Court of its burdens, but everyone understood that the

[23] K Whittington, *Constitutional Construction: Divided Powers and Constitutional Meaning* (Cambridge, MA, Harvard University Press, 1999). In 1970 Representative Gerald Ford, supporting a resolution to impeach Justice William O Douglas, asserted that the grounds for impeachment were 'whatever a majority of the House of Representatives considers them to be at a given moment in history'. Ford's resolution went nowhere because the house was controlled by liberal Democrats, but also in part because his assertion seemed legally erroneous.

[24] In 1989 the Senate convicted Judge Alcee Hastings for conspiracy to accept a bribe even though he had been acquitted of accepting a bribe and perjury in a criminal trial held in 1981. Hastings was elected to the House of Representatives in 1992, and as of 2014 continues to serve there.

plan was aimed at ensuring that the Court would uphold Roosevelt's New Deal programs. After a hard-fought political battle, in which the justices themselves intervened to say that they were not overworked, the Court-packing plan was defeated in the Senate. That seems to have established a convention that the Supreme Court's size, actually fixed only by statute, shall permanently be set at nine, and certainly established a convention that the Court's size cannot be changed simply to change the results expected from the Court.

Restricting the Court's Jurisdiction

As noted earlier, the written Constitution clearly leaves it to Congress to create courts. It also gives Congress the power to make 'Exceptions' to the appellate jurisdiction of the Supreme Court. Taken together, these provisions seem to authorize Congress to deny the national courts the power to rule on specific constitutional questions if Congress wishes to keep the questions away from those courts. Suppose, for example, that Congress believed that the Supreme Court might mistakenly interpret the Constitution to prevent it from including the phrase 'under God' in the national Pledge of Allegiance. Exercising its power to structure the lower federal courts, it could deny jurisdiction in the federal trial-level courts to hear cases raising constitutional questions about the Pledge's constitutionality. And, exercising its power to make exceptions to the Supreme Court's appellate jurisdiction, it could eliminate appellate jurisdiction over the same questions (as well as the question of the constitutionality of eliminating trial-level jurisdiction), even when the questions were raised in state courts.

Congress responded to a Supreme Court decision that detainees in Guantánamo Bay were entitled to have their claims that their constitutional rights were being denied heard in the lower federal courts by exercising its power to regulate jurisdiction. The Military Commissions Act of 2006 placed sharp limits on the claims the lower courts could hear, and completely denied them the power to rule on some constitutional claims. In 2008 the Supreme Court held that this statute violated the constitutional guarantee that the writ of habeas corpus should not be suspended except when Congress specifically found that emergency conditions required such a suspension.

There is a huge scholarly literature on whether controlling the Supreme Court's jurisdiction to control the outcomes of controversial cases is constitutional, with the weight of scholarly opinion being that such restrictions are unconstitutional.[25] The controversy is almost entirely scholarly, though. For all practical purposes, only a single Supreme Court opinion comes close to addressing the issue, and everyone concedes that the decision in fact settles nothing of interest.[26] The more recent *Boumediene* case does establish that Congress cannot eliminate the writ of habeas corpus indirectly, by failing to provide an adequate alternative remedy if it does not expressly indicate that it wishes to suspend the writ's operation. That holding, though, is of quite limited general significance. The reason that there is no decisional law on the issue is that Congress has, again for all practical purposes, never exercised the power it might have to restrict the courts' jurisdiction in a constitutionally troubling way. It has refrained from doing so for reasons that blend politics and commitments to a vision of the Constitution. Denying the Supreme Court jurisdiction in controversial cases actually cannot ensure specific outcomes, because everyone agrees that Congress cannot deny jurisdiction to state courts to address the issues that Congress might be concerned about. To continue the example, by denying jurisdiction to the federal courts to decide the Pledge of Allegiance question, Congress still runs the risk that some state court will find the Pledge's use of 'under God' unconstitutional, and members of Congress will then not receive the political benefits they sought. But, almost certainly more important, members of Congress understand that selective denials of jurisdiction, even if licensed by the written Constitution's words, are in severe tension with a long tradition in US constitutional law of treating constitutional questions as open for judicial consideration, with limited exceptions devised by the courts themselves (discussed in the next section of this chapter). We can call this understanding political if we want: members of Congress do face political costs if they act against this

---

[25] For a discussion that cites the literature as of 1984, see M Tushnet and J Jaff, 'Why the Debate on Congress' Power to Restrict the Jurisdiction of the Federal Courts Is Unending' (1984) 72 *Georgetown Law Journal* 1311. For a recent treatment focusing on issues raised by congressional limitations on jurisdiction in connection with detentions at Guantánamo Bay, see RH Fallon Jr and DJ Meltzer, 'Habeas Corpus Jurisdiction, Substantive Rights, and the War on Terror' (2007) 120 *Harvard Law Review* 2029.

[26] *Ex p McCardle* 74 US 506 (1869).

tradition. Describing it as a normative commitment to a vision of what US constitutionalism means is more accurate.

Strategic Nominations

Presidents can use Supreme Court appointments to bring the Court into line. Strategic appointments can be targeted at a specific decision or at a confined set, or more generally at ensuring that the president's constitutional vision be represented and eventually prevail on the Court. In 1870 and 1871 the Supreme Court decided the *Legal Tender* cases, which raised the question of whether Congress had violated the Constitution when, during the Civil War, it enacted a statute requiring that creditors accept payments in paper money—'greenbacks'—rather than insisting on payment in gold specie. In 1869 the Supreme Court held by a four-to-three vote that the statute was unconstitutional. Justice Robert Grier voted with the majority, although he was senile and may not have understood what he was doing. Justice Grier resigned immediately after the first *Legal Tender* case was decided. President Grant then appointed two new justices. The Court then reconsidered the constitutionality of greenbacks and, in 1871, upheld the statute by a five-to-four vote.

After the failure of the Court-packing plan, Roosevelt used strategic appointments to entrench the expansive vision of national power associated with the New Deal. He had to wait until vacancies occurred, but they came in relatively rapid succession after 1937, and Roosevelt filled each position with a justice who, he knew, was committed to the New Deal. By 1943, there were seven Roosevelt appointees on the Court. Notably, Roosevelt was concerned only with protecting the New Deal against constitutional challenge, but his nominees tended to be liberal more generally, with the exception of South Carolina's James F Byrnes, and the effect of the Roosevelt appointments was to entrench a general liberal viewpoint on constitutional law.

Roosevelt's entrenchment of liberalism on the Court was perhaps inadvertent. With the rise of criterion-based appointments in which judicial philosophy was an important criterion, strategic nominations became a broader tool for partisan entrenchment.[27] In a period of

---

[27] See JM Balkin and S Levinson, 'Understanding the Constitutional Revolution' (2001) 87 *Virginia Law Review* 1045.

unified government, as occurred under Roosevelt, nominations need not be strategic. The ordinary political considerations that a president takes into account will result in creating a Supreme Court whose members agree with the broad contours of the party controlling the other branches. Partisan entrenchment matters more when government is divided, and matters even more when a political regime is vulnerable and its adherents seek to salvage something of their constitutional vision by ensuring that the federal courts perpetuate that vision even after they have become a minority in the political branches. That was the Federalist strategy in 1800, and it may be the best description of the Republican strategy in the nominations of Chief Justice Roberts and Justice Alito.

Politics, then, can help coordinate the judiciary with the other branches, but in some configurations politics can exacerbate rather than reduce conflict. Further, some of the mechanisms described here operate through politics, without judicial enforcement, yet probably are more accurately described as constitutional conventions that have normative force as politicians consider what they want to, can, and should do.

DOCTRINAL CONSTRAINTS ON THE JURISDICTION OF THE FEDERAL COURTS

The Supreme Court has been sensitive to the countermajoritarian difficulty. It has developed some doctrines aimed at preserving what Justice Lewis F Powell called the 'proper—and properly limited—role of the courts in a democratic society'.[28] Gathered together under the general label 'justiciability' rules, these doctrines have been formally justified as flowing from the fact that judicial review in the United States is concrete and a posteriori. The Constitution gives the federal courts the power to decide 'Cases or Controversies'. The Supreme Court has taken this to mean that the courts can decide constitutional questions only in the context of real controversies between parties whose legal and practical interests would be affected by a judicial resolution of those questions. These doctrines have a smaller scope than some of their formulations might suggest. Here we examine two—the political question

---

[28]   *Warth v Seldin* 422 US 490, 498 (1975).

doctrine and the standing doctrine—whose analysis exposes the ways in which the doctrines serve to coordinate actions by the three branches.[29]

The Political Question Doctrine

Chief Justice Marshall in *Marbury* distinguished between the questions the courts would address in exercising their duty to interpret the Constitution, and political questions:

> The province of the court is, solely, to decide on the rights of individuals, not to inquire how the executive … perform duties in which they have a discretion. Questions in their nature political, or which are, by the constitution and laws, submitted to the executive, can never be made in this court.[30]

This is a rich statement, which could support a distinction between constitutional questions implicating individual rights, which the courts would decide, and those involving constitutional structure but not (directly) individual rights, which the courts might not decide. It could support a distinction between questions of constitutional interpretation, all of which the courts would decide, and questions about the exercise of discretionary authority, none of which the courts would decide. The history of the political questions doctrine reflects all the possibilities that can be teased out of Marshall's statement.

The phrase 'political questions' was picked up by later courts to describe some questions of constitutional interpretation that for some reason courts would not decide. But, as all scholars understand, the term 'political' is somewhat misleading. It certainly cannot refer to questions of constitutional interpretation that raise important questions of public policy, or questions about which political leaders and the public have strong opinions. Otherwise the Supreme Court could not have

---

[29] Other justiciability doctrines include 'ripeness', a doctrine asserting that the federal courts cannot decide cases before they have fully matured into actual controversies, and 'mootness', a doctrine barring the federal courts from deciding constitutional questions once the parties have resolved all their actual disputes. Henry Monaghan accurately described these two doctrines as 'standing set in a time frame' and so detailed attention to them would add little to the overview offered here: H Monaghan, 'Constitutional Adjudication: The Who and When' (1973) 82 *Yale Law Journal* 1363. Justiciability also prevents the federal courts from offering advisory opinions, although some state courts do.

[30] *Marbury v Madison* 5 US, 170.

decided *Brown v Board of Education*, invalidating racial segregation of the public schools, or *Bush v Gore*, resolving the 2000 election.

What, then, is a political question? Attempting to summarize a century's worth of decisions, Justice William Brennan identified six features of cases involving political questions:

> Prominent on the surface of any case held to involve a political question is found a textually demonstrable constitutional commitment of the issue to a coordinate political department; or a lack of judicially discoverable and manageable standards for resolving it; or the impossibility of deciding without an initial policy determination of a kind clearly for non-judicial discretion; or the impossibility of a court's undertaking independent resolution without expressing lack of the respect due coordinate branches of government; or an unusual need for unquestioning adherence to a political decision already made; or the potentiality of embarrassment from multifarious pronouncements by various departments on one question.[31]

We can understand Justice Brennan's list by examining some cases where the Court did—and did not—find a political question presented.

Foreign Affairs Cases

As Justice Brennan's list suggests, cases implicating foreign affairs, where there might be a special need for the nation to speak with a single voice, sometimes seem to be at the heart of the political questions doctrine. Consider *Goldwater v Carter* (1979).[32] The United States had a mutual defense treaty, approved by the Senate, with the Republic of China (that is, the government on Taiwan). As part of the negotiations leading to US recognition with the People's Republic of China (the mainland government), the Carter administration agreed to abrogate the mutual defense treaty. Senator Barry Goldwater sued, arguing that the Constitution required that the Senate participate in the abrogation of a treaty just as it required that the Senate participate in making treaties. In a confusing decision without a controlling opinion, the Supreme Court held that the courts should not decide the question Senator Goldwater raised, with four justices saying that the case posed a political question.

Yet, the courts regularly decide cases implicating foreign policy, even when that category is narrowly defined. For example, *Japan Whaling*

[31] *Baker v Carr* 369 US 169, 217 (1962).
[32] 444 US 996 (1979).

Association v Cetacean Society (1986) involved questions about whether an executive agreement between the president and Japan regarding whaling was consistent with two federal statutes.[33] According to the Court, the case did not implicate the political questions doctrine even though it involved foreign affairs. All that was at stake was an ordinary question of statutory interpretation. The Court reached a similar result in *Zivitofsky v Clinton* (2012), in which the Court held that no political question was presented by a case in which a child born in Jerusalem to American parents sought an order requiring the Department of State to identify Israel as his place of birth, as a statute required.[34]

Luther v Borden *(1849)*

Through the Jacksonian period the state of Rhode Island's political system remained organized by a charter granted by the British kings. Unsurprisingly, the rising surge of democracy generated a movement to change Rhode Island's constitution. Failing to negotiate constitutional changes, the democratic movement became a rebellion. The rebellion failed, and in the aftermath, the state constitution finally having been changed, a suit reached the Supreme Court in which the issue was whether, before the rebellion, Rhode Island had lacked the 'Republican Form of Government' that, the Constitution said, the United States had to 'guarantee' to the state. The Supreme Court held that the Guarantee Clause claim presented a political question.[35] Whether a state had a republican form of government was to be determined by Congress and the president, not the courts. Put another way, interpreting the term 'republican form of government' by determining whether a state had such a government was a task for the political branches.

Powell v McCormack *(1969)*

Adam Clayton Powell was a flamboyant member of Congress, an African American representing the heavily black Harlem area of New York City. He got embroiled in a number of public scandals, though he had not been convicted of any crimes. Outraged at Powell's

---

[33]   478 US 221 (1986).
[34]   132 SCt 1421 (2012). The Court later considered whether the statute was an unconstitutional restriction on the President's power to conduct foreign relations.
[35]   *Luther v Borden* 48 US (7 How) 1 (1849).

behavior, the House of Representatives voted to deny him his seat. Its justification was that the Constitution makes each house the 'sole judge' of its members' qualifications. The House's action amounted to a determination that Powell was not qualified to be a member of the House. Powell sued, arguing that, properly interpreted, the Constitution gave the House only the power to determine whether a person satisfied the standards of age and residency set out in the Constitution itself. The Supreme Court agreed.[36] Judicial review meant that the Court had the power to decide what the Constitution meant in giving the House the sole power to determine members' qualifications. The House's view of the scope of its own power was irrelevant.

Nixon v United States *(1993)*

Walter Nixon was a federal judge. He was convicted of a federal crime, after which the House of Representatives presented articles of impeachment to the Senate. Following one of its internal rules, the Senate referred the articles to a special committee for a hearing at which the House and Judge Nixon presented evidence. After the hearing the committee prepared a report in which it summarized the evidence and recommended that Judge Nixon be convicted and removed from office. Relying on the report, the Senate did convict Judge Nixon. He challenged his conviction on the ground that the Senate's procedures denied him the 'trial' to which he was entitled under the Constitution. The Senate responded that under the Constitution it had the 'sole power' to try impeachments and the power to makes its own rules, and together those powers implied that it had given Judge Nixon the trial to which he was entitled. The Supreme Court agreed with the Senate.[37] There was no single meaning to the word 'try', the Court held, and the 'sole power' clause meant that the Senate had the unreviewable power to decide was counted as a trial.

Making sense of all these decisions is not easy. They probably should be understood in truly political terms rather than in doctrinal ones. Two concurring opinions in Judge Nixon's case point in that direction. Responding to the suggestion that the Senate certainly could not say

---

[36] *Powell v McCormack* 395 US 486 (1969).
[37] *Nixon v United States* 506 US 224 (1993).

that flipping a coin to decide whether to convict or acquit amounted to a trial, Justice John Paul Stevens said: 'Respect for a coordinate Branch of this Government forecloses any assumption that improbable hypotheticals ... will ever occur.' Justice David Souter's opinion hinted that the courts might have the power to intervene if the Senate adopted a wildly unconstitutional procedure. These opinions suggest the following, which does make sense of a fair amount of the cases, those finding that no political question was presented as well as those finding that one was: political questions are those satisfying two criteria. First, there is good reason to think that the political branches have strong incentives to *address* the question of what the Constitution means in the circumstances. These reasons may be directly political, as when the Senate has to decide what its prerogatives are in the process of treaty abrogation, or normative and so indirectly political, when politicians internalize the proposition that they should take the Constitution seriously if only because their constituents expect them to do so. Second, there is good reason to think that those same factors give the political branches incentives to come up with reasonable albeit contestable constitutional interpretations.

On this view, the political questions doctrine is tightly linked to the way in which ordinary politics operates. It thereby serves to coordinate the judicial branch and the political branches through judicially developed doctrine.

STANDING

Chief Justice Marshall's reference in *Marbury* to the courts' role in vindicating individual rights generated what became known as the private-rights model of judicial review. In that model the courts' power of judicial review could be invoked only by parties who suffered individualized injuries analogous to those redressed in ordinary common-law actions (akin to trespasses, for example, or a breach of contract, as in *Marbury*), although sometimes those injuries could be widespread. Legislators who, in some other systems of judicial review, have privileged access to the courts, are no different from ordinary citizens in this regard; they too must allege that the statute or executive action they are challenging somehow injures them in their capacity as legislators.[38] The doctrine of standing identifies those who are entitled to invoke the power of judicial review.

Through the early twentieth century the private-rights model worked reasonably well, allowing the courts to determine the constitutionality of nearly every claim presented to them. The rise of the regulatory state posed new problems. Suppose a regulatory agency unlawfully granted a permit to a company's competitor. At common law the loss of business from competition was not an injury the courts would redress. The private-rights model would thus allow unlawful action to go unremedied. In response the Court expanded the notion of injury. Instead of injury to some interest analogous to those protected at common law, the courts required only 'injury in fact'. In addition, they recognized that legislators could create new interests, the violation of which would give rise to standing. So, for example, when legislatures enacted laws authorizing and sometimes requiring executive officials to designate some sites as worthy of historic preservation, someone 'interested in' historic preservation gained an interest in ensuring that designations occur pursuant to the criteria the legislature specified. On the private-rights model someone who could not alter her building because it was mistakenly designated a historic site would readily have standing; under the newer model someone who sometimes viewed a historic building would have standing to challenge the executive's failure to designate the building as a historic site.

By the late twentieth century standing was quite widely available, particularly in cases involving environmental law. The Supreme Court became concerned that its expansive standing doctrines were obstructing executive officials from exercising their lawful discretion. No matter what an official proposed to do, someone would have standing to challenge the action, thereby at least delaying the implementation of entirely lawful policies. The Court attempted to develop some restrictions on standing, but it was unable to come up with rules that struck the right balance, even in the Court's view, between allowing the government to operate efficiently and ensuring that it operated lawfully.

[38] See, eg, *Raines v Byrd* 521 US 811 (1997), which denied standing to legislators who challenged the Line Item Veto Act on the ground that it unconstitutionally shifted power from Congress to the president, because they had not alleged that they had voted for a bill that would have received sufficient votes in Congress but was not enacted because of Congress's understanding that the president would veto a specific appropriation.

The Court's canonical statements about standing doctrine were that a plaintiff had to allege that he or she suffered injury in fact, that the injury was caused by the challenged action, and that a judicial ruling in the litigant's favor would redress the injury. Applying that doctrine sensibly has proved impossible. As before, considering several cases is illuminating.

Allen v Wright *(1984)*

Direct resistance to the Supreme Court's desegregation decisions became transformed in the 1960s and 1970s into indirect resistance. Parents who did not want their children to attend racially desegregated schools set up private schools. Such schools were eligible for tax-exempt status—that is, those who donated money to them would be able to reduce their federal tax payments—if they did not discriminate in admissions on the basis of race. After a substantial political flap, the tax administrators decided to enforce the non-discrimination requirement by requiring only that schools submit a statement that they did not discriminate; that statement would be conclusive unless the administrators had other information indicating that a particular school did discriminate.

Parents in school districts subject to desegregation orders believed that the agency's enforcement mechanism was so feeble that private schools that did discriminate continued to operate, and thereby it made it more difficult for their districts to have truly desegregated schools. The Supreme Court disagreed.[39] According to the Court, the chain of causation between the agency's enforcement decisions and the interference with the desegregation orders was too attenuated. As Justice John Paul Stevens pointed out in dissent, the Court's position seemed to be that markets do not operate: The parents were claiming that the agency's enforcement policy unlawfully lowered the cost of operating a discriminatory school, which one would have thought would imply that the available supply of such schools would be larger than otherwise, which would in turn imply that there would be fewer children available to desegregate the schools.

---

[39] *Allen v Wright* 468 US 737 (1984).

Lujan v Defenders of Wildlife *(1992)*

The federal Endangered Species Act requires executive officials in one agency to consult with the Secretary of the Interior when it plans some action that might threaten an endangered species. The Secretary interpreted this provision to be inapplicable to projects outside the boundaries of the United States. A federal agency proposed to provide financial assistance for the Aswan High Dam on the Nile River in Egypt. The Defenders of Wildlife believed that constructing the dam would threaten the habitat of the endangered Nile River crocodile, and, alleging that the Secretary of the Interior's interpretation of the consultation requirement was inconsistent with the Endangered Species Act, sued to force the agency to consult with the Secretary. Among the plaintiffs was a woman who had traveled to Egypt five years earlier, to observe the Nile River crocodile, and who asserted that she hoped to do so again. The Supreme Court held that she did not have standing.[40] Her inchoate hope, 'without any description of concrete plans', did not show that she faced actual or imminent injury. Yet, as other opinions in the case made clear, had she actually purchased a ticket to go to Egypt, she would have had standing. No one thinks that such a formalistic distinction makes much sense.

Global Warming

The state of Massachusetts challenged the failure of the federal environmental agency to regulate carbon dioxide emissions from automobile tailpipes. The failure to do so, the state said, contributed to global warming, which had already caused sea levels to rise in a way that took away some of the coastal land the state owned. The Supreme Court agreed that the state had standing.[41] Four dissenters argued, plausibly enough, that the chance that US regulation of tailpipe emissions would have any effect at all on sea levels, or even on the rate of global warming, was so small that it could hardly be said that getting the agency to

---

[40] *Lujan v Defenders of Wildlife* 504 US 555 (1992).

[41] *Massachusetts v Environmental Protection Agency* 549 US 497 (2007). Although the Court's opinion at points emphasized the importance of the fact that a state was suing the national government, the injury it identified—loss of coastal land—would be suffered by individual owners of property on the coast as well.

regulate those emissions had any prospect of redressing the sea-level rise that caused the loss of coastal land.

The Court's standing rules operate erratically. The Court's most prominent decisions tend to restrict rather than expand standing—but not always. Ingenious lawyers can of course come up with accounts that reconcile the disparate cases, but the legal theories they develop have an air of unreality to them. Sometimes one gets a sense that the Court is worried about excessive interference with the discretion of executive officials in administering the law, as in *Allen v Wright* and *Lujan*. But other cases, such as the global warming decision, seem to pose at least as great a threat to administrative discretion. Nothing seems to make sense of standing doctrine in all its applications. A well-advised group that seeks to challenge the constitutionality of legislation ordinarily should be able to identify a plaintiff who satisfies the Court's standing requirements. Other procedural rules allow litigants to obtain 'preliminary' relief that has the effect of blocking the legislation from going into effect until the courts resolve the constitutional questions. And, at least when the litigant is challenging legislation on the ground that it violates the right of free expression, the courts will assess the statute 'on its face'. That is, they will decide whether the statute covers so many constitutionally protected activities that it cannot be enforced at all.[42] Nominally the federal courts exercise only concrete and a posteriori review, but these doctrines mean that they also, and not merely occasionally, exercise the functional equivalent of abstract and a priori review. Once again, the efficient Constitution differs from a version of the written Constitution focusing on the latter's use of the term 'case or controversy'.

CONCLUSION

The oldest constitutional court in the world, the US Supreme Court has become an important participant in the nation's overall system of government. Important, but not dominant. Many political matters raise no constitutional questions. The Court's justiciability doctrines keep some, though few, questions out of court. The mechanisms by

---

[42] The Court has sometimes entertained facial challenges to statutes regulating abortion as well, but the extension of facial challenges beyond the First Amendment and free expression is controversial.

which the courts are coordinated with the political branches mean that the courts' independent contribution to governance is smaller than the rhetoric of judicial independence suggests. When political circumstances are configured 'correctly', the Supreme Court can play a large role in governance, although the coordination mechanisms mean that its role gradually, and sometimes not so gradually, diminishes.

FURTHER READING

American Judicature Society, 'Methods of Judicial Selection', available at http://www.judicialselection.us/judicial_selection/methods/index. cfm?state= (describing judicial selection methods in the states).

Chemerinsky, E, *Federal Jurisdiction* (5th edn New York, Aspen Publishers, 2007) (containing a comprehensive discussion of the justiciability doctrine).

Friedman, B, *The Will of the People: How Public Opinion Has Influenced the Supreme Court and Shaped the Meaning of the Constitution* (New York, Farrar, Straus & Giroux, 2009).

Goldman, S, *Picking Federal Judges: Lower Court Selection from Roosevelt through Reagan* (New Haven, Yale University Press, 1997).

Kramer, LD, *The People Themselves: Popular Constitutionalism and Judicial Review* (New York, Oxford University Press, 2003) (an account of the history of departmentalism, with the author describing his preferred version as 'popular constitutionalism').

Snowiss, S, *Judicial Review and the Law of the Constitution* (New Haven, Yale University Press, 1990) (describing the early uses of departmentalism).

5

Federalism and the Reach of National Power

State Governments and the US Constitution – The Emergence
of (Nearly) Plenary National Power – The So-Called 'Federalism
Revolution' of the 1990s and Beyond – Federalism and the
Spending Power – Conclusion

THE UNITED STATES is a federal system. The powers of the
national government are listed in Article I, and were said by
James Madison to be 'few and defined'.[1] Few, perhaps: Article I,
section 8 has 18 clauses, though some have subdivisions. And defined,
to some extent: the clause giving Congress the power 'To Establish
Post Offices and Post Roads' is not subject to much interpretation.[2]
Other provisions are not as obviously well defined; the meaning of the
clause giving Congress the power 'To regulate Commerce ... among
the several States' has been contested almost continuously since 1789.

The Constitution also contains a residual clause, in the Tenth
Amendment: 'The powers not delegated to the United States by the
Constitution ... are reserved to the States respectively, or to the people'.
Upholding the federal minimum wage law, Justice Harlan Fiske Stone
observed that textually this provision 'states but a truism that all is
retained which has not been surrendered'.[3] It does not help us identify

---

[1] *The Federalist* 45.
[2] Chief Justice John Marshall did argue that the clause did not clearly give Congress the power to punish postal thefts, and that such a power had to be found in
the clause giving Congress the power 'To make all Laws which shall be necessary
and proper for carrying into Execution the foregoing Powers': *McCulloch v Maryland*
17 US (4 Wheat) 316, 417 (1819).
[3] *United States v Darby* 312 US 100, 124 (1941).

what has been surrendered to the national government. Yet, it certainly suggests that the states are the primary repository of governing power. Again, Madison provides a useful statement: 'The powers reserved to the several States will extend to all the objects which, in the ordinary course of affairs, concern the lives, liberties, and properties of the people, and the internal order, improvement, and prosperity of the State'.[4]

The efficient Constitution is quite different from this. The national government is today essentially a government of plenary power over all subjects. Over the past decades the Supreme Court has imposed modest and controversial limits on national power in the name of federalism, but the modesty is far more important than the restrictions. Defenders of state authority regularly cite family law, ordinary criminal law and land use regulation as areas where the states are the primary lawmakers and over which the national government has quite limited power. Yet, as scholars have shown, national law pervades the regulation of families and land use, and federal criminal law reaches deep into the states, for example making it a federal crime to rob a neighborhood grocery store.[5] Congress does not exercise all the power it has under the efficient Constitution, but the reasons lie in politics rather than constitutional law.

STATE GOVERNMENTS AND THE US CONSTITUTION

The US Constitution says nothing about the powers state governments have. Some provisions expressly limit state power, for example by barring states from issuing 'bills of Credit'. In addition, the national government has the power to displace state laws by enacting legislation that falls within the powers granted to the national government. In general, though, the Constitution assumes that state governments will have significant governing power, able to pursue whatever policies state voters prefer. The Supreme Court has identified a nontextual principle of the 'sovereign equality' of the states,[6] confirming as a matter of constitutional doctrine the long-standing principle in the efficient Constitution that the United States has a system of symmetrical federalism in which

---

[4] *The Federalist* 45.
[5] See JE Hasday, 'Federalism and the Family Reconstructed' (1998) 45 University of California Los Angeles *Law Review* 1297; 18 USC § 1851, known as the Hobbs Act.
[6] *Shelby County v Holder* 133 SCt 2612 (2013).

all states are assumed to be identical in their governing capacity—though, of course, states may vary in the extent to which they exercise the powers they have. The existence of states is a predicate of the overall constitutional system in the United States even though the US Constitution says relatively little about the states as such. Justice Louis Brandeis famously asserted that 'a single courageous State may, if its citizens choose, serve as a laboratory; and try novel social and economic experiments without risk to the rest of the country'.[7] And indeed, states have originated innovative policies regarding openness in government, environmental protection, and much more—policies that sometimes have spread to other states and then were adopted or adapted by the national government.

State governments mirror the national government in structure: an elected chief executive (the state's governor), two houses in the legislature (with the exception of Nebraska, whose legislature consists of a single house), and a judiciary. Aside from the fundamental proposition that state governments have plenary power—that is, can legislate on any subject whatever—whereas the national government has only enumerated powers, state governments differ from the national government structurally in two other ways. In many states some important executive officials are elected independent of the governor. Sometimes even the second-in-command, the lieutenant-governor, is elected separately, which occasionally leads to an uncomfortable partnership, with the governor reluctant to go out of the state and leave its government in a rival's hands. And, even more important, judges in almost every state are elected or appointed subject to subsequent 'retention' elections. Neither the similarities nor the differences across states in their structures of government, nor the similarities to and differences from the national structure, are required by the national Constitution; they result from political choices made at varying times within the states. The only constraint imposed by the national Constitution is that states must have a 'republican' form of government, a requirement enforced not by the courts but by Congress in its decisions about whether to seat a legislator who might have been chosen in a 'non-republican manner', or by the executive branch in using national military force to displace a non-republican state government.[8] Neither contingency has arisen in the

---

[7] *New State Ice Co v Liebmann* 285 US 262, 311 (1932) (Brandeis J dissenting).
[8] *Luther v Borden* 48 US 1 (1849).

United States because the concept of 'republican form of government' is capacious enough to accommodate all the institutional innovations generated within the states.[9]

Judicial elections pose important questions about judicial independence. Judicial elections became popular as a way of freeing judges from control by political bosses who previously controlled their appointment. By the late twentieth century, new concerns had arisen. As with other elections, money flowed into contested judicial elections, as businesses, trial lawyers, and labor unions all vied to secure the election of judges who would favor their positions in ordinary civil litigation. The Supreme Court held that there were no special attributes of judicial elections that justified stricter limits on campaign finance for judicial than for legislative and elections. Extreme cases, though, might raise due process concerns, when a judge who benefited from a large expenditure by a litigant before the court ruled in that litigant's favor. 'Good government' efforts to replace judicial elections with selection by judicial nominating commissions made some progress in the twentieth century but were far from universal.[10]

Each state develops its own budget. The US Constitution does not require that the national government operate in fiscal balance, and in recent years it has rarely done so. State constitutions, in contrast, generally require that each year the state's expenditures match its revenues. State governments are financed through taxes on real property and through sales taxes, supplemented by grants from the national government to implement national policies. Balanced-budget requirements mean that state governments attempt to have a surplus of revenues over expenditures in good economic times, accumulating 'rainy day' funds that can cover what would otherwise be fiscal deficits in bad economic times. In the second half of the twentieth century, though, strong local movements to restrict tax increases placed state governments under real pressure, as voters treated 'rainy day' funds not as prudent planning but as resulting from taxes that were higher than needed to cover current expenditures.

---

[9] See *Pacific States Telephone & Telegraph Co v Oregon* 223 US 118 (1912), treating as a political question the compatibility of direct popular legislation through initiative and referendum with the 'republican form of government' clause.

[10] *Republican Party v White* 536 US 765 (2002); *Caperton v AT Massey Coal Co* 556 US 868 (2009).

Disparities in resources and differences in citizen preferences—for low taxes rather than substantive policies, for example—can lead to wide differences among the states in how much each spends on education, prisons, roads, consumer protection and all the other objects of government policy. Some of these differences reflect the federal system operating through its 'laboratories' of social experimentation, but sometimes the differences are so large and troubling as to bring the value of federalism into question—consider, for example, the inadequate investment in protecting the city of New Orleans from flooding during a large hurricane. Notably, nothing in the US Constitution requires that the national government do anything to address these disparities; doing so is simply a matter of policy choice at the national level.

THE EMERGENCE OF (NEARLY) PLENARY NATIONAL POWER

Federalism questions arise only when Congress enacts a statute that defenders of state and local authority contend falls outside the scope of the powers granted Congress. That simple statement reveals an important point. Federal questions arise only when Congress acts. If Congress sits back passively, or does relatively little, federalism questions will not arise. And that describes reasonably accurately the first century of the nation's history under the Constitution.

The motor of constitutional development in the United States was the economy, which means that Congress's power to regulate 'Commerce ... among the several States' was the provision most often invoked. Newspapers and legislative debates in the founding era show a conventional triumvirate of economic activities: manufacturing, agriculture, and commerce, the latter pretty clearly referring to the actual exchange of goods for goods or money—trade in the ordinary sense. Chief Justice John Marshall seized the opportunity in the first great Commerce Clause case to substitute a much broader notion of commerce for the founding era one, giving the term, as Justice Robert Jackson put it a century later, 'a breadth never yet exceeded'.[11]

Marshall's case involved a challenge to the monopoly the state of New York had given to Robert Fulton, the inventor of the steamship, to

---

[11] *Wickard v Filburn* 317 US 111, 120 (1942).

operate between New York and New Jersey.[12] The challengers asserted that they were entitled to operate their own steamships along the same routes because they had a license from Congress to do so. As Marshall saw the problem, the first question the Court had to answer was whether the Commerce Clause gave Congress the power to issue licenses to operate ships along the coast—or, as he put it, whether 'navigation' was encompassed within the term 'commerce'. The categorical approach suggested by the founding era triumvirate made it at least coherent to ask whether 'navigation' might be yet a fourth category, different from 'commerce'. Marshall had little trouble coming to the conclusion, obvious to modern readers, that navigation is a form of commerce. Marshall's definition of 'commerce' was quite expansive: Commerce, for Marshall, was 'intercourse' broadly understood. What of commerce 'among the several States'? 'Among' meant 'intermingled with' and did not 'stop at the external boundary line of each State, but may be introduced into the interior'. Were there any limits on Congress's power to regulate interstate commerce? Here, Marshall offered several formulations. The most comprehensive was this: the grant of power did not cover 'that commerce which is completely internal, which is carried on between man and man in a State, or between different parts of the same State, and which does not extend to or affect other States'. A few lines later, Marshall referred to 'the exclusively internal commerce of a State'.

What ended up mattering was the conjunctive form of Marshall's definition: Congress lacked power to regulate commerce that was both completely internal to a state *and* that did not affect other states. As the national economy became increasingly interconnected, the domain of the 'completely internal' shrank and, more important, even completely internal commerce began to affect other states. In 1789 a person might sell a horse to a neighbor without much effect anywhere else, but once a national market for horses developed, local sales inevitably affected the national market. The Jacksonians who dominated the national government in the 1830s were opposed to the expansion of national power, though, and were disinclined to take advantage of the power Congress had under the Constitution.

It took the Civil War to demonstrate to politicians that the national government could actually operate on a reasonably large scale. And, after the war, economic expansion and the concomitant disruptions it

---

[12] *Gibbons v Ogden* 22 US (9 Wheat) 1 (1824).

occasioned generated political pressure on Congress to do something. Constitutional historians conventionally date the real beginning of aggressive congressional use of the power to regulate interstate commerce from 1887, when Congress created the Interstate Commerce Commission to regulate the rates charged by railroads to their customers, the politically relevant group of which was farmers shipping their products to urban centers for processing. But, on any coherent theory of the Commerce Clause's meaning, regulation of rates charged for interstate transportation of goods counted as commerce, and no one raised serious questions about congressional power here.

The situation changed when Congress enacted the Sherman Antitrust Act in 1890. One early enforcement action was against the so-called Sugar Trust, which resulted from the acquisition by one sugar company of four competing refineries. The Sugar Trust controlled 98 per cent of the nation's sugar refining capacity, and of course had the power to set the prices consumers paid for sugar. The Supreme Court held that the Sherman Act did not prohibit the creation of the Sugar Trust—because if it did, it would be unconstitutional.[13] The Court relied on the founding-era distinctions to hold that sugar refining was manufacturing, not commerce. The pre-New Deal Court invoked a similar conceptual framework in barring Congress from regulating labor relations in the mining industry: 'Mining brings the subject matter of commerce into existence. Commerce disposes of it'.[14]

Simultaneously with these restrictive interpretations of the commerce power, the Court developed more expansive interpretations. And necessarily so. Congress had enacted a large number of regulatory statutes. In 1922 Chief Justice William Howard Taft listed the most important ones in addition to the Interstate Commerce Act and the Sherman Act: 'the Railroad Safety Appliance Law, the Adamson Law, the Federal Trade Commission Law, the Clayton Act, the Federal Employers' Liability Law, the Pure Food Law, the Narcotic Law, and the White Slave Law'.[15] The Court could hardly set its face against all of these statutes, and it developed doctrinal tools that allowed it to uphold them all, at least in

---

[13] *United States v EC Knight Co* 156 US 1 (1895).

[14] *Carter v Carter Coal Co* 298 US 238 (1936).

[15] W Howard Taft, 'Three Needed Steps of Progress' (1922) 8 *American Bar Association Journal* 34 (Jan).

their most common applications. Congress could prohibit the interstate transportation of goods—except when it could not.[16] It could regulate local activities that affected interstate commerce—except when the effects were 'indirect'.[17] By the early years of the twentieth century the Court had developed a doctrinal toolkit that seemingly could be used to uphold or invalidate anything Congress did. Clever lawyers could, of course, reconcile the apparently inconsistent cases, but the public certainly got the impression that the courts were implementing their own vision of how a modern economy ought to be organized and regulated rather than interpreting the Constitution.

Matters came to a head when the conservative-dominated Supreme Court confronted Franklin Roosevelt's New Deal legislation. The so-called 'Sick Chicken' case triggered the strongest response. Roosevelt had supported the creation of the National Recovery Administration, which authorized industries to create and enforce codes of 'fair competition'. Most industry codes, including that for the poultry industry, contained provisions requiring that employers pay prescribed minimum wages and employ workers for no more than a specified maximum number of hours. The code also required that retail purchasers accept a full 'run' of chickens offered to them, without picking out the best from the run. The New Deal's economic theory, almost certainly mistaken, was that managing competition would stabilize production and give the country a chance to restore the economic prosperity lost during the Depression.

The Schechter brothers were retail purchasers in Brooklyn, New York, who, after slaughtering the chickens they purchased, would sell the chickens to butchers for sale to consumers. They bought their chickens from shippers who got them from farms scattered around the country and sent them by rail to New York. They violated the code's wage and hour provisions, as well as the 'entire run' requirement by refusing to accept sick chickens out of a full run. They challenged the

---

[16] *Champion v Ames* 188 US 321 (1903) (upholding a congressional ban on the interstate transportation of lottery tickets); *Hammer v Dagenhart* 247 US 251 (1918) (invalidating a congressional statute prohibiting the interstate transportation of goods produced by child labor).

[17] The *Shreveport Rate Cases* 234 US 342 (1914) (upholding congressional power to regulate the rates charged for shipments within a single state because such rates had effects on interstate commerce); *EC Knight* 156 US 1 (1895) (holding that the effects on prices of the creation of a monopoly were indirect).

penalties imposed on them on the ground that their activities were not part of interstate commerce.

The Supreme Court unanimously agreed.[18] Chief Justice Charles Evans Hughes wrote the lead opinion. The chickens were no longer 'in' interstate commerce when the Schechters purchased them. And, more important, these local activities had only an indirect effect on interstate commerce:

> If the commerce clause were construed to reach all enterprise and transactions which could be said to have an indirect effect upon interstate commerce, the federal authority would embrace practically all the activities of the people, and the authority of the State over its domestic concerns would exist only by sufferance of the federal government.

Even the relatively liberal Justice Benjamin Cardozo agreed that the NRA reached too far into local matters, writing more pungently than Hughes:

> The law is not indifferent to considerations of degree. Activities local in their immediacy do not become interstate and national because of distant repercussions. What is near and what is distant may at times be uncertain. There is no penumbra of uncertainty obscuring judgment here. To find immediacy or directness here is to find it almost everywhere. If centripetal forces are to be isolated to the exclusion of the forces that oppose and counteract them, there will be an end to our federal system.

Roosevelt fumed at the decision, fearing that it cast into doubt large aspects not only of the New Deal but also of well-established federal regulatory schemes. At a press conference shortly after the decision was announced, Roosevelt criticized the Court for 'relegat[ing]' the nation 'to the horse-and-buggy definition of interstate commerce'.[19] Responding to the *Schechter* case and related decisions, Roosevelt developed his Court-packing scheme. Meanwhile, his lawyers prepared to defend other major New Deal programs.

The Court-packing plan failed, but the lawyers' defense succeeded, partly because they were able to manage the litigation better. The key case involved one of the nation's major steel companies, not a small slaughterhouse, and the National Labor Relations Act, a real center-piece of the modern administrative state, not the NRA—an odd and badly designed response to the Depression. The problem, or so it might

---

[18] *ALA Schechter Poultry Corp v United States* 295 US 495 (1935).

[19] Press Conference of May 31, 1935 SI Rosenman (ed) *Public Papers and Addresses of Franklin D Roosevelt*, vol 4, (New York, Random House, 1938-), p. 221.

have seemed, was the old triumvirate of 'agriculture, manufacturing, and commerce': Steel production was clearly manufacturing. The Court, with Chief Justice Hughes again writing the opinion, had no problem sustaining the National Labor Relations Act.[20] As he put it, 'The question is necessarily one of degree'. Simply reciting the scope of the operation was enough to show that Congress clearly could regulate it. Some activities, like the Schechters', might have only small and indirect effects on the national economy. But, Hughes wrote:

> We are asked to shut our eyes to the plainest facts of our national life and to deal with the question of direct and indirect effects in an intellectual vacuum. Because there may be but indirect and remote effects upon interstate commerce in connection with a host of local enterprises throughout the country, it does not follow that other industrial activities do not have such a close and intimate relation to interstate commerce as to make the presence of industrial strife a matter of the most urgent national concern.

The NLRB case purported to operate within the doctrinal framework established in earlier cases. A few years later, the Court abandoned the effort to limit congressional power under the Commerce Clause. *Wickard v Filburn* involved a regulation that penalized a wheat farmer for growing both some wheat for sale in the interstate market and additional wheat for consumption on his own farm.[21] The Court had difficulty figuring out how to resolve the case within existing doctrine, and in the end it gave up. First it rejected the classical triumvirate:

> Whether the subject of the regulation in question was 'production,' 'consumption,' or 'marketing' is ... not material for purposes of deciding the question of federal power before us.'

Then, reciting the facts of the national market for wheat, Justice Robert Jackson observed that, in economic terms, wheat consumed on the farm substituted for wheat purchased on the market, reducing demand and depressing prices. The constitutional question turned on whether on-farm consumption in the aggregate affected interstate commerce, and it did:

> That appellee's own contribution to the demand for wheat may be trivial by itself is not enough to remove him from the scope of federal regulation where, as here, his contribution, taken together with that of many others similarly situated, is far from trivial.

---

[20] *NLRB v Jones & Laughlin Steel Corp* 301 US 1 (1937).
[21] 317 US 111 (1942).

With *Wickard*'s aggregation technique in hand, the doctrinal game was over. Congress had effectively plenary power, and only politics mattered. Or, as Justice Jackson put it more elegantly:

> The conflicts of economic interest between the regulated and those who advantage by it are wisely left under our system to resolution by the Congress under its more flexible and responsible legislative process.

The doctrinal structure created by the New Deal Court eliminated controversy over the scope of congressional power for several generations. Again conventionally, the illustrative case is *Perez v United States*, which upheld against constitutional challenge a statute making loan-sharking—lending money at very high interest rates and enforcing the loans by threats of violence—a federal crime.[22] This was a paradigmatic local crime, not different in principle from mugging a pedestrian, and yet the Court, over a single dissent, found the case easy: loan-sharking transactions in the aggregate had a substantial impact on the national economy, and that was enough for the Court.

The Supreme Court's Commerce Clause doctrine fit comfortably within the presuppositions of the New Deal, that the national government had the power and indeed the responsibility to ensure the smooth functioning of the national economy. And, because everything was connected to the economy, the national government became one of plenary power. Its authority would be exercised whenever national politicians believed it to their advantage to do so, the constraints becoming purely political rather than constitutional—or, more precisely, the constraints arising from the efficient rather than the written Constitution.

When the New Deal regime began to deteriorate and faced the Reagan Revolution, the Court's doctrine came under increasing pressure, which culminated in a series of decisions in the 1990s that were the Reagan Revolution's equivalent to cases like *Wickard v Filburn*—exemplifications of the constitutional principles underlying the newer regime.

THE SO-CALLED 'FEDERALISM REVOLUTION' OF THE 1990s AND BEYOND

Several Supreme Court decisions in the 1990s led observers to declare that a 'Federalism Revolution' had begun. And, indeed, the Court found

[22] 402 US 146 (1971).

a few statutes unconstitutional because they violated principles of federalism for the first time since 1936. Yet, to this point the 'revolution' looks more like a group of farmers with pitchforks than a serious effort to overturn the expansion of national power that followed the New Deal. That expansion is so deeply embedded that the most we can expect are some rare skirmishes over unimportant additional extensions of national power—or, if the Court does decide to take on some important matter, a constitutional crisis akin to that of 1937.

The cases said to constitute the Federalism Revolution fall into four categories.

National Power Under the Commerce Clause

In 1990 Congress enacted the Gun-Free School Zones Act. The brain-child of Wisconsin Senator Herbert Kohl, the statute made it a federal crime to possess a gun near any school. Gun possession in and near schools may have been a real social problem, but the states were already dealing with it through their own laws. There is little reason to think that additional legislation by Congress was needed, except insofar as Senator Kohl and his colleagues thought there was political advantage to be gained by showing that they were 'tough on crime'. Federal prosecutors understood how pointless the statute was, and devoted their resources to other matters. But one federal prosecutor did file charges against a student who brought a gun to school as a favor to a friend who was in a gang.

When the case reached the Supreme Court in 1995, for the first time since 1936 the Court invalidated a national statute on the ground that it did not deal with 'commerce among the several States'.[23] Chief Justice William Rehnquist's opinion for the Court contains several themes. Two had some enduring impact. First, what has been called the 'non-infinity' principle: examine the interpretation of the Commerce Clause the government uses to defend the statute's constitutionality.[24] If that interpretation would also support the constitutionality of every imaginable

---

[23] *United States v Lopez* 514 US 549 (1995).

[24] The term was first used in GH Reynolds and BP Denning, 'Lower Court Readings of *Lopez*, or What if the Supreme Court Held a Constitutional Revolution and Nobody Came' (2000) 2000 *Wisconsin Law Review* 369, 376.

statute, the courts should reject the interpretation and hold the statute at issue unconstitutional. Or, in Chief Justice Rehnquist's words, '[I]f we were to accept the Government's arguments, we are hard-pressed to posit any activity by an individual that Congress is without power to regulate'. Second, the 'commercial activity' rule: the New Deal approach of upholding regulations of local activities if, in the aggregate, those activities have a significant or substantial effect on interstate commerce can be used only when the local activity is itself a commercial one.

The non-infinity principle is clearly an important one, but it is equally clearly not a significant limit on congressional power. It may prune away some excesses of centralization, but with respect to nearly everything Congress does we will be able to come up with some limiting principle.

The 'commercial activities' rule might have been more important, although much would turn on how the courts went about 'individuating' activities, as philosophers might put it. That is, suppose Congress required that everyone who transfers a gun to someone else report the transaction. Should a transfer of a gun between friends be treated as a non-commercial activity because no money changes hands, or should the regulated activity be described as 'gun transfers', most of which are clearly commercial? The Court did not have to explore that problem, because a decade after it decided the Gun-Free School Zones Act case it came up with an analysis that converted that decision from a potentially significant harbinger of things into an odd aberration.[25]

Gonzales v Raich was a challenge to the application of the national law making possession of marijuana a crime.[26] In addition to its psychotropic effects, marijuana can be an effective pain-killer. Angel Raich suffered from debilitating illnesses, and was able to relieve her pain only by using marijuana. She grew marijuana in her home in quantities sufficient only for her own use.[27] Concerned that she might be prosecuted for violating the national criminal law, she sought a declaration that if the law applied to her activities, it was unconstitutional because it was a local activity beyond Congress's power to regulate under the Commerce

---

[25] The Court followed *Lopez* only once, in invalidating a provision of the Violence Against Women Act that made a federal remedy available for physical assaults motivated by the victim's gender: *United States v Morrison* 529 US 598 (2000).

[26] 545 US 1 (2005).

[27] I have simplified the facts for expositional purposes, but the simplification does not affect the application of the Court's rule to the facts as they actually were.

Clause. The Court rejected her argument. It treated what she did as a non-commercial activity but, Justice John Paul Stevens wrote, 'Congress can regulate purely intrastate activity that is not itself "commercial" … if it concludes that failure to regulate that class of activity would undercut the regulation of the interstate market in that commodity'. The problem in the gun possession case, then, now turns out to be that it was a free-standing statute, not part of a larger regulatory scheme the effectiveness of which would be undercut by excluding gun possession near schools from regulation.

After *Raich* it would appear that Congress can regulate local and non-commercial activities as long as it embeds that regulation in a larger regulatory program. Again, some tricky questions might arise. Suppose Congress enacts a rather broad system of gun controls at one time, and several years later comes to believe that its system is being weakened by the fact that it is not a crime to possess guns near schools. It enacts a specific statute dealing with the latter problem. Should the new statute be treated as a freestanding statute, in which case it might be unconstitutional, or as part of a multi-statute regulatory system, in which case it probably would be constitutional under *Raich*? The *Raich* analysis gives Congress incentives to be more intrusive on state authority rather than less intrusive, because it says that broad regulatory systems will be easier to defend than narrower ones.

A constitutional challenge to President Barack Obama's major legislative accomplishment, the Affordable Care Act, produced yet another doctrinal innovation in the federalism revolution, but once again the challenge seems likely to have little enduring impact. This is particularly true because, although a majority of the Supreme Court endorsed a new limitation on congressional power, a differently composed majority actually upheld the Act by invoking Congress's power to tax and spend for the general welfare. The Commerce Clause challenge, which five justices accepted, was that the Affordable Care Act's 'individual mandate,' a requirement that every individual with the financial resources to do so obtain health insurance either from an employer or by purchasing it from a private insurance company, regulated 'inactivity' rather than commercial activity. The Affordable Care Act also required insurance companies to provide insurance for people who had 'preexisting conditions,' that is, medical conditions that existed before they purchased the insurance, and charge such people only the general ('community') rate. In another doctrinal innovation, the majority also held that, although the individual mandate might be a 'necessary' means for guaranteeing that a system of privately purchased health insurance covering preexisting conditions and community rating would not unravel as people waited to buy insurance at low rates when they became seriously ill, it was not a 'proper' means for doing so because of the innovative nature of regulating inactivity.[28]

Congress rarely if ever regulates inactivity, and indeed, had the 'inactivity' restriction been known before the statute was enacted, it would have been relatively easy to draft a statute imposing the individual mandate on people who engaged in any activity that increased the risk that they would become ill or have an accident requiring medical care. The new doctrine separating the 'Necessary and Proper' Clause into two distinct parts might be more generative, yet here too what made the statute not 'proper' was that it was independently unconstitutional, that is, because there was already another constitutional objection to the individual mandate. In the end, the fact that the Affordable Care Act went into effect is likely to dwarf the fact that a Supreme Court majority articulated new constitutional doctrines that seemed designed to invalidate only that statute, and no others.

The details to one side, the larger picture is clear. After *Raich* and *NFIB* the only national statutes likely to be held unconstitutional are small policy initiatives that may well have little justification other than political grandstanding. Anything important Congress wants to do, it can.

The 'Anti-Commandeering' Principle

The Supreme Court also developed a new principle to meet a new form of congressional legislation. The Court said that Congress could not 'commandeer' the resources of a state legislature or, more important, its executive branch to enforce national law. A national statute required that the backgrounds of people who purchase guns—their mental health and criminal histories—be checked before they could actually obtain the guns. After complex political maneuvering, Congress set up a computerized national system that would allow these background checks to be done at the moment of purchase. Implementing the

---

[28] *National Federation of Independent Business v Sebelius* 132 SCt 2566 (2012).

computerized system, though, would take several years. In the interim, Congress required that the chief law enforcement officer in the area where the gun transaction occurred conduct the background check. The Supreme Court held that this commandeering of local law enforcement resources was unconstitutional.[29]

Much of the Court's opinion dealt with the *arcana* of the Constitution's drafting and adoption, with the majority and dissenting opinions dissecting in minute detail a few passages in *The Federalist Papers*. The Court also offered a functional justification for the anti-commandeering principle. The gun control policy was unpopular in many jurisdictions, and its opponents might blame the local sheriff for doing the background checks when he or she really had no choice. Commandeering, that is, blurred the lines of political responsibility in ways that could not be overcome by statements by sheriffs that they were doing the background checks only because Congress forced them to.

The anti-commandeering principle might have the perverse effect—from the standpoint of someone interested in keeping the national government as small as possible—of encouraging the growth of a national enforcement bureaucracy. Blocked from using state resources already in place, a Congress forcefully committed to implementing a specific program might create a new bureaucracy, as indeed it did with the national computerized background check. Yet, this is often only a theoretical possibility. The commandeering technique offers three, not two, choices to Congress: a cheap enforcement mechanism by means of commandeering, an expensive one through a national bureaucracy, and ineffective enforcement. With the cheap mechanism barred by the anti-commandeering principle, the depth of Congress's political commitment to the program will determine the choice between an expensive effective method and a cheap, ineffective one.

As Justice Scalia's majority opinion in the gun control case noted, congressional efforts to recruit support from state officials were a new phenomenon, and, he sensibly argued, one would have thought that were the technique truly important for effective operation of the national government, Congress would have used it more often. The anti-commandeering principle, then, might have some small effects—positive and negative—on the size of the national government and so

---

[29] *Printz v United States* 521 US 898 (1997).

on federalism, but it plays a trivially small role in the actual distribution of power between the nation and the states.

Sovereign Immunity

The Eleventh Amendment provides:

> The Judicial power of the United States shall not be construed to extend to any suit in law or equity, commenced or prosecuted against one of the United States by Citizens of another State, or by Citizens or Subjects of any Foreign State.

Textually, the Amendment is something of a puzzle in cases that became increasingly important as Congress enacted statutes regulating the activities of state governments. Suppose a citizen of New York sued New York to force it to comply with some national statutory or constitutional requirement. By its terms, the Eleventh Amendment is inapplicable, because it refers to 'citizens of another State'. Yet, why bother to amend the Constitution to deal only with cases brought by out-of-staters? This question is particularly puzzling when one realizes that a suit by an out-of-stater to enforce a national statute is barred by the Amendment's language but precisely the same lawsuit by an in-stater is not.

In 1890 the Supreme Court interpreted the Eleventh Amendment to bar the in-stater's suit. Later decisions clarified the underlying rationale: the Eleventh Amendment embodied a principle of sovereign immunity, insulating state governments from liability for their non-compliance with national law. Stated broadly, though, that principle threatened the supremacy of national law. Consider this case, which came to the Court in 1908. According to then-applicable constitutional doctrine, the Constitution prohibited states from setting rates for railroad services that were excessively low. Minnesota enacted a statute that, according to the railroads, did exactly that, and threatened every railroad employee who collected any larger charge with enormous fines and jail terms. How could the railroads challenge this statute, which in their view was unconstitutional? One way would be to violate the law, go to trial in state court, defend against conviction by asserting the statute's unconstitutionality as a defense, and if convicted appeal to the Supreme Court. But, the railroads said, the size of the penalties made it completely unreasonable to expect that any employee would expose himself to the risk of conviction and eventual defeat. Instead, the railroads went into the national court system and asked for an order barring the state's Attorney-General from enforcing the rate regulation. The Supreme Court held that the Eleventh Amendment did not bar the railroad's lawsuit.[30] Suing a state official was different from suing the state, according to the Court, and only the latter fell under the Eleventh Amendment.

Everyone understands that this is a legal fiction, but its effect is to create a system in which there is some way to use the courts to ensure that state governments follow national law as the Supremacy Clause requires. This system—suing state officials but not the state—worked reasonably well, but it was not perfect. Notably, it gave states no reason to comply with national law until they were sued and enjoined to do so. In the meanwhile ordinary citizens would not get the benefits of national law. And those benefits could be substantial. National law, for example, requires all employers to pay minimum wages. Eventually the state government will be forced to pay those wages, when its officials are directed to do so. But until then the state government gets to operate on the cheap. The remedy is obvious: make the state government liable for monetary damages for failing to pay the minimum wage.

The Supreme Court in the 1990s held that the Eleventh Amendment precluded Congress from adopting this remedy. The Court held that the later-enacted Eleventh Amendment overrode any power Congress might have had under Article I to 'abrogate'—that is, deny effect to— the states' sovereign immunity.[31] And, though the Eleventh Amendment by its terms has nothing to do with state courts, the Supreme Court also held that Congress could not force states to entertain suits against themselves in their own courts, because sovereign immunity was presupposed in the constitutional scheme.[32]

These decisions undoubtedly weaken the supremacy of national law, and to that extent undermine the centralization of national power that occurred during the twentieth century. Their effects should not be over-estimated, though. States remain under a constitutional duty to comply with national law, and that duty can be enforced in the national courts by the fiction of suing a state official rather than the state itself. Indeed,

[30] *Ex p Young* 209 US 123 (1908).
[31] *Seminole Tribe of Florida v Florida* 517 US 44 (1996).
[32] *Alden v Maine* 527 US 706 (1999).

the Court has said that the national government itself can enforce national law directly in the national courts.

Perhaps more important, state governments have political and normative incentives to comply with national law. The same interest groups that press Congress to enact laws exist on the state level, and they influence state governments as well—perhaps somewhat less effectively in some states than in others, and less effectively than they can influence Congress, but with some effects nonetheless. Largely for that reason, many states have their own laws setting minimum wages or banning workplace discrimination that parallel national law, albeit sometimes differing in detail. And, normatively, state officials tend to believe that they ought to comply with national law. Cases arise not primarily because state governments contend that they do not have to comply with clearly applicable national law (after all, they know that they will be forced to do so in one of the fictitious 'officer' suits), but rather because they and plaintiffs disagree over whether national law applies in the first place.

The facts of one of the Supreme Court's cases are instructive.[33] The national minimum wage laws set minimum wages but exempt law enforcement officers. The state of Maine contended that its probation and parole officers were exempt because they were law enforcement officers. After a lower court rejected Maine's position, the state began to pay the required wages to its probation and parole officers. What was left to the lawsuit was a claim for back wages. The Supreme Court held that Maine was within its rights to assert sovereign immunity in its own courts against that claim. No doubt, the probation officers did not get what they were entitled to under national law. At the same time, though, the case is hardly one of straight-out state defiance of national law. Again, the Federalism Revolution evidenced by the sovereign immunity cases is smaller than one might have thought.

Congressional Power to 'Enforce' the Fourteenth Amendment

The Fourteenth Amendment gives Congress the power to 'enforce' the rights it provides individuals against state violation. The idea of enforcement seems clear enough. Congress has the power to create judicial remedies when states deny equal protection of the laws, for

[33] *Ibid.*

example. That formulation conceals some difficulties, though. No problems arise when the courts themselves agree that a state law denies equal protection. There the courts are enforcing constitutional rights the courts themselves recognize. What, though, if Congress thinks that the Constitution confers *broader* rights than the Court recognizes?

The problem arose after the Supreme Court held that the Free Exercise Clause of the First Amendment was not violated by generally applicable state laws that nonetheless had a significant adverse impact on the ability of a group to comply with its religion's precepts. The case upheld the constitutionality of applying a state's ban on the consumption of peyote, a psychoactive drug, to members of the Native American Church, for whom peyote consumption during religious rituals was required.[34] Disagreeing with the Court's interpretation of the Free Exercise Clause, Congress enacted the Religious Freedom Restoration Act, which prohibited governments from 'substantially burdening' religious practices even by generally applicable laws unless the burden advanced a compelling state interest and was the least restrictive means to do so—a test the Court itself had applied in cases decided before the peyote case.

Congress interpreted the Free Exercise Clause to protect individuals against certain state regulations; the Court interpreted the Clause differently. Which interpretation was to prevail? Not surprisingly, the Court's. Using the language of judicial supremacy rather than that of departmentalism, the Court held that Congress lacked the power under the Fourteenth Amendment to enact the statute:

> If Congress could define its own powers by altering the Fourteenth Amendment's meaning, no longer would the Constitution be 'superior paramount law, unchangeable by ordinary means.'[35]

The Court did allow for the possibility that Congress's power to enforce the Fourteenth Amendment meant more than that Congress could confer jurisdiction on the courts to decide whether a constitutional violation had occurred. But, it said, Congress's response had to be 'congruent with and proportional to' the extent of state violations of constitutional rights as the courts would define them. Confronted with a national law purporting to enforce the Equal Protection Clause

---

[34] *Employment Div, Dept of Human Resources of Oregon v Smith* 494 US 872 (1990).
[35] *City of Boerne v Flores* 521 US 507 (1997).

by requiring state employers to provide reasonable accommodations to their workers with disabilities, the Court held that the reasonable-accommodation requirement was not proportional to the record of state violations of the employment rights of disabled people.[36] In contrast, it upheld the application of the Family and Medical Leave Act to the states.[37] The act required employers to provide up to 12 weeks of unpaid leave to take care of ill spouses, children, or parents, and was justified as a proportionate response to employment decisions predicated on stereotypes about the proper role of women as caretakers.

The significance of the Court's decisions providing limits on Congress's power to enforce the Fourteenth Amendment should not be overestimated. Their most important feature is their endorsement of judicial supremacy in constitutional interpretation, not their practical effects. Congress can use its power to regulate interstate commerce to impose all sorts of requirements on states as employers, for example. What was really at stake in the employment cases was back pay. Recall that the Eleventh Amendment, adopted after Article I, vindicated a principle of sovereign immunity that limits Congress's ability to force states to pay monetary damages. By parallel reasoning, the Fourteenth Amendment, adopted after the Eleventh, overrides that principle and makes back pay available—although only when Congress is actually enforcing the Fourteenth Amendment.

The limits on Congress's enforcement power have some bite, of course. Not everything state governments do comes under the umbrella of interstate commerce. They conduct elections, for example, and Congress has required that states develop reasonable accommodations in the voting process for people with disabilities. Even here, though, there is another support for congressional action: the power conferred in Article I to regulate the 'Times, Places and Manner of holding Elections for Senators and Representatives'. As of 2008 the 'hottest' cases involving the scope of Congress's power to enforce the Fourteenth Amendment dealt with challenges to special fees—usually quite small,

---

[36] *Board of Trustees v Garrett* 531 US 356 (2001).

[37] *Nevada Dept of Human Resources v Hibbs* 538 US 721 (2003). But see *Coleman v Court of Appeals of Maryland* 132 SCt 1327 (2012) (holding the self-care provisions of the FMLA unenforceable against state governments because of a lack of evidence that self-care was a typically gendered activity, unlike child care and care for family members).

ranging from $5 to $20—charged to those who sought special tags that allow people with disabilities to park more easily. Without disparaging the importance of the problem these cases raise, we can still see that the Court's restrictions on congressional power to enforce the Fourteenth Amendment operates around the edges of an expansive national government, and even if vigorously developed would not do much to reduce the effective reach of national power.

Taken as a whole, these four sets of cases impose only rather modest restrictions on national power in the name of federalism. Most of the Court's decisions affect the states only in their managerial capacities, and even then do not place strong limits on what Congress can do: States must still comply with the substantive requirements of federal employment laws, for example, even if they are protected against monetary liability under some of those laws by sovereign immunity. National power could be restricted substantially only if the Court held that Congress lacked power to adopt the regulatory initiatives characteristic of late twentieth century government. The *Lopez* decision might have been pushed in that direction, restricting some national environmental laws such as applications of the Endangered Species Act that protect tiny insects that never cross state lines. That might yet occur. The *Raich* decision, though, puts in place a doctrine into which *Lopez* fits as a narrow exception to expansive national power. The Supreme Court's decisions since the 1990s do not amount to a real Federalism Revolution.

FEDERALISM AND THE SPENDING POWER

The main lines of centralization of power in the national government were laid down through congressional use of the power to regulate interstate commerce. Congress has others powers, of course, and as the twentieth century proceeded, one in particular became increasingly important. Congress has the power 'To lay and collect Taxes ... and provide for the common Defence and general Welfare of the United States'. James Madison and Alexander Hamilton engaged in a theoretical debate about the meaning of the 'general Welfare' clause. Both agreed that the overall provision referred to how taxes could be used. To the locally oriented Madison, the clause added nothing to Congress's other powers; Congress could use the money raised by taxes only in the service of one of the other enumerated powers. To the nationalist

Hamilton, the clause gave Congress the power to spend money for the general welfare without tying the idea of 'general welfare' to anything other than congressional judgment.

This dispute was largely theoretical in the nation's early years, when its fiscal resources were relatively limited, drawn almost entirely from tariffs, and the national government made few expenditures in the service of the general welfare. The growth of the national government and especially the adoption of the Sixteenth Amendment (1913), authorizing Congress to collect an income tax, opened up the possibility of a more vigorous use of the taxing and spending powers. And Congress took advantage of the money it now had available. In 1936 the Supreme Court endorsed Hamilton's view of the power's scope.[38] Thereafter Congress did not have to justify an expenditure by pointing to some other enumerated power whose purposes were served by the expenditure.[39] Indeed, a majority of the Supreme Court upheld the constitutionality of individual mandate in the Affordable Care Act (2010) on the ground that it was a penalty administered through the tax system rather than a pure regulatory requirement; the constitutional restrictions on regulatory requirements were inapplicable to taxes and tax-like penalties.

Spending programs proliferated. Their most important implications for the division of effective governing power between the states and the national government came from 'conditional spending' programs. In these programs Congress gives the states money, on condition that the states follow national regulatory requirements not only with regard to spending the money itself but also with regard to other, sometimes tangentially related matters. The Supreme Court took the position that as long as states were free to refuse the federal grants, the conditions rarely raised serious constitutional questions.

Federal grants have become a substantial part of state budgets, but until 2012 the courts never held that the grants were so large or so

---

[38] *United States v Butler* 297 US 1 (1936).

[39] In *Butler* the Court invalidated a New Deal program to stabilize agricultural production, not because it fell outside the scope of Congress's power to spend for the general welfare but because it violated independent constraints imposed on Congress's power by the idea of federalism.

attractive that states were coerced into accepting them.[40] Then, in the Affordable Care Act case the Court did find a spending condition coercive. In addition to the individual mandate, the Act expanded the system by which poor people obtained health insurance, a system known as Medicaid. The cost of providing this insurance was shared between state governments and the national government, with significant portions of state budgets devoted to their share of the Medicaid program. The Affordable Care Act required states to expand Medicaid so that it would cover a significant number of people with incomes above the formal 'poverty' line, on the theory that many people with low incomes could not afford to purchase health insurance from private companies. The national government promised to cover all of the additional costs of coverage for several years, and then to cover 90 per cent of the costs permanently. This requirement was enforced by the threat that states that did not expand Medicaid would lose not merely the money the national government provided for the Medicaid expansion but the far larger amounts the national government provided for the existing Medicaid program. According to the Supreme Court, that threat was indeed coercive, probably on the view that states were extremely unlikely to sacrifice insurance coverage for the poor simply because of objections to expanding that coverage above the poverty line. The majority acknowledged that Congress could have accomplished the same result by repealing the existing Medicaid system and replacing it with the expanded one, but that was of course politically unrealistic by the time the Court issued its decision. The result was that states with large numbers of people just above the poverty line, controlled by Republican legislatures, refused to expand Medicaid.[41]

In light of the national government's fiscal resources, the conditional spending power has become almost as important a tool for centralizing governing authority as the Commerce Clause. With the exception of the highly politically charged Affordable Care Act case, the Court has

---

[40] See, eg, *Steward Machine Co v Davis* 301 US 548 (1937), upholding the federal unemployment compensation system, which provided funds to states if their unemployment systems conformed to national requirements. The case presented possibly the strongest case for finding coercion, because given the way the system operated corporations in states that rejected the federal funds were likely to be at a serious competitive disadvantage. Local legislators therefore had very strong incentives to accept the federal funds and the accompanying conditions.

[41] *National Federation of Independent Businesses v Sebelius* 132 SCt 2566 (2012).

shown no interest in developing serious limitations on the conditional spending power.

CONCLUSION

Judicially enforced doctrine under the written Constitution has done little to place real limits on the expansionist tendencies of the national government, although such doctrine may have occasionally and erratically slowed the centralizing trend. The written Constitution, as interpreted by the Supreme Court, gives Congress almost plenary regulatory authority, and the Tenth Amendment's residuary clause is indeed no more than a truism imposing no real limits on congressional power.

The United States is not, though, a nation in which all governing power is in fact exercised by a national government that, when it chooses, allows state and local governments to pursue whatever policies they want. Despite the presence of national laws dealing with the environment that affect local land-use policies, enormous amounts of land-use planning occurs on the local level; despite the presence of national laws affecting the way in which states, cities and towns provide elementary and secondary education, large portions of the curriculum and a wide array of pedagogic techniques are determined on the local level; and so on through many important areas of public policy. The efficient Constitution, that is, does limit congressional power. As a classic article written in the 1950s put it, there are 'political safeguards of federalism'.[42] The Supreme Court briefly endorsed this view, in an opinion by Justice Harry Blackmun that observed: '[T]he fundamental limitation that the constitutional scheme imposes on the Commerce Clause to protect the "States as States" is one of process, rather than one of result.'[43]

Identifying those safeguards proves to be difficult. Herbert Wechsler, who first used the phrase, wrote of structures built into the written Constitution: the power of state legislatures to draw district lines for the House of Representatives in ways that gave state legislatures real

---

[42] H Wechsler, 'The Political Safeguards of Federalism: The Role of the States in the Composition and Selection of the National Government' (1954) 54 *Columbia Law Review* 543.

[43] *Garcia v San Antonio Metropolitan Transit Auth* 469 US 528 (1985).

influence on Representatives once elected; the selection of Senators by state legislatures in the original Constitution; the influence of the electoral college in ensuring that presidential candidates pay attention to the interests of states throughout the nation; and a general background assumption in the national legal and political culture that state legislatures are the front-line developers of public policy, with Congress playing a secondary role. Even in 1954, though, those structures were no longer effective in safeguarding federalism. Indeed, by 1954 the selection of Senators by state legislators had been abolished by constitutional amendment, and by then or shortly thereafter it probably was inaccurate to say that the legal and political culture treated state lawmakers as the front line for policy development.

More plausibly by the end of the twentieth century, the political safeguards of federalism were more purely political. As we have seen, political parties continue to be organized primarily on the state level. Many members of Congress gain experience by serving in state or local office before they move to Washington, although, as noted in chapter two, there are now other ways of becoming politically prominent. In addition, while it is easy to understand why a mayor or governor would care that Congress keep out of local matters, it is unclear why a member of Congress who once served as a mayor or governor would continue to care about that. Still, there are enough examples of Senators who returned to their home states to serve as governors to suggest that at least some Senators will think about preserving some scope for local governance.

Further, the incentives national legislators have do not push uniformly in the direction of grasping more power. National legislators might burnish their reputations and increase their chances for re-election by enacting policies that centralize power—but only if those policies work. And some policy initiatives fail. A Representative who pushed the limits of national power to get the initiative enacted will have to take the blame for the failure. Then, too, a single Representative will rarely be able to take full credit, even with his or her constituents, for successful policy initiatives. That reduces the 'supply' of centralizing proposals that get introduced and adopted. (But, of course, no single Representative will bear the full blame for failures, which reduces the pressure to refrain from offering policy proposals and increases the supply.)

Wechsler and other students of federalism sometimes used the 'political safeguards' argument to suggest that the political safeguards did a good enough job in producing a normatively attractive distribution of power between the national government and state and local governments. In *Garcia*, for example, Justice Blackmun said that the states' success in obtaining federal funds and exemptions from federal regulatory requirements demonstrated the 'effectiveness of the federal political process in preserving the States' interests'.[44] Moving from the descriptive claim that there are political safeguards to the normative one that those safeguards are 'effective' is almost certainly a mistake. Normative defenses of federalism typically assert that there are good reasons for organizing a government as a federal one. Federalism, it is said, limits the possibility of tyranny by making it possible for people to move easily from one location to another, thereby giving rulers an incentive to develop freedom-promoting policies that keep people from moving. It also helps achieve greater social welfare by allowing people with different values to live in subnational units and enact the policies that they like even though people living elsewhere, with different values, like different policies. And it is said to be a useful way of experimenting with various social policies until we see which policy works best, at which point the national government can scale-up a policy that succeeded locally. Notably, though, these defenses of federalism tell us almost nothing about how much centralization is too much—other than, perhaps, that complete centralization of all policies at the national level is a bad idea. That federalism is a good idea does not help us decide whether any particular distribution of power between state and nation is normatively desirable or 'effective'.

What we do know is that efforts to develop sensible doctrinal limits on centralization have not succeeded. The reason may lie in the specifics of US constitutionalism: The words of the Constitution, or the nation's constitutional tradition, may be inadequate to generate sensible doctrine. What is left are the political safeguards of federalism. We can note that they operate without contending that the safeguards work 'well' in some normative sense. The political safeguards of federalism arise out of ordinary political calculations about what course of action increases a national legislator's chances of reelection or a candidate's chances for election. No doubt the twentieth century saw centralization of power on a large scale, and a concomitant whittling down of state

---

[44] 469 US at 552.

and local governing authority. And that trend might well continue. Politics and economics probably explain the centralizing trend. An increasingly interconnected economy produces problems that nearly everyone thinks are better addressed at the national level. National politicians do not have to grab power, because, to overstate the point, no one really resists them. In the absence of some coherent normative account of the distribution of authority created by the US Constitution, the political safeguards simply are how the efficient Constitution implements federalism.

FURTHER READING

Choper, JE, *Judicial Review and the National Political Process: A Functional Reconsideration of the Role of the Supreme Court* (Chicago, University of Chicago Press, 1980) (restates Wechsler's argument with more recent evidence).

Frankfurter, F, *The Commerce Clause under Marshall, Taney, and Waite* (Chapel Hill, NC, University of North Carolina Press, 1937) (describes the development of commerce clause doctrine through the nineteenth century).

Jackson, VC, 'Federalism and the Uses and Limits of Law: *Printz* and Principle' (1998) 111 *Harvard L Rev* 2180 (analyzes the 'anti-commandeering' principle).

Kramer, L, 'Putting the Politics Back into the Political Safeguards of Federalism' (2000) 100 *Columbia L Rev* 215 (updates Wechsler's argument and emphasizes the role political parties play today).

Lessig, L, 'Translating Federalism: *United States v. Lopez*' (1995) 1995 *Supreme Court Rev* 125 (analyzes the beginnings of the 'Federalism Revolution').

Levinson, SL, *Framed: America's 51 Constitutions and the Crisis of Governance* (New York, Oxford University Press, 2013).

Shugerman, J, *The People's Courts: The Rise of Judicial Elections and Judicial Power in the United States* (Cambridge, Harvard University Press, 2012).

6

The Substance of Individual Rights under the Constitution

The Starting Point – Pragmatic and Realist Critiques – The New Deal Reconstruction – The Emergence of Modern Liberalism: Autonomy and Accommodation – Lawyers and Rights Litigation: The Development of Support Structures – Political Parties and Social Movements – From Congress to the Courts: The Venues for Rights Protection – The 'Backlash' Thesis – Constitutional Rights in the Twenty-First Century

THE IDEA OF rights has been central to US political and constitutional discourse from the beginning. The Declaration of Independence appealed to 'inalienable rights' and the first amendments to the Constitution were universally described as a Bill of Rights. The central place rights have in US constitutional culture would make it foolish to attempt to survey the substantive law of individual rights under the US Constitution. Instead, we can examine what happened to the idea of rights over the course of the twentieth century. By the end of the century rights-claims were being asserted in locations, such as schools and prisons, where they had not been found at the century's beginning, and they were being asserted on behalf of claimants, such as fetuses and new arrivals to the United States, who were outside the domain of rights earlier. And, perhaps most important, the content of rights-claims changed from assertions of classical liberal rights to property and contract to modern liberal rights to autonomy.

This transformation in rights occurred because of the relation between the Constitution and the political order. People find themselves facing material conditions that they wish would be different. Some people put themselves forward as leaders, and provide an account of how the material conditions could be changed.[1] This account provides the glue that transforms the discontented into a social movement.[2] And, importantly, sometimes the movement's leaders articulate some right as an important part of their account of why things are bad and how they could be changed.[3]

If the social movement becomes large enough, politicians take notice. Some see the possibility of political advantage in seeking the movement's support. They appropriate, rearticulate and transform the rights-claim associated with the movement. If these political leaders are successful, the rights-claim becomes part of a party platform, and indeed, sometimes, part of the platforms of both major political parties. Legislative recognition of the rights-claim may follow, although again we have to note the times at which and the ways in which the political versions of rights-claims differ from the social movement's version. The right, no longer a claim, then can become embedded in executive and, sometimes, corporate bureaucracies, where lawyers take its enforcement as part of their duty to comply with the law.

Alternatively, the rights-claim may be vindicated in courts. A political party that sees the social movement as an important constituent will ensure that the judges its leaders appoint or confirm are sympathetic to the rights-claim. Or, particularly when leaders in both major parties

---

[1] These movement entrepreneurs can but need not be members of the disaffected group.

[2] Sometimes it is useful to think of this group more narrowly as an interest group. With respect to most aspects of the argument here, nothing analytically important turns on whether we describe the group as a social movement or an interest group. I suspect that leaders of relatively narrow interest groups have to do somewhat more work to develop a rights-based defense of their claims than do leaders of social movements, but I am confident that they can do so and have sometimes done so.

[3] As I suggested at the outset, appeals to rights have a particular valence in US political culture, and so can—although they need not always—serve as a more effective rhetoric for mobilizing support than appeals to 'mere' interests. When social movement leaders make their strategic choices, rhetoric is one dimension of choice, and sometimes they will choose the rhetoric of rights.

offer support for the rights-claim, judges already on the bench may begin to think that a rights-claim that they previously had not thought valid actually has more force than they earlier believed.[4]

These institutional factors provided the basic support for changes in ideas about rights. The changes in ideas involved a shift from classical liberalism to modern liberalism. At the outset of the twentieth century the prevailing idea of rights defined them with reference to the doctrines of classical liberalism with its emphasis on choice and contract in the market, supplemented by an ideal of equality expressed in hostility to class legislation that departed from neutral treatment of all groups in the economy and society. At the end of the century rights were associated with a modern liberalism adding to the classical liberal account a concern for individual autonomy in all spheres of life, supplemented by a more substantive ideal of equality that extended, again, into all spheres of life.

Ideas about rights are always complex when they are brought to ground in law. Elaborating the details of a particular right inevitably raises questions about the scope of the right, whether it should be limited by other rights, the extent to which general social policies can limit rights, and more. At one time one understanding of rights, and of specific rights, may prevail, and then be displaced in the legal culture by other ideas. The older ideas do not disappear, though. They hang on, sometimes serving as one basis for criticizing the new order and sometimes offering an alternative to which the nation might return. What follows attempts to identify the central tendencies of rights discourse through the twentieth century, but older ideas never disappear, and sometimes affect the way in which newer ones develop.[5]

---

[4] Here I rely on the insights of Reva Siegel and Robert Post. See, eg, R Siegel, 'Constitutional Culture, Social Movement Conflict and Constitutional Change: The Case of the de facto ERA' (2006) 94 *California Law Review* 1323; R Seigel and R Post, 'Popular Constitutionalism, Departmentalism, and Judicial Supremacy' (2004) 92 *California Law Review* 1027.

[5] For a conceptualization of the ways in which changing ideas and institutions overlap, see the discussion of 'intercurrence' in K Orren and S Skowronek, 'Institutions and Intercurrence: Theory Building in the Fullness of Time' in I Shapiro and R Hardin (eds), *NOMOS 38: Political Order* (New York, New York University Press, 1996).

THE STARTING POINT

Among lawyers at the end of the nineteenth century the conceptual framework for addressing rights questions was reasonably well developed. Deploying that framework in particular cases was less stable, although some approaches clearly predominated over others. The instability in application provided the opening wedge for critiques that began early and became increasingly credible in the first decades of the twentieth century. Meanwhile, popular discourse about rights did not respect the lawyers' categories, but precisely because it was popular had less coherent conceptual underpinnings.

Lawyers sorted rights into three categories:

— Civil rights: These were rights that arose from the mere existence of organized society. Drawing on the social contract tradition, lawyers treated the right to physical security, the right to own property and the right to enter into contracts (and some associated rights essential to protecting those basic rights, such as the right to sue in court and to present evidence in support of one's claims) as civil rights. The Civil Rights Act of 1866, which provided that 'citizens, of every race and color, without regard to any previous condition of slavery or involuntary servitude ... shall have the same right, in every State and Territory in the United States, to make and enforce contracts, to sue, be parties, and give evidence, to inherit, purchase, lease, sell, hold, and convey real and personal property ... as is enjoyed by white citizens', used this idea of civil rights.

— Political rights: These were rights that arose from the political organization of particular societies. A society might not have jury trials, but if it did, the right to sit on juries was a political right—as, of course, was the right to vote.

— Social rights: In many ways this was a residual but extremely important category, covering all the activities of daily life that did not implicate contract or property. As Rebecca Scott points out, the term social equality functioned in the late nineteenth century as a pejorative, identifying areas of life in which close associations between whites and other racial groups were regarded—by whites—as especially to be avoided.[6]

---

[6] RJ Scott, 'Public Rights, Social Equality, and the Conceptual Roots of the Plessy Challenge' (2008) 106 *Michigan Law Review* 777.

With important qualifications, governments could not deny anyone either civil or political rights, but had no duty to protect social rights.[7] They could limit social rights by exercising their traditional police powers, defined expansively to include not only promotion of safety and health, but public morals as well. Indeed, governments might be barred from seeking to advance social rights if protecting one person's social rights would limit another's civil rights.

Because they were baseline rights, civil and political rights had notions of equality built into them. How, then, did late nineteenth-century lawyers justify denying the right to vote to women, for example? By invoking the qualifications on the basic rights. These rights were available to everyone who satisfied requirements of capacity, defined in terms of the ability to deliberate and choose rationally, and independence, defined as a person's ability to come to conclusions without being unduly influenced by another who held economic power over the person. Women could be denied the right to vote on grounds of both capacity and dependence: To some, their more emotional responses to problems of public policy meant that they did not have the capacity to participate in making public policy; to others, the economic dependence of women on their fathers or husbands meant that they were subject to undue influence.[8]

Ideas of equality played an additional role. Drawing on roots going back at least to the Jacksonian period, late nineteenth century constitutional theory was hostile to what was described as 'class legislation'. Such legislation promoted the interests not of the people as a whole, but only the interests of a segment of the people. Discerning when a statute was merely class legislation was of course difficult. Opponents of a statute might call it class legislation, but its proponents ordinarily could deploy arguments aimed at demonstrating that the proposal advanced the general interest. Hostility to class legislation was therefore more a cast of mind that lawyers brought to their consideration of particular statutes, than a doctrine uncontroversially invoked to explain why a statute was unconstitutional.[9]

---

[7] For a discussion, see MV Tushnet, 'Political Aspects of the Changing Meaning of Equality in Constitutional Law: The Equal Protection Clause, Dr. Du Bois, and Charles Hamilton Houston' (1987) 74 *Journal of American History* 884.

[8] For discussion, see W Wiecek, *The Lost World of Classical Legal Thought: Law and Ideology in America, 1886–1937* (New York, Oxford University Press, 1998).

[9] See generally H Gillman, *The Constitution Besieged: The Rise and Demise of Lochner Era Police Powers Jurisprudence* (Durham, NC, Duke University Press, 1993).

Several important cases illustrate these categories.

—   *Plessy v Ferguson* (1896) upheld a state law requiring that railroads maintain separate cars for white and African American travelers. According to the Supreme Court, the right to ride in a particular car was merely a social right.[10]

—   *Holden v Hardy* (1898) upheld a state law limiting the hours miners could work to eight hours a day. Mining was risky and unhealthy, and the government could use its police powers to protect miners. In addition, according to the Court, there was reason to think that miners were not sufficiently independent to have a civil right to sign contracts requiring that they work long hours: 'the proprietors lay down the rules and the laborers are practically constrained to obey them. In such cases, self-interest is often an unsafe guide, and the legislature may properly interpose its authority.'[11]

—   *Lochner v New York* (1905) struck down a state law limiting bakers to 10 working hours a day. The Supreme Court found insufficient evidence that limiting working hours made it more likely that bakery products would be safe for consumers, or less likely that bakery workers would be healthy. And there was no reason to think that bakers were less able than any other workers to make good decisions about their own interests—that is, no reason to think that bakery workers either lacked capacity to contract or were too dependent on others.[12]

—   *Muller v Oregon* (1908) upheld a state law limiting to eight the hours women could work in laundries. The Court's decision invoked both the police power—the ability of the state to intervene in a contractual relation because of women's distinctive physical capacity—and women's dependence on men: 'history discloses the fact that woman has always been dependent upon man.... Though limitations upon personal and contractual rights may be removed by legislation, there is that in her disposition and habits of life which will operate against a full assertion of those rights.... It is impossible to close one's eyes to the fact that she still looks to her

---

[10]   163 US 537, 552 (1896).
[11]   169 US 366, 397 (1898).
[12]   198 US 366, 397 (1905).

brother, and depends upon him ... The two sexes differ in ... the self-reliance which enables one to assert full rights...'[13]

— *Buchanan v Warley* (1917) invalidated a Louisville ordinance requiring residential segregation. The ordinance prohibited African Americans from buying houses on blocks where whites were a majority and whites from buying houses on blocks with African American majorities. The Court's opinion emphasized that the ordinance interfered with the owner's ordinary right to sell his property at the price he chose to the person he chose.[14]

— *Meyer v Nebraska* (1923) struck down a state law prohibiting instruction in German, even in private schools. The Court offered two reasons for its decision. The first fit easily into the existing conceptual framework: The statute 'attempted materially to interfere with the calling of modern language teachers' and thereby deprived them of their right to enter into contracts with parents who wanted their children educated in German. The second was broader, more compatible with modern liberalism's emphasis on personal autonomy, here the autonomy of parents from the state: The Constitution protected 'the right of the individual to contract, to engage in any of the common occupations of life, to acquire useful knowledge, to marry, establish a home and bring up children, to worship God according to the dictates of his own conscience, and generally to enjoy those privileges long recognized at common law as essential to the orderly pursuit of happiness by free men.'[15]

Many of these cases have an undoubted libertarian flavor, but classical liberalism was not modern libertarianism or mere laissez faire. When private contracts had effects on third parties—people who were not part of the contractual relationship—the Court upheld a wide range of regulatory statutes as valid exercises of the government's police powers, even when those regulations might have been characterized as interfering with someone's right to property or contract. No one seriously questioned the constitutionality of provisions in New York's law regulating bakeries that required that prohibited workers from sleeping at their workplace, for example. The reason is that such a practice might well render the workplace unsanitary, and so affect the quality and safety

---

[13] 208 US 412, 422 (1908).
[14] 245 US 60, 74–75 (1917).
[15] 262 US 390, 401, 399 (1923).

of the bread the workers made. *Plessy* provides another example: railroads and African Americans might have been happy to make contracts allowing the latter to ride on any car they wished, but, as the legislature and the Court saw things, those contracts affected the social rights of whites who wanted to ride in segregated cars. The contracts between the railroads and African Americans could therefore be regulated.

The Court got its back up only with respect to statutes it regarded, in a phrase used in *Lochner*, as a 'labor law pure and simple'—that is, as legislation resting on the assumption that ordinary workers could not bargain effectively with their employers. Nor did the Court write the common law's definitions of capacity and dependence into the Constitution. No one thought that courts could refuse to enforce miners' agreements to work long hours in states without a maximum hours law—that is, that miners lacked capacity under the common law. Rather, the Court recognized some power in the legislature to alter traditional common-law definitions, at least to some extent.[16]

Most of the constitutional issues at the heart of late nineteenth century discourse were bound up with economic regulation, and not with the issues of free expression and equality that came to dominate rights discourse in the twentieth century. But the libertarian tendencies associated with the earlier discourse had implications for those issues as well. As political scientist Mark Graber and legal scholar David Rabban have shown, while courts were unsympathetic to free speech claims during this period, a vigorous libertarian jurisprudence of free expression developed, and was available when political liberals began to worry about government regulation of speech.[17] And, to the extent that Jim Crow was a system of legal regulation that extended into the domain of social rights, *Buchanan v Warley* showed how libertarian tendencies could support claims for racial equality.[18]

The discourse of civil, political and social rights was a *lawyer's* discourse. Ordinary citizens, and particularly those associated with the late

---

[16] For a discussion, see DE Bernstein, 'Lochner's Legacy's Legacy' (2002) 92 *Texas Law Review* 1.

[17] M Graber, *Transforming Free Speech: The Ambiguous Legacy of Civil Libertarianism* (Berkeley, University of California Press, 1992); D Rabban, *Free Speech in Its Forgotten Years* (New York, Cambridge University Press, 1997).

[18] On *Buchanan* as a libertarian decision, see DE Bernstein, 'Philip Sober Controlling Philip Drunk: Buchanan v Warley in Historical Perspective' (1998) 51 *Vanderbilt Law Review* 797.

nineteenth century labor movement, talked of rights more diffusely. For them, the rights of labor were whatever seemed necessary or appropriate to ensure that workers were able to lead decent lives. The voluntarist elements in the labor movement were actively hostile to judicial enforcement of rights, because they believed that the courts would inevitably side with employers. William Forbath describes voluntarism as teaching 'that workers should pursue improvements in their living conditions through collective bargaining and concerted action in the private sphere rather than through public political action',[19] As Samuel Gompers put it, the 'best thing the State can do for Labor is to leave Labor alone'.[20]

Gompers had reason for his belief. Voluntarists were willing to bargain with employers to obtain maximum hours, desirable conditions of work and, of course, guaranteed wages. To get employers to the bargaining table and then to agree to terms, though, workers had to be able to use economic force by withholding their labor and discouraging others from talking their place. Courts in the late nineteenth and early twentieth centuries regularly applied common law doctrines about interference with contractual relations to restrict unions' ability to conduct effective strikes. Put another way, the rights courts enforced were employers' rights, not the rights of labor. Better, to the voluntarists, for the courts to step aside—and, if abandoning the idea of rights was necessary to that end, so be it. The craft unions that were Gompers' main constituency believed their economic power vis-à-vis their employers was great enough to allow them to accomplish more than courts were willing to see done by legislation.

Voluntarists were not entirely comfortable with securing the rights of labor through legislation either. In part that flowed from the idea of voluntarism itself. In addition, the lawyers' conceptual categories pushed in the direction of defending labor legislation by asserting that some workers, at least, did not have the capacity to contract—an assertion that no labor leader could afford to make with respect to workers generally.

---

[19] WE Forbath, *Law and the Shaping of the American Labor Movement* 1–2 n 3 (Cambridge, MA, Harvard University Press, 1991).
[20] S Gompers, 'Judicial Vindication of Labor's Claims' (1901) 7 *American Federationist* 283, 284.

Other supporters of the labor movement, though, believed that the rights of labor could be secured through legislation. They had no need to develop careful conceptual categories to sort out what the rights of labor were, or how they related to the rights already recognized and described by the lawyers' categories. That would be a task for the future. For the present, what was needed was legislative recognition of the rights of labor, whether those rights be protection against judicial interference with collective bargaining or substantive guarantees of good working conditions and the like. Workers then could enforce the rights of labor directly, by pressure on employers in negotiations or through public criticism.

Yet, the lawyers' conceptual categories, while widely used, were not self-defining. In nearly every case the categories themselves could have been developed to reach the result the Court rejected. The notion of limited capacity used in *Holden* was available in *Lochner*. In the former, the Court assumed that people who worked in mines had to accept the terms offered them by mine-owners. Why people who worked in bakeries were different is unclear.[21]

Maximum hours laws (and their counterpart, minimum wage laws) were an important part of the political agenda of organized labor and its Progressive allies. In addition, *Lochner*'s doctrine placed a great deal of Progressive legislation under a cloud. The courts might eventually uphold regulatory legislation, but it would take time and additional effort to defend the legislation. These concerns fueled the effort to develop a critique of the way in which rights protection was conceptualized at the turn of the twentieth century.

PRAGMATIC AND REALIST CRITIQUES

Political progressives in the early years of the twentieth century were pragmatists philosophically, not in any formal sense but in the sense that a rough pragmatic approach was the working philosophy of political progressivism. The pragmatic philosophers, led by John Dewey,

---

[21] The Court seems to have assumed that bakers faced with unattractive terms could simply walk away and take some other employment, but that seems true of miners as well. It is not obvious that miners' alternative employment opportunities were more limited than bakers'.

developed a jurisprudence, sometimes described as sociological jurisprudence, that placed the idea of rights under real pressure. To pragmatists, social policy—and constitutional law—rested in the end on a
careful balancing of interests.[22] Yet, the very point of identifying something as a constitutional right was to block consideration of some social
interests. Pragmatism weakened the distinction between rights and mere
social policy, at a time when legal pragmatists were insisting that courts
had given inadequate attention to social policy by erecting strong and
pragmatically indefensible barriers to legislation in the name of rights.

Meyer v Nebraska provides a good example. Justice James McReynolds's
opinion conceded that the nation had an interest in ensuring that its
people understood 'American ideals' and would be 'prepared to understand current discussions of civic matters'. For legal pragmatists, the
real question was whether restricting instruction to English would assist
in promoting that interest. But *Meyer* said nothing about that question.
At the point where a legal pragmatist would have taken it up, McReynolds asserted, in conclusory terms, 'Perhaps it would be highly advanta-
geous if all had ready understanding of our ordinary speech, but this
cannot be coerced by methods which conflict with the Constitution—a
desirable end cannot be promoted by prohibited means'.

From the perspective of the late twentieth century, the legal pragmatists' approach to free speech may be more interesting. Governments
at every level tried hard during World War I to regulate speech because
its dissemination would interfere with the war effort. Advocates of free
speech rights insisted that remote consequences of speech, such as the
possibility that some listener might conclude from the speech that some
illegal action to interfere with the war effort was desirable, should be
ignored, and only proximate effects considered. For the pragmatists,
that was a mistake. Constitutional law might discount remote effects but
it could not ignore them completely.

John Dewey wrote several essays for the progressive journal *The
New Republic* on rights during wartime. He saw the war as a chance to
displace 'the individualistic tradition' of the United States and assert
'the supremacy of public need over private possessions'. Dewey's own
judgments on free speech were temperately supportive of wartime dissenters, although as legal historian David Rabban observes, he did not

---

[22] Rabban, above n 17 at 184 (describing the connection between Roscoe
Pound's sociological jurisprudence and pragmatism).

'express any concern for the dissenters themselves' and criticized them for an individualism that he associated with the idea of rights. Harvard Law School dean Roscoe Pound was even more skeptical about dissenters' claims that their rights were being violated. Law, even constitutional law, involved a balancing of interests, and rights-claims were simply one among many interests. His published writings were even more moderately in support of dissent in wartime, although in a private letter he observed that 'in time of insurrection, riot, or war the general interest in public security may require us to put the lid on for the time being'.[23]

Legal pragmatists focused more on the interests of labor than on other rights. And there their critique of rights had more bite. They disdained the rhetoric of 'the rights of labor', turning their attention to the fact that the rights courts were enforcing against labor were employers' rights. Legal pragmatists were more sympathetic than the *Lochner* court to empirical evidence showing that police power regulations served social purposes. But, even more, they contended that there was nothing wrong with a labor law 'pure and simple'. There were, legal pragmatists believed, social interests in ensuring that workers were well off enough—an interest in preserving social peace if material conditions were truly desperate, and an interest in promoting collective bargaining on more equal terms once some basic needs were secured. The rights of labor could be secured only by affirmative government action.

The pragmatists' sociological jurisprudence of competing interests left little room for constitutional rights. As historian Eric Foner puts it, '"Freedom" was not the most prominent word in the vocabulary of Progressivism'.[24] Pragmatists could accept a practice in which the result of the consideration of all the relevant interests got the label 'right', as long as the label did not lead people to believe that concepts given that label had some force beyond the balance of considerations already built into particular rights. But, wary of the possibility that labels misled, legal pragmatists were generally unsympathetic to the rhetoric of rights.

World War I saw a concerted assault on what we now think of as free-speech rights. Liberals and Progressives were divided over the merits of

---

[23] J Dewey, 'The Social Possibilities of War', quoted in D Kennedy, *Over Here: The First World War and American Society* 50 (New York, Oxford University Press, 1980); Rabban, above n 17, 246, 184–9 (Pound's letter is quoted at 189).

[24] E Foner, *The Story of American Freedom* (New York, WW Norton, 1998) 140.

the free speech claims made by political radicals and opponents of the war. In part that was because American participation in the war was the project of President Woodrow Wilson, himself a progressive, who depicted the war as one whose goal was the extension of democracy. And in part it was because radicals with whom liberals and Progressives were at odds in politics made the rights-claims. But in part it was because liberals and Progressives had developed a jurisprudence in which rights were associated with conservatism and the status quo, and in which the rights people had were the result of a careful balancing of competing social interests. In Foner's words:

> Civil liberties, by and large, had never been a major concern of Progressivism, which had always viewed the national state as the embodiment of democratic purpose and insisted that freedom flowed from participating in the life of society, not standing in isolated opposition.[25]

The discomfort with the idea of rights associated with pragmatism and sociological jurisprudence found expression in the characteristic form of Progressive-era legislation. Instead of enacting statutes creating rights enforced in courts, progressives created agencies to administer workers' compensation laws and gave experts a central role in administering new systems of juvenile justice. Progressives looked to experts and new institutional forms because they believed that the conceptual categories lawyers and courts used were inconsistent with the more nuanced set of values that good public policy—and therefore good constitutional law—required.

Progressive discomfort with the courts found its way into constitutional theory as well. Progressives spent a great deal of political energy defending labor's legislative victories against constitutional challenge. Picking up a theme extending far back into US constitutional history, they worried about the relative roles of courts and legislatures in assessing when legislation violated the Constitution. Pragmatism required the consideration of many facts about the world, and the balancing of competing social interests. Pragmatists questioned whether courts were better at assessing those facts and balancing those interests than legislatures. Writing in the progressive journal of opinion, *The New Republic*, law professor Felix Frankfurter regularly invoked institutional

---

[25] *Ibid* at 178.

considerations in his criticisms of the Supreme Court's use of the due process clause to invalidate progressive legislation.[26]

Technical expertise and empirical examinations of social reality were not the only contributions that university-affiliated pragmatists made to constitutional theory in the early decades of the twentieth century. Insights drawn from the nascent field of political science cast doubt on classical liberalism's hostility to class legislation. Arthur Bentley redescribed class legislation as the ordinary product of groups operating in the legislative process.[27] Stripped of some of Bentley's quasi-philosophical excesses, an interest-group approach to legislation helped progressives explain why laws that seemed to benefit only part of society should be regarded as standard and obviously constitutional. Eventually, interest-group influences on legislation expanded and became, once again, a source of concern. When that happened, a further transformation of constitutional thinking occurred as well.

Some in the pragmatic tradition took the critique even deeper. Some legal realists worked with the lawyers' categories of civil, political, and social rights, to the end of demonstrating that the categories had *no* determinate content. *Plessy* could have been a case about the civil right to contract, *Lochner* a case about the legislature's power to expand the concept of capacity to contract beyond its common law boundaries. And, on the other side, *Buchanan* could have been reconstructed as a case about the social right to select those with whom one would associate: Those who wished to exercise their social right to live far away from African Americans found that right undermined by a few people—about to leave the neighborhood anyway—who were willing to sell houses to African Americans. They solved what we would today call a collective action problem by securing legislation to prevent others from interfering with their social rights.

Legal realists found the lawyers' traditional categories empty. Much in the realists' arguments about constitutional law arose first in their critiques of the common law. According to the realists, courts applying the common law purported to invoke seemingly obvious propositions, such

---

[26] See, eg, 'The Red Terror of Judicial Reform' (1924) *The New Republic*, Oct 1, 110 (unsigned but written by Frankfurter).

[27] AF Bentley, *The Process of Government: A Study of Social Pressures* (Chicago, University of Chicago Press, 1908).

as that courts should not interfere with the agreements people made. But, the realists pointed out, common law judges did not in fact endorse those propositions. They qualified them: Courts should indeed interfere with contracts predicated on fraud, or where one party was so deficient that the contract could not fairly be attributed to his own choice. These qualifications undermined the claim that courts applying the common law were simply enforcing neutral and non-political criteria.[28]

The realist critique could extend to constitutional law. The qualifications found within the common law were relevant as well to the standard conceptual categories, and particularly to the idea of civil rights. So, for example, that category could make sense of unquestionable legal rules such as the denial of rights to children and the insane only by including a qualification that civil rights could be held only by those with the capacity to make contracts and own property. Defenders of the traditional categories then had to spell out exactly what constituted that capacity. In doing so they imported criteria such as rationality and independence from their common law counterparts. The realists then pushed their criticisms of the common law into new terrain. And, importantly, defenders of the traditional categories did not have the resources—within the law itself—to resist that development. All they could do was assert what all came to see were merely political objections, not conceptual ones.

Alternatively, legal realists showed how particular problems posed conflicts between rights. Sometimes the conflicts were between rights in the same category. One person's civil right to own property conflicted with another person's right to enter into contracts. The aftermath of *Buchanan v Warley* provides an example. Deprived of the ability to secure legislation guaranteeing racially segregated neighborhoods, property owners wrote restrictions on the power to sell one's property, known as racially restrictive covenants, into their deeds. Restrictive covenants presented problems within property theory, but also within constitutional law: Property law allowed some contractual provisions—some restrictive covenants—to qualify the ordinary property right to sell to whoever one chose, but not all conceivable restrictive covenants. Into which class

---

[28] RL Hale, 'Coercion and Distribution in a Supposedly Non-Coercive State' (1923) 38 *Political Science Quarterly* 470, 478.

did the racially restrictive covenant fall? Legal realists argued that legal analysis, on its own, could not provide an answer.[29]

Sometimes the conflicts were between categories, as in *Plessy* where the railroads' right to contract conflicted with white customers' social right of association. The legal realist critique, on the first level, simply demanded that the courts *address* the existence of a conflict, something entirely absent in *Plessy*. But, what were courts to do once they noticed a conflict? Ranking rights—treating social rights as more important than civil rights, or vice versa—was not a promising strategy, because the categories contained widely diverse particular rights, and the grounds for ranking were quite unclear. Instead, the realists insisted that all the courts could do was choose which right to treat as more important in the circumstances.

The legal realist approach to rights provided some leverage on the institutional concerns Frankfurter articulated. Because the legal concepts used to analyze rights claims had no content at all, everyone called upon to participate in the processes of constitutionalism simply had to make choices that were not legal but political or ideological. At least as long as judicial review existed, judges could only choose—and they were at no disadvantage relative to legislatures with respect to choice alone. The legal realist analysis did not significantly diverge from sociological jurisprudence while progressives were out of power, but it came to have real bite once the Supreme Court's composition shifted to favor progressivism.

THE NEW DEAL RECONSTRUCTION

Once progressives gained firm control of the Supreme Court in the late 1930s, they had to make a strategic choice, described by political scientist Martin Shapiro as a choice between dismantling the weapons the Supreme Court had developed and which their opponents had

---

[29] The Supreme Court avoided the question by asserting in 1926 that the mere presence of racially restrictive covenants in property deeds did not implicate the Constitution at all. Twenty years later, it said that the state's enforcement of such covenants did violate the Constitution: *Corrigan v Buckley* 271 US 323 (1926); *Shelley v Kraemer* 334 US 1 (1948).

used against them, or turning those weapons against their opponents.[30] The debate over that choice persisted through mid-century, with the advocates of dismantling the weapons—that is, a systematic pursuit of judicial restraint—gradually losing ground to those who sought to reconstruct a jurisprudence based on individual rights that was somehow stripped of the libertarian leanings of classical liberalism.

The choice was closely connected to the construction of the New Deal Democratic coalition. On the level of ideas, the pragmatists' attraction to replacing the language of rights with the language of social interests served well to defend the New Deal's major initiatives, such as the creation of the Social Security system and the general regulatory thrust of New Deal interventions in the economy. And, indeed, in selecting nominees for the Supreme Court, Franklin Roosevelt paid attention only to whether they would uphold these initiatives. Inevitably, then, pragmatic balancing and suspicion of rights-based claims would have a foothold on the Supreme Court.

Pragmatism, though, provided few resources in the areas of modern civil liberties such as freedom of speech and racial equality. Notably, by the mid-1930s the categories of classical constitutional theory had disappeared completely from constitutional discourse. The term 'civil rights' now referred to the constitutional interest in securing racial equality, the term 'political rights' had been replaced by 'civil liberties' and the idea that there were social rights had no more than a residual influence in political rhetoric. Pragmatic balancing was unsuited to determining whether civil rights and civil liberties were at risk, because it gave no special analytic status to those interests.

The key move made in the judicial theory of constitutional rights in the 1930s had two components: a sharp differentiation between the economic interests at the heart of the New Deal and civil liberties and civil rights, which were at most of collateral and long-term interest to New Dealers, accompanied by a justification for that differentiation that brought the earlier institutional concerns about judicial capacity to the fore. Justice Harlan Fiske Stone provided the classic formulation of this move in a case that would otherwise have remained obscure, a constitutional challenge rooted in classical liberalism to a New Deal regulation

---

[30] M Shapiro, 'Fathers and Sons: The Court, the Commentators, and the Search for Values' in V Blasi (ed), *The Burger Court: The Counterrevolution that Wasn't* (New Haven, Yale University Press, 1983).

prohibiting the sale of 'filled milk', a cheap and nutritious substitute for whole milk. The New Deal Court had little difficulty upholding the statute (*United States v Carolene Products* (1938)).[31] The case became famous because of its 'Footnote 4'. Attached to a sentence saying that courts would defer to legislative judgments on matters of economic regulation, Footnote 4 asserted that there might be room for more aggressive judicial intervention when litigants claimed either that a statute violated a specific prohibition in the Bill of Rights or, more important for the development of the modern liberal idea of rights, if they claimed that legislation interfered with or resulted from defects in the democratic process, with prejudice against 'discrete and insular minorities' counting as such a defect.

Obvious on the surface of Footnote 4 jurisprudence was a new concern for the constitutional rights of African Americans, and a concern for freedom of expression derived from liberals' reflections on the experience of World War I and its aftermath (and on the effects of attacks on the free speech rights of labor organizers and political radicals, who were at least for the moment the allies of the New Deal). But the implications of that jurisprudence were far more extensive.

The liberalism associated with the New Deal defended deference to legislative judgments with respect to economic regulation on institutional grounds. According to the emerging theory of constitutional rights, economic regulation raised complex questions of fact and value. Legislatures had better resources to determine facts than did courts. More important, legislative judgments of value reflected the values held by legislators' constituents. The pragmatic critique of classical liberal constitutional law established, to the satisfaction of mid-century liberals, that value judgments about economic regulation were 'essentially contested'.[32] New Deal liberalism contended that in an area where value disagreement was inevitable, courts should defer to the decisions of representative legislatures because whatever might be said on the merits of the value judgments, those decisions had a warrant in the theory of majority rule that judicial value choices lacked, or at least had in much weaker form.

---

[31] 304 US 144 (1938).

[32] That term was appropriated in the 1960s from its use in a major article about moral and political philosophy, but the concept was roughly available to New Deal jurisprudence earlier.

All well and good, for the matters New Dealers were most concerned about. There was another theme in New Deal and legal realist jurisprudence, with implications for the new civil rights and civil liberties. The legal realist critique of libertarian-leaning protections of property and contract was that those categories gained content only through substantive analysis, which had to take into account the distribution of power between employers and workers. Overruling earlier decisions invalidating minimum wage and maximum hours laws, Chief Justice Charles Evans Hughes suggested that the government had an affirmative duty to protect 'liberty' against 'the evils which menace the health, safety, morals, and welfare of the people'. Employers who paid less than the minimum wage were 'in effect' receiving 'a subsidy' from the public that was called upon to support the needy.[33] This perspective linked constitutional law to background rules of property law, with the former responding to inadequacies of the latter. Hughes probably did not understand that his approach thrust constitutional rights into every space in society, and forced courts to determine the merits of every constitutional claim without the deference to the legislature to which New Dealers were also committed.

Footnote 4 jurisprudence, though, brought that implication to the fore. That jurisprudence argued that courts could identify situations in which legislation lacked the democratic warrant that New Dealers relied on to explain judicial deference on economic regulation. Here the emerging theory of constitutional rights could also draw on the sharper edged legal realist critiques of economic rights as well. Generalized to all rights, those critiques suggested that there were no 'democratic institutions' that existed independent of the courts' determination that a particular institution was indeed democratic. The point was obvious in cases like *Colegrove v Green* (1946), a challenge to the malapportionment of the Illinois congressional delegation.[34] Justice Frankfurter argued that the courts should stay out of apportionment controversies because they could be resolved only if one adopted a substantive theory of democratic representation, the kind of value judgment that courts were unsuited for. But, although the Court refused to intervene in *Colegrove*, Frankfurter's colleagues understood that his argument did not fit the

---

[33] *West Coast Hotel v Parrish* 300 US 379, 399 (1937).
[34] *Colegrove v Green* 328 US 549 (1946).

issue before them: He was asking them to defer to the judgments of Illinois's legislature because those judgments had a warrant in democratic representation that a judicial choice of a theory of democracy would not, in a context where the claim was precisely that the legislative judgment could not be defended by referring to the legislature's democratic credentials.[35]

From the New Deal through the early 1960s, the jurisprudence of Footnote 4 explained nearly everything the Supreme Court did, as law professor John Hart Ely showed in one of the leading works of constitutional theory in the late twentieth century.[36] The Court refrained from striking down economic regulations, but developed an elaborate law of free expression and racial equality. Ely showed that judicial practice and constitutional theory had accepted the jurisprudence of Footnote 4, even when particular results were controversial.

Footnote 4 jurisprudence would run into trouble near the end of the twentieth century, when the simple New Deal vision of how democracy worked came under pressure from political scientists, who emphasized the way in which interest groups could disconnect legislative value judgments from the judgments held by legislators' constituents, and from economists working in the field of 'public choice', who developed more formal models explaining why that disconnect occurred.[37] Interest-group accounts of the legislative process generated a proliferation of 'discrete and insular minorities'. Any interest group could be so characterized, at least with the exercise of a bit of ingenuity. The proliferation of such 'minorities' opened up two possibilities. One could follow Footnote 4 faithfully, and allow judicial intervention in every case that an analyst could describe as the result of an interest group deal in which some discrete and insular minority—typically, the consumer or general interest—was disregarded. Or, one could urge

---

[35] Technically, one might respond to this criticism by noting that the legislature drawing Illinois's congressional district lines was not itself under challenge as malapportioned. Still, Frankfurter and his colleagues clearly understand that Frankfurter intended his analysis to extend to all apportionment cases: 'The policy with respect to federal elections does mean that state legislatures must make real effort to bring about approximately equal representation of citizens in Congress. Here the legislature of Illinois has not done so' 328 US at 572 (Black J, dissenting).

[36] JH Ely, *Democracy and Distrust: A Theory of Judicial Review* (Cambridge, MA, Harvard University Press, 1980).

[37] B Ackerman, 'Beyond Carolene Products' (1985) 98 *Harvard Law Review* 713.

the courts to abstain from intervention in all cases, arguing that discrete and insular minorities might have lost on a particular question, but certainly were in a position to bargain and win on other issues. By the 1960s, for example, the political power of African Americans, the group for whom the category 'discrete and insular minority' had been invented, was large enough to make questionable the use of Footnote 4 jurisprudence as a basis for striking down laws on the ground that they discriminated against African Americans—unless, of course, one used a fancy enough Footnote 4 theory, with all sorts of implications for the theory's general scope.

Other modes of analysis were coming to displace Footnote 4, though, and these difficulties remained largely theoretical. For the most part, criticisms of the legislative process as excessively influenced by narrow interest groups undermined the case for judicial deference to legislative judgments about economic regulation—that is, about the text to which Footnote 4 was attached—and, if anything, provided even greater support for the judicial interventions suggested by the footnote itself.

Footnote 4 jurisprudence, resting as it did on an account of the relative capacities and incapacities of courts and legislatures, could not coherently be a jurisprudence for rights discussions by politicians and their constituents. Unavailable within the discourse of Footnote 4 jurisprudence, appeals to economic rights continued in politics. The New Deal's commitment to ensuring the possibility of collective bargaining was regularly described as 'Labor's Bill of Rights', for example, and once again in a context where the entire point of securing the rights was to get away from the courts and their intrusions on bargaining between labor and management. The New Deal embedded government social provision into the world of statutory rights. The Social Security Act, national unemployment compensation legislation and, eventually, a general system of public assistance to the poor were statutory 'entitlements', that is rights. Often limited in scope by racism and sexism—federal minimum wage laws excluded agricultural workers from coverage, for example, because too many such workers were African Americans—these statutory rights nonetheless became an important component of the rights revolution.

Franklin Roosevelt's State of the Union address in 1944 urged that the nation should adopt a 'Second Bill of Rights' which would guarantee jobs with decent wages, medical care, homeownership, and more.[38] These were offered as rights for legislative implementation. Congress responded with the feeble Employment Act of 1946, which watered down the jobs guarantee, and then killed President Harry Truman's proposal for universal medical care. The language of rights continued to have some hold on the public imagination in legislative settings, but that hold was clearly weaker than the idea of rights as objects of special judicial attention. That the Second Bill of Rights would have been a social democratic document, guaranteeing what came to be called second-generation rights, of course mattered too for its enervation, in light of the weakness of the social democratic tradition in the United States. Late in the century, some aspects of social provision came under attack, under the name of 'entitlement reform'. The very term, though, suggests that rights ideas still mattered. And, though some entitlement reforms did occur, they ran up against a wall when the reforms threatened to eliminate entirely the safety nets for the poor, and to threaten income support for the elderly. With some reason, we can say that as a practical matter the United States did recognize these statutory provisions as rights guarantees.[39]

THE EMERGENCE OF MODERN LIBERALISM:
AUTONOMY AND ACCOMMODATION

The transformation of liberal rights discourse in the New Deal persisted through the end of the twentieth century. Older themes continued, of course. African Americans secured civil rights in the modern sense, both through sustained litigation culminating in the Supreme Court's decision invalidating racial segregation in schools in *Brown v Board of Education*, followed up with a series of decisions making it clear that all forms of public segregation were unconstitutional. Direct action protesting discrimination taken by the civil rights movement of the 1960s led Congress to adopt a series of Civil Rights Acts in 1964, barring racial discrimination in employment and in hotels and restaurants; in 1965, protecting voting rights; and, in 1968, dealing with housing

---

[38] CR Sunstein, *The Second Bill of Rights: FDR's Unfinished Revolution and Why We Need It More than Ever* (New York, Basic Books, 2004).

[39] *See* E Young, 'The Constitution Outside the Constitution' (2007) 117 *Yale Law Journal* 408.

discrimination. The Supreme Court began what some called a revolution in criminal procedure, requiring that government provide criminal defendants with lawyers early in their confrontation with public prosecutors, and that police officers read the famous *Miranda* warnings to suspects in custody. Applied in all criminal proceedings, these requirements and the others imposed in the criminal procedure revolution were largely motivated by the justices' perception that African Americans were being treated unfairly throughout the criminal process.

Eventually these developments—the criminal procedure revolution, the civil rights statutes, their judicial enforcement, and the enforcement of the Court's desegregation rulings—generated a backlash, but for much of the late twentieth century 'civil rights' was a rallying cry for liberal activists, whose cultural resonance was such that even conservatives began to frame their claims as ones for civil rights as well. For example, the Christian Right of the 1980s and after sought public recognition of and support for religion as a 'civil right' flowing from its adherents' position as equal citizens in the community.

But, in the last third of that century, modern liberalism took on a new cast. In addition to guarantees of rights associated with democracy, modern liberalism reintroduced libertarian themes, not in the first instance in connection with economics, but rather with respect to personal autonomy. Concern for personal autonomy generated support for rights not previously recognized within New Deal jurisprudence—a development that some liberals such as Ely found both baffling and unprincipled—but also injected new elements into previously recognized rights. Developments in constitutional law and in legislation led constitutional law to incorporate the idea that, sometimes, equality could be achieved in markets and through legislative mandates only if those subject to regulation were required not only to refrain from discriminating against certain groups but were required as well to accommodate those groups. These developments were sufficiently widespread—arising in connection with the extended process of desegregation, with affirmative action, with pregnancy discrimination, with discrimination against persons with disabilities—as to provoke a broader rethinking of what equality required. By the end of the century, the idea that equality was a matter of substance and not only of form had become embedded in American constitutionalism. Embedded, but not firmly implanted, because substantive equality inevitably pushes in the direction of recognizing entitlements to social and democratic rights.

At the same time, classical liberalism staged a comeback, but in a new form. The libertarian strand of classical liberalism resurfaced as a concern that legislatures oppressed minorities. The right to keep and bear arms became an exemplary right associated with citizens' autonomy, when the Supreme Court held that people had a right to own widely used weapons for the purpose of self-defense.[40] In the economic domain oppression took the form of regulations that prevented ambitious entrepreneurs from starting their own small businesses. Elsewhere oppression took the form of affirmative action programs that were said to disadvantage white members of immigrant groups who came to the United States after slavery had been abolished. Even those in the new Christian Right who sought to infuse public policy with specifically religious content framed some of their claims in terms of rights to equal participation in the democratic process, and not as justifiable efforts to create a nation committed to religious belief.

Autonomy became an important component of modern liberalism for several reasons. Political philosophers reminded legal theorists that classical liberalism and the democratic commitments arising from it rested, in the end, on the idea of individual autonomy. Modern liberals responded by adding a direct recognition of autonomy to the indirect recognition of autonomy expressed in their commitment to democracy, thereby creating the possibility of a clash between the direct protection of autonomy and intrusions on autonomy licensed by democratic decision-making. Modern liberals resolved the conflict in two ways. They denied democratic legitimacy to decisions by legislatures that failed Footnote 4's requirements; this dissolved the conflict. Creative reconstructions of Footnote 4 could go a long way here, as we will see in a moment, but such reconstructions raised their own problems. In addition, when push came to shove, modern liberals insisted that the direct protection of personal autonomy prevail over the expressions even of well-functioning democratic legislatures.

World War II and the Cold War supported the development of direct protection of personal autonomy as well.[41] It seemed feeble to identify the problem with totalitarianism simply with the absence of democracy in Nazi Germany and the Soviet Union. George Orwell's image

---

[40] *District of Columbia v Heller* 554 US 570 (2008).

[41] *See* Note, 'A Brooding Omnipresence: Totalitarianism in Postwar Constitutional Thought' (1996) 106 *Yale Law Journal* 423.

of a boot stamping on a human face forever, and of Winston Smith's 'agreement' after enhanced interrogation that two plus two might indeed equal five, were more potent and accurate, but they were images of intrusions on human autonomy. Scholarly studies of totalitarianism suggested as well that totalitarian governments could elicit simulacra of consent, like Winston Smith's, from their populations. Coupled with studies of advertising in the late 1940s and 1950s, this raised worries about the possibility that what appeared to be consent-based support for nominally democratic governments and their policies might be similarly ill founded. Only direct protection of personal autonomy could guard against that possibility.

The proximate source of modern liberalism's concern for personal autonomy was the mid-century sexual revolution. Constitutional law first became concerned with government restrictions on sexual activity in challenges to laws prohibiting marriages across racial lines, which could have been addressed merely as problems of race discrimination. After avoiding decision on those questions to avoid heightening existing tensions over desegregation, the Supreme Court ultimately held such restrictions unconstitutionally discriminatory in 1964 and, definitively, in 1967.[42] When personal autonomy emerged as a theme in modern liberalism, these cases were reconstructed as cases about the fundamental importance of one's ability to choose a marriage partner.

Meanwhile, *Griswold v Connecticut* (1965) marked that theme's arrival in constitutional law. There the Supreme Court held unconstitutional a Connecticut statute, one of only two in the country, that made it a crime to provide contraceptives even to married couples. The statute was never enforced, but for decades it had deterred family planning advocates from opening clinics that would supply contraceptives to their clients. Justice William O Douglas's opinion for the Court purported to avoid reviving notions of substantive due process by drawing on a range of decided cases that showed that the Court had girded specific constitutional rights with 'penumbras' that were essential to ensure that people could effectively exercise the enumerated rights. Other opinions in the case referred to the Ninth Amendment's recognition that the people retained rights not listed in the Bill of Rights. *Griswold* described the right it protected as a right to privacy, but it rapidly became clear that the right at issue was better described as a right to personal autonomy

---

[42] *McLaughlin v Florida* 379 US 184 (1964); *Loving v Virginia* 388 US 1 (1967).

in making important decisions related mostly to sexual conduct—a right, that is, to insulate one's own decisions from regulation by the government.[43] Eventually the case came to be understood as resting on an idea of autonomy that was not explicitly enumerated in the Constitution, but that found a reasonably comfortable home in the Due Process Clause of the Fourteenth Amendment, which as we have seen always had some substantive content.

Within a decade *Griswold* became the basis in precedent for the Court's controversial decisions sharply restricting the ability of governments to regulate a woman's decision (in consultation with her doctor) to carry a pregnancy to term or to have an abortion. And just after the new century began the Court extended these precedents to invalidate state laws making consensual sexual contact between persons of the same sex unlawful.[44] Confirming the power of the idea of personal autonomy, state courts in Massachusetts and California relied on state constitutions to create a right to marriage for homosexual partners.

What is striking is how deeply embedded the constitutional protection of personal autonomy rapidly became. The legal theory supporting *Griswold* was controversial among scholars committed to the New Deal paradigm of constitutional law, but *Griswold*'s holding soon came to seem obviously correct to the public. Judge Robert Bork's nomination to the Supreme Court foundered on his principled position that he could find no basis in the Constitution for a freestanding right to privacy, which his opponents effectively presented to the public as a criticism of *Griswold*'s outcome. Thereafter nominees who disagreed with the Court's abortion decisions were careful to say that they did not challenge that holding, although they rarely presented an account of how they would justify overturning the abortion decisions without casting doubt on *Griswold* as well.

The rapid development of gay rights, and in particular marriage equality, as a constitutional issue, demonstrates how deeply embedded the defense of autonomy had become in US constitutional culture. In 1986 a narrow majority of the Supreme Court declared that the claim that restrictions on homosexual sodomy were inconsistent with deep American traditions was 'at best facetious.' The Supreme Court overruled that

---

[43] 381 US 479 (1965).
[44] 539 US 558 (2003).

decision in 2003, specifically invoking a right of personal autonomy.[45] Similarly, critics of that decision focused not on its specific holding, which seemed uncontroversial by that point, but on the decision's doctrinal implications for challenges to laws denying homosexuals the right to marry. In the 1990s and early 2000s many states adopted statutes and constitutional amendments purporting to insulate 'traditional' marriage between one man and one woman from constitutional attack. Congress enacted a related statute, the Defense of Marriage Act, which defined the term 'marriage', as used in every federal statute, in that way. The Supreme Court held the statute unconstitutional in 2013, in an opinion that blended concerns about federalism (because national statutes had previously tracked state-law definitions with respect to issues of family law) with concerns about equality. Although the Supreme Court on the same day refused to consider whether a state ban on gay marriage was unconstitutional, lower courts rapidly held it unconstitutional for states to deny marriage equality.[46]

Modern liberalism's attention to personal autonomy resonated broadly within the culture of late twentieth century America. Of the trilogy 'Sex, drugs, and rock-and-roll', constitutional law came to give significant protection to the first and third (the latter through the First Amendment). The symbolic and perhaps even doctrinal high point of the integration of constitutional law with a culture valorizing personal autonomy may have been *Cohen v California* (1971), where the Court, in an opinion by the strait-laced Justice John Marshall Harlan, held it unconstitutional to convict for disorderly conduct a young man protesting the war in Vietnam by displaying on the back of his jacket the phrase 'Fuck the Draft'. (Some justices were uncomfortable with printing the word 'Fuck' in the Supreme Court Reports, and later cases invalidating similar convictions sometimes used the cosmetic 'F—'.)[47] On the doctrinal level, *Cohen* recognized the importance of personal autonomy when it explained why the state could not insist that Cohen use some more polite way of expressing his opposition to the draft: 'One man's vulgarity is another's lyric', Justice Harlan wrote.

---

[45] *Bowers v Hardwick* 478 US 186 (1986); *Lawrence v Texas* 539 US 558 (2003); *Windsor v United States* 133 SCt 2675 (2013).

[46] The Supreme Court agreed to review some of these lower court decisions, with opinions to be issued too late for discussion here.

[47] *Cohen v California* 403 US 15 (1971); *Rosenfeld v New Jersey* 408 US 901 (1972); *Lewis v New Orleans* 415 US 130 (1974).

Occasionally scholars attempted to defend these personal-autonomy decisions in Footnote 4 terms, and in doing so revealed another source of the direct protection of personal autonomy. The reason Connecticut retained its ban on contraception, these scholars observed, was the disproportionate power of the Catholic Church in state politics.[48] More commonly, scholars defended the abortion decisions on the ground that restrictive abortion laws were implicitly discriminatory, imposing burdens on women that were not paralleled by the imposition of similar burdens on men and that resulted from the under-representation of women in state legislatures and from the disproportionate influence of the Catholic Church and Protestant fundamentalists in those legislatures.

These arguments were cast in the form provided by Footnote 4, but they were quite substantial extensions of the original. The arguments shifted attention from the formal characteristics of statutes defining the democratic process to the actual operation of politics in the United States. Footnote 4 was designed to license some limited judicial intervention after the collapse of classical liberal constitutional theory under the pragmatist and legal realist critiques. Shifting attention to the real world of politics would license judges to supervise public policy across an enormous range of issues. Some constitutional theorists were not dismayed by that prospect, though even they ordinarily preferred to defend judicial activism on the ground that it advanced substantive justice.

Notably, the Footnote 4 reconstruction of the personal-autonomy cases focused on what its proponents identified as the improper influence in the political process of traditionalism generally and religion specifically. Modern liberalism, with its concern for personal autonomy, was a political philosophy, translated into constitutional law, of legal elites that were increasingly secular as the century advanced. Though the association was not logically required, elite secularism was associated with opposition to the presence of religion in the making of public policy. In part this opposition was the residue of a long-standing anti-Catholicism among Protestant elites, which diminished somewhat with the election of John F Kennedy but which retained a hold on the imagination of liberals that surfaced in connection with issues dealing

---

[48] See, eg, D Garrow, *Liberty and Sexuality: The Right of Privacy and the Making of Roe v Wade* (Berkeley, University of California Press, 1998).

with sexuality and reproduction. In part it was a residue as well of a similar anti-fundamentalism among elites, dating back at least to HL Mencken's mocking of William Jennings Bryan during the 1925 trial of John Scopes for teaching evolution, and that revived with the growing political influence of religious fundamentalists in the politics of the late twentieth century.[49]

In addition to incorporating a direct concern for personal autonomy, modern liberalism began to redefine equality in a way loosely linked to issues of autonomy, although the movement here was more halting. Classical liberalism was committed primarily to formal equality, in which legislation refrained from using what came to be known as 'suspect' categories such as race, religion, and national origin. Statutes that did not use these terms could not be class legislation, because they applied to everyone equally.

Modern liberalism placed pressure on formal equality from several directions. Its proponents asked, Why were only *some* classifications 'suspect'? The answer they received was cast in Footnote 4 terms: When legislation allocated burdens by using these classifications, there ordinarily was reason to believe that something had gone wrong in the representative process. Modern liberals then made two moves.

— They argued that other groups suffered the same kinds of political disadvantage. The revived women's rights movement made Footnote 4 arguments to support its claim that legislation singling out gender as a basis for allocating burdens should be treated with as much suspicion as legislation using racial classifications. Then the claims on behalf of additional groups flooded in: the poor, because their poverty disabled them from effective political participation; people with disabilities such as mental retardation, because their disabilities restricted their ability to get to the polls; gays and lesbians, because social stigmatization forced them into the closet.

The courts gradually accepted the claims made by the women's movement and, to a significantly smaller degree, those made by gays and lesbians. They resisted the claims made by persons with disabilities, but those groups made significant progress in legislation. The problem with this move was that it had no obvious limits.

---

[49] See generally JC Jeffries and JE Ryan, 'A Political History of the Establishment Clause' (2001) 100 *Michigan Law Review* 229.

The political disadvantages to which modern liberals pointed were pervasive. Indeed, by the end of the century some conservatives had begun to sign on to the same arguments, but now on behalf of white ethnics, the objects of prejudice expressed, in their view, in affirmative action programs, and on behalf of small business-people, who could not effectively resist the power of big business and labor to obtain regulations that forced small businesses into bankruptcy.

— Modern liberals also argued that Footnote 4 problems did not occur in on-and-off form. Rather, they were matters of degree. Constitutional law should therefore develop more nuanced approaches to questions of equality. Justice Thurgood Marshall offered the most comprehensive alternative, a 'sliding scale' approach that took account both of the degree to which a group suffered from political disadvantage and the size and importance of the burdens placed on the group by the challenged legislation.[50]

These moves in equality theory reinforced concerns, arising at roughly the same time, that formal equality—the framework within which the moves were made—was itself an inadequate account of constitutional equality. Terminology varied: Within constitutional law, the typical formulation called for achieving substantive equality; in popular media, the phrase was 'equality of outcome'. As the law of racial equality began to develop, advocates of racial equality could and did reasonably contend that formal and substantive equality went hand-in-hand: Eliminate laws requiring racial discrimination, and equality of outcome would follow relatively quickly.

Experience proved that the easy equation of substantive equality with the practical outcome of achieving formal equality was mistaken. From mid-century on, cases and statutes proliferated that made more sense as expressions of a constitutional vision of substantive equality than of formal equality. That vision, though, was controversial, and by the end of the century formal and substantive equality had become almost entirely decoupled.

In the immediate aftermath of the New Deal transformation of constitutional law, categories for dealing with equality concerns were fluid. The Court developed the doctrine of the 'public forum', which required

---

[50] *Dandridge v Williams* 397 US 471 (1970), 521 (Marshall J, dissenting).

that the government make available some of its facilities—streets and parks—to people who lacked the financial resources to disseminate their messages through other means. The doctrine rested, though only implicitly, on concern about the implications of economic inequality for free speech. The restrictive covenant cases of 1948, mentioned earlier, involved legal rules that were formally neutral, barring inter-racial sales of all types, but the rules were unconstitutional because of their real-world effects on racial equality.

Substantive equality eventually cropped up in many areas.

— *Racial equality: Brown v Board of Education* (1954) held that laws segregating students by race were unconstitutional. The remedy for such laws was obvious: Eliminate race as a basis for assigning students to schools. That could have been done within a year of the decision. Instead, anticipating resistance to desegregation, the Supreme Court allowed schools to desegregate 'with all deliberate speed'. Yet, the Court could not acknowledge openly that it was giving Southern schools time to desegregate because it knew that they did not want to. The gap between the theory justifying *Brown* and the remedy order was eventually filled by the view that the Constitution required, not merely the desegregation that the Court's remedy order allowed states to defer, but integration, which indeed could only be accomplished gradually.

The Court confirmed the shift from desegregation to integration in *Green v School Board of New Kent County* (1968). There it said that the time for deliberate speed had ended, and that school boards were required to develop plans that 'promise[d] realistically to work, and promise[d] realistically to work *now*'. The only account that makes sense of the term 'work' is one requiring integration.[51]

— *Affirmative action.* Never constitutionally mandated, programs of affirmative action adopted by legislatures, school boards, and universities also sought to achieve substantive outcomes—in general, allocation of government benefits in proportion to the racial composition of the relevant population. Applying doctrines of formal equality, the Supreme Court whittled away at justifications that expressly invoked concern for substantive equality. By the end of the century, it seemed as if the only justification left was 'diversity',

[51] 391 US 430, 439 (1968).

a concept applicable in some settings such as education but not obviously applicable in others such as government contracting. Yet, even as the Court erected higher and higher barriers to affirmative action, political support for such programs remained reasonably strong.

Affirmative action programs brought out the connection between substantive equality and accommodation. Until the Supreme Court ruled them out, the most straight-forward explanations for affirmative action were that such programs adjusted the present-day allocation of government controlled resources to rectify the continuing effects of past discrimination by governments, and that they did so to offset the effects of on-going societal discrimination. These explanations rest on the observation that the beneficiaries of affirmative action come to the programs with material resources and human capital endowments that make them less able to take advantage of the programs than others. That in turn implies that affirmative action is a mechanism for accommodating the programs to the endowments people bring to them.

— *Explicit accommodation requirements.* By the 1980s the proposition that equality required that institutions adjust their prior operations to make the operations fully available was firmly embedded in the law. The first appearance of the language of accommodation seems to be in the employment discrimination provisions of the Civil Rights Act of 1964. The statute's provisions on religious discrimination required that employers make 'reasonable accommodations' for their employees' religious practices. Once the idea of accommodation entered the law, it spread. Employers were required to make accommodations to deal with pregnancies and with employees' needs to care for close relatives. Employers and public agencies had to make reasonable accommodations in their operations for persons with disabilities.

Relatively early in its development of the law of free exercise of religion, the Supreme Court indicated that the Free Exercise Clause required governments to adjust their programs to take account of religious practices, when it held that the Free Exercise Clause was violated by a state law denying unemployment compensation to a person whose religious beliefs made it impossible for her to accept work on Saturday, the only work available to her in her locality. The Court rapidly retreated from the widest implications of this holding, and eventually returned to the idea that, in the context of religious practice, the Constitution required only formal neutrality. But, if accommodation, like its cousin affirmative action, was not constitutionally required, it could be mandated by statute. Indeed, unlike affirmative action with respect to race, which was limited by the invocation of the idea that formal equality barred the use of race as a classifying device except in extremely unusual circumstances, accommodation in the context of religion relatively easily overcame the constitutional barrier that might have been posed by the non-establishment principle. In general the Court construed statutory requirements of 'reasonable' accommodation rather narrowly. Some degree of substantive equality was nonetheless required once accommodation was required to any extent.[52]

In 2013 conflicts between accommodation requirements and modern liberal's agenda of substantive equality emerged, and the consensus about the value of accommodation began to crumble, when religious conservatives sought and obtained an exemption from a requirement that the health insurance policies they maintained for their employees cover several forms of contraception that, the employers believed, were equivalent to abortion. Similar efforts to obtain exemptions from requirements that all businesses open to the public, including wedding photographers, make their services available to everyone, including gay couples, generally failed. But the controversies exposed two kinds of tensions: those internal to a regime of substantive equality, because women, gays, and religious employers all claimed to seek substantive equality, and those between substantive equality and some of traditional liberalism's commitments to individual autonomy.

Finally, the development of an accommodation-focused account of equality fit comfortably with the rise of identity politics. Indeed, on one view the entire point of identity politics was to achieve accommodations in public policy to the distinctive characteristics of identity-based groups, such as multiculturalism and multilingualism in education. Opponents of identity politics understood the point when they characterized as multiculturalists as seeking 'special rights.'

Substantive equality was a controversial account of constitutional equality, of course. The political and moral valence of accommodations

[52] *Sherbert v Verner* 374 US 398 (1963); *Employment Division v Smith* 494 US 872 (1990); *Corporation of Presiding Bishop v Amos* 483 US 327 (1987).

varied. They were largely positive when invoked in cases involving disability and age discrimination, negative in affirmative action cases. Accommodations could be expensive, and identity-politics threatened the vision some held of a culturally unitary United States. In addition, substantive equality was the guiding theory of social democracy, always weak in the United States. In paying attention to the actual distribution of social goods, substantive equality immediately raised questions about the interaction between the laws structuring market transactions and the laws seeking to alter the outcome of results reached through such transactions. In the end, substantive equality could not be a theory about regulatory or redistributive laws alone; it had to be a theory about markets as well. The political support for such a theory was weak in the United States.[53]

Yet, by the end of the twentieth century no significant alternative to modern liberalism was on the scene. Even the resurgence of fundamentalist religion did not pose a serious challenge to the conceptual basis of modern liberalism. Here there was an elective affinity between modern liberalism's ideal of personal autonomy and Protestant fundamentalism's ideal of a personal relationship with Jesus Christ: Both ideals worked from the inside out. In the constitutional domain, liberalism was so strong that those who sought to advance religion in the public sphere regularly relied on liberal rights-based arguments. Denying them access to public places to proselytize, for example, was said to violate the right to free speech as interpreted in standard liberal doctrine.[54] Placing statutes under a cloud merely because many of their proponents invoked religious arguments to explain why the statutes should be adopted was an even greater inroad on ordinary free speech ideas. Public financial support for parents who wanted to send their children to religiously affiliated schools, it was argued, was required so that those parents

---

[53] One indication of the difficulties associated with an explicit theory of substantive equality is the short story 'Harrison Bergeron' by Kurt Vonnegut, a person whose political sympathies were clearly to the left of center, offering a critique of substantive equality that was frequently cited by those to the right of center: K Vonnegut, 'Harrison Bergeron' in *Welcome to the Monkey House* (New York, Dell, 1968). For a conservative use of the reference, see *PGA Tour, Inc v Martin* 532 US 661, 705 (2001) (Scalia J, dissenting).

[54] *Capitol Square Review Board v Pinette* 515 US 753 (1995).

would be treated equally—substantively equally, note—to parents who could afford to make that choice by paying tuition from their personal resources.[55]

The Institutions for Protecting Constitutional Rights

Like constitutional ideas, the institutions of constitutional law change—slowly, sometimes randomly, and always leaving a residue that continues to affect the development of constitutional law. Here I discuss three institutions and one general process associated with the twentieth century rights revolution.

— The first institution is what political scientist Charles Epp calls the support structure for rights claims: the lawyers who put rights claims forward, and the organizations that finance them.[56] Here the story is of organizational innovation and imitation, and of political conflicts within the institutions supporting the rights revolutions.

— The second are the political parties, and groups within them, that find political advantage, either against the opposing party or within their own party, in supporting rights claims. Here the story is of the way in which the rights revolution assisted in the transformation of the two dominant political parties.

— The third are the institutions for articulating and vindicating constitutional rights. Here, the story is of a dramatic shift in institutional energy, from a world in which legislatures played a significant role relative to courts, to one in which courts were overwhelmingly dominant.

— The process is 'backlash', in which judicial decisions favouring one right are met with resistance, sometimes leading to political responses to the decisions, such as proposed constitutional amendments and partisan mobilization around the composition of the courts.

---

[55] For an argument to this effect, see C Bolick, *Voucher Wars: Waging the Battle over School Choice* (Washington, Cato Institute, 2003).

[56] CR Epp, *The Rights Revolution: Lawyers, Activists, and Supreme Court in Comparative Perspective* (Chicago, University of Chicago Press, 1998).

LAWYERS AND RIGHTS LITIGATION: THE DEVELOPMENT
OF SUPPORT STRUCTURES

Prior to the twentieth century, lawsuits were occasionally used to advance innovative positions on constitutional rights. Advocates of women's rights, for example, used a test case strategy to argue, unsuccessfully, that the Fourteenth Amendment guaranteed women the right to vote. *Plessy v Ferguson* resulted from outrage among New Orleans's community of *gens du couleur*—the city's middle-class community of African Americans with white ancestry—who organized a group specifically to support a challenge to the state's Jim Crow law, hired a lawyer and recruited Homer Plessy to become the plaintiff whose case would be carried, again unsuccessfully, to the Supreme Court.[57]

Beginning as an organization to support draft resisters during World War I, the American Civil Liberties Union (ACLU) took on the defense of free speech for left-wing activists in the 1920s. The ACLU had a 'legal committee' operating out of its national office, but at first did not directly represent defendants. The legal committee screened requests for assistance. It sent those it found worth supporting to volunteer lawyers closer to the ground, usually in the area where the case arose. Although it articulated a general vision of free speech, most of the ACLU's efforts through the 1960s were on behalf of people on the left, largely because the free speech rights most under assault were those of leftists. Nonetheless, the ACLU self-consciously refrained from defending the rights of Nazi sympathizers before and during World War II, and was quite ambivalent about, and no more than lukewarm in support of, the free speech rights of Communists during the early years of the Cold War.

A conceptual innovation occurred early in the twentieth century, although the innovative device was lost to historical memory and had to be reinvented independently two decades later. Earlier test case litigation, and the ensuing activities of the ACLU, was generally defensive— that is, constitutional challenges were raised only when the government took action against the litigants—and focused solely on the outcome of the case at hand. A group of management lawyers shifted from defense to offense, and from episodic litigation to sustained litigation

---

[57] CA Lofgren, *The Plessy Case: A Legal-Historical Interpretation* (New York, Oxford University Press, 1988).

with relatively long-term goals. Seeking to use the courts as a defense against labor organizing, employers supported systematic efforts by lawyers to use common law rules to bar strikes, to get the courts to construe antitrust laws to cover worker-organized boycotts, and to obtain rulings that state laws supporting labor unions by making it illegal for employers to insist that their employees not join unions were unconstitutional.[58]

These 'lawyers against labor' were largely successful. But, perhaps because their successes came just as classical liberalism was losing hold in constitutional law, the importance of the innovation was not immediately appreciated. The National Association for the Advancement of Colored People (NAACP), founded in 1909, had a legal department from its early years. At the start, the NAACP had a single lawyer on the organization's payroll, and used the ACLU model—which developed at the same time—of relying on lawyers in local communities who had independent legal practices and contributed their efforts to the NAACP. Unlike the ACLU's volunteer lawyers, though, the NAACP's local counsel typically received at least a modest fee, in light of the usually tight economic conditions of their legal practices.[59]

At first the NAACP's lawyers adopted the defensive posture. In the mid-1920s, though, the possibility of gaining foundation support for a broader litigation effort opened up when the NAACP's chief executive, James Weldon Johnson, obtained a grant from a left-leaning foundation, the American Fund for Public Service. With the first installment of the grant in hand, the NAACP hired Nathan Margold, a recent graduate of Harvard Law School, to develop a plan. Margold's report, which became legendary within the NAACP and eventually beyond, was overly ambitious, but contained the seeds of an important perception: Segregation could be undermined step by step. His successor, Charles Hamilton Houston, transformed Margold's plan. Houston realized that the NAACP did not have the resources to support the kinds of direct challenges to overall inequalities in funding that Margold targeted. Instead, Houston narrowed the focus to cases challenging the exclusion of African Americans from state graduate and professional schools, and

---

[58] DR Ernst, *Lawyers Against Labor: From Individual Rights to Corporate Liberalism* (Urbana, University of Illinois Press, 1995).

[59] M Tushnet, *The NAACP's Legal Strategy Against School Segregation, 1925–1950* (revd edn, Chapel Hill, University of North Carolina Press, 2004).

to cases challenging salaries for the African American teachers in segregated schools, which were universally lower than the salaries for white teachers of equivalent training and experience. Houston encouraged teachers, who would benefit from winning lawsuits, to join the NAACP and strengthen it organizationally. Litigation turned out to be more catch-as-catch-can than the official account of systematic, planned litigation would have had it.

The official account prevailed in the legal imagination, though. The reason was *Brown v Board of Education*. Looking back from 1954, lawyers saw a series of NAACP Supreme Court cases undermining *Plessy*'s premises. And, in the NAACP's official account, that had been their point all along.[60]

Defensive litigation persisted, and even took on an enhanced role during the civil rights and antiwar movements of the 1960s. But the vision of affirmative and strategic litigation became central to the institutional culture of rights. The idea that lawyers, consulting and to some extent influenced by social movements, could sit down and write out a plan of litigation that, once implemented, would achieve the movements' rights-based goals, was certainly seductive to the lawyers, and the cultural power of *Brown* meant that the movements themselves were captivated, sometimes fleetingly and sometimes in the longer term, by the same idea. And, indeed, the vision of strategic litigation did not even require that the lawyers have the discipline of pre-existing clients or a social movement. So, for example, some aspects of the prisoners' rights movement were almost entirely lawyer-developed and driven.

By the late 1960s, a substantial public interest bar existed to support the kinds of rights-claims asserted by political liberals. It took longer for conservatives to develop a parallel structure, because the possibilities for conservative successes arose later.[61] In 1971 Lewis F Powell wrote a memorandum to a friend at the United States Chamber of Commerce urging the business community to create institutions to challenge what Powell described as the domination of the left in the academy and in

---

[60] *Missouri ex rel Gaines v Canada* 305 US 337 (1938); *Sipuel v Board of Regents* 332 US 631 (1948); *Sweatt v Painter* 339 US 629 (1950); *McLaurin v Oklahoma State Regents* 339 US 637 (1950).

[61] S Teles, *The Rise of the Conservative Legal Movement: The Battle for Control of the Law* (New Haven, Yale University Press, 2008), provides an insightful overview.

the 'public interest' bar. The business community's first effort was a false start. The Pacific Legal Foundation, the first conservative public interest law firm, was established in 1973. Several others followed on soon after. This first group of public interest law firms achieved some modest successes, but relatively few. The reason was that business interests dominated them. They could not effectively present themselves as representing the public interest under those conditions. And, even more, the business community was often divided over the merits of many government programs. Some businesses—typically, large ones—benefited from government regulations that helped organize their markets and made it difficult for smaller competitors to achieve a foothold.

Conservative public interest law came into its own when it broke free from direct support from the business community and, like its liberal counterparts, began to be funded by conservative-leaning foundations. The most effective conservative public interest law firms revived classical liberal constitutional theory with its libertarian leanings. Their difficulty was that their successes—in limiting egregious environmental regulations, and similarly egregious regulations of small businesses, for example—were too narrow to have much effect. They could induce the courts to strike down regulations that were quite difficult to defend, and they could invoke libertarian constitutional theories that had some potential for doctrinal expansion in doing so. The most successful of these groups focused on religious liberty issues, seeking exemptions from regulations that, in their clients' view, intruded on religious liberty. Notably, these 'accommodation' claims resonated with some themes in modern liberalism as well. But the regulatory state was so entrenched by the end of the twentieth century that libertarian doctrines and accommodationist adjustments could make only small inroads on the government's reach.

The government also provided support for rights-claims. One might think this unlikely, because rights-claims are asserted against the government. Why would a government provide resources to challenge its own programs? Because sometimes the national government had an interest in challenging state and local governments, because sometimes the Constitution was interpreted to require the government to do so, and because government support for some constitutional challenges had the largely unintended result of supporting an account of substantive justice that generated political support for constitutional challenges to government programs more broadly.

In the early 1940s the Department of Justice created a Civil Rights Section, whose purpose was to enforce the relatively few existing criminal laws against violations of civil rights. These laws prohibited violent interferences with exercises of constitutional rights. Lacking enthusiasm and the political capital for the enactment of a federal law against lynching, the Roosevelt administration created the Civil Rights Section as a way of addressing lynch law in the South. The Section gradually grew, and was converted into a full-fledged 'Division' within the Department by the Civil Rights Act of 1957. Over the next decades, the Division's responsibilities expanded, to include enforcement of voting rights laws, anti-discrimination laws, and more. Here, the national government intervened to enforce civil rights guarantees against state and local governments.[62]

Starting in the 1930s, the Supreme Court held that sometimes criminal defendants were entitled to legal representation at public expense. At the outset, as in the Scottsboro cases, the private bar provided representation, with lawyers with general practices occasionally representing clients whose fees were paid by the government. Gradually, larger cities adopted public defender systems where the only services the lawyers provided were to those unable to afford private representation. The expansion of legal services of this sort was fueled by the Supreme Court's decision in 1963 that every defendant facing substantial time in jail if convicted was entitled to a lawyer.[63]

Despite the limitations on private and public support for rights-oriented organizations, by century's end the organizations had become a seemingly permanent part of the structure of rights-protection in the United States. What mattered was not whether they would exist, but how robust they would be, and how they would interact with each other and with the rest of the political system.

POLITICAL PARTIES AND SOCIAL MOVEMENTS

Constitutional law provides the structure within which politics occurs, but it also figures in the strategies political parties adopt. Social

---

[62] See RL Goluboff, *The Lost Promise of Civil Rights* (Cambridge, MA, Harvard University Press, 2007).

[63] *Gideon v Wainwright* 372 US 335 (1963); A Lewis, *Gideon's Trumpet* (New York, Vintage, 1981).

movements can threaten to disrupt existing party structures, as insurgencies within one party or as vehicles of social disorder that makes an opposition party's claim that it can restore order credible. Political leaders respond to these difficulties by attempting to incorporate the social movements' ideals, and then some elements of the movements themselves, into their political agendas. A platform plank on a constitutional issue can reach out to voters; an administration policy position dealing with constitutional rights can appeal to a constituency within the party or undermine the position taken by the administration's opponents either in the party or outside it. Notably, this can occur on both sides of the political aisle, and indeed is likely to so occur. What may differ between the parties is not their willingness to seek support from a constituency interested in a particular rights-claim, but rather the particular way in which the parties—or, more precisely, leaders within the parties—accommodate the rights-claim in policy proposals that fit comfortably within their party's broader approach to public policy. Politicians thereby build new visions of the Constitution into politics.

Of many possible examples, I use the Warren Court to illustrate the ways in which parties and rights interact. The Warren Court's support for modern liberalism, coupled with congressional civil rights initiatives, simultaneously enhanced the position of modern liberals within the Democratic party and weakened the party's support in more traditional venues, including the South. The effect is captured in the comment Lyndon Johnson reportedly made on signing the Civil Rights Act of 1964: 'There goes the South for a generation',[64] meaning 'There goes Southern support for the Democratic party'. Johnson's commitment to civil rights was both principled and political. As he saw it, Northern liberals, mainly urban and including many African Americans, were a more important component of the party coalition than the Southern conservatives who, Johnson accurately predicted, would sooner or later lose their seats to a resurgent Republican party in the South.

The Warren Court shaped the Republican party in another way. Its decisions expanding constitutional rights in criminal proceedings occurred just as crime rates increased dramatically. Richard Nixon campaigned for the presidency as a law-and-order candidate who would reshape the Supreme Court by appointing justices who would

---

[64] For a reference to this statement, see T Noah, 'Forget the South, Democrats', *Slate*, 27 Jan 2004: http://www.slate.com/id/2094552.

support what Nixon called the forces of peace rather than the forces of disorder.[65]

The Republican challenge to the Warren Court initially took the form of advocacy of a general theory of judicial restraint. The Warren Court had gone wrong, Republicans contended, by interfering with the policies elected representatives endorsed. This was a theory that worked as long as its advocates controlled legislatures but not the courts. As Republican appointees came to dominate the courts, the rhetoric of judicial restraint became less attractive, although it never entirely lost its hold.

The reason is that the United States experienced an extended period of divided government at the end of the twentieth century. Republicans controlled the presidency for 20 of the 24 years between 1969 and 1993, and only Republicans nominated Supreme Court justices during that period because no vacancies occurred during Jimmy Carter's presidency. But Democrats controlled Congress during the entire period (except for six years when Republicans had a majority in the Senate but not the House of Representatives). From a political point of view, what Republicans needed was a constitutional theory that *supported* judicial intervention when their political adversaries prevailed politically. A general posture of judicial restraint would not do.

Republicans solved their problem by insisting that the courts could intervene when—but only when—legislation was inconsistent with constitutional provisions as they were understood at the time they were adopted.[66] Departing from an interpretive tradition in which original understandings figured as one among many bases for constitutional interpretation, the constitutional theory of the Republican party at the end of the twentieth century was almost exclusively originalist. Judicial restraint mattered, within originalist accounts, only when the original understanding supported restraint; judicial restraint was a category within originalist theory, not the principle that should always guide constitutional interpretation. Like the Footnote 4 jurisprudence it replaced, at least among Republicans, originalism was sufficiently flexible to do the political jobs for which it was used.

---

[65] FP Graham, *The Self-Inflicted Wound* (New York, Macmillan, 1970).

[66] J O'Neill, *Originalism in American Law and Politics: A Constitutional History* (Baltimore, Johns Hopkins University Press, 2005).

Divided government persisted into the twenty-first century.[67] In those circumstances, the political uses of constitutional rights would inevitably be confused. Democrats defended a constitutional right to choice with respect to abortion because women committed to the right to choose had become an important constituency within the party. Republicans challenged the constitutionality of affirmative action programs because white men who believed themselves to be disadvantaged by affirmative action had become an important constituency within *that* party. Divided government made fights over constitutional rights increasingly intense.

FROM CONGRESS TO THE COURTS: THE VENUES FOR RIGHTS PROTECTION

The American discourse of rights underwent a substantial institutional reallocation during the twentieth century. In part because of the typically defensive nature of rights-assertions, and in part because of the institutional thinness of the support structure of rights-assertions in courts, the language of rights was widely used in ordinary political discourse—in addition, of course, to being deployed in courts. Outside the courts, though, the lawyer's conceptual structures—the division of rights into three categories, for example—played a much smaller role. Advocates of the rights of labor, in the labor movement or in progressive political circles, were uninterested in determining whether the rights of labor were civil or social rights. They were, simply, rights. If they could be secured in the courts, well and good, but securing them through legislation was just as good—and seemingly easier.

The growth of the support structure began a process of change. The ACLU and the NAACP both started out interested as much in influencing legislation and educating the public about their rights-concerns as in winning court cases. The ACLU rapidly and the NAACP more gradually began to focus on courts. The federal income tax law restricted lobbying by organizations that received donations exempt from taxation, but that was only a minor reason for the shift. The

---

[67] M Tushnet, *A Court Divided: The Rehnquist Court and the Future of Constitutional Law* (New York, Norton, 2005).

more important one was that the organizations could almost never win anything in the legislature or through influencing executive officials, but could occasionally win something in the courts. The NAACP's repeated failures to obtain anti-lynching legislation from a New Deal Congress controlled by Democrats, because of the strategic positions occupied by conservative Southern Democrats, showed that the organization had no influence outside the courts.

One should not exaggerate the rate at which the courts in fact protected rights, but getting something from them was better for the organizations, and for rights, than getting nothing from legislatures. In a political version of Say's Law—the (questionable) economic theory that supply elicits demand—successes in courts gave lawyers increasing prominence within the communities interested in rights, and their increased prominence made it easier for the lawyers to make the case that their activities deserved an increasing share of the funds available for all rights-oriented activities. Here too, the institutional thickening of the support structure made lawyers who focused on the courts a group within each organization and social movement whose interests had to be accommodated.

The content of the rights courts protected, compared to the rights of labor and the like, also affected the shift of resources into the courts. Courts were good at protecting rights that fit easily into a classical liberal framework, such as rights to free expression and equality understood in formal terms. The courts could reverse convictions for making assertedly dangerous speeches, or direct executive officials to refrain from enforcing statutes that discriminated on the basis of race. Through most of the twentieth century the remedies available for violations of rights that swept more broadly—roughly speaking, second generation rights to social and economic well-being, and third-generation rights to a desirable physical and cultural environment—were not well developed. What law professor Abram Chayes called public law litigation emerged in the late twentieth century with remedies aimed at forcing public bureaucracies to reform and behave in a constitutionally acceptable manner.[68] The reign of public law remedies was relatively brief, though. Not surprisingly, there was a strong political backlash against public law remedies.

---

[68] A Chayes, 'The Role of the Judge in Public Law Litigation' (1976) 84 *Harvard Law Review* 1281.

As law professor Risa Goluboff has shown, civil rights lawyers in the 1940s, inside the government and in the NAACP, saw the possibility of constructing an ideal of civil rights in which economic security played a large role.[69] They chose a different path, partly because the precedents with which they had to work made it easier to develop a race-related ideal than an economic security one, and partly because they worried that the association of economic security with unions and, in particular, the Communist Party would limit what they could achieve with respect to economic security and, even more, impair their overall efforts with respect to racial equality.

Interest in protecting economic well-being as a right enjoyed a brief revival in the late 1960s, but this time almost exclusively through efforts to obtain judicial rulings that the Constitution protected such a right. Occasionally, advocates would push legislation forward with rhetoric like 'Health care is a human right', but far more commonly they supported their proposals as good social policy, not as the implementation of a right. In the final quarter of the century, Congress enacted a large number of statutes dealing with environmental protection. Each was defended as good social policy. Near the end of the century, environmental activists looked back at their accomplishments, and began to describe what they sought—a decent environment—as a human right. Environmental legislation also began to produce judicial remedies that were more nuanced than the traditional injunction, even the public law structural injunction. But these developments at their incipient stages when the twenty-first century began, and whether they would spread, in the environmental field or beyond, remained unclear.[70]

Social movements did not abandon legislatures, of course. They sought, and sometimes obtained, rights-protective statutes. And, while an important feature of such statutes was that they provided remedies in courts for rights violations, the statutes—or perhaps more precisely the mobilization that secured their enactment—sometimes helped change social understandings about the practices the statutes made unlawful. On the liberal side, statutes like the Family and Medical Leave Act (1993) reinforced the sense that women and men should share duties of family caretaking; on the conservative side, state legislation restricted

[69] Goluboff, above n 61.

[70] R Lazarus, *The Making of Environmental Law* (Chicago, University of Chicago Press, 2004).

the power of cities to condemn property for purposes of economic development reinforced the sense that people's homes were particularly important to them. Describing these statutes disparagingly as merely symbolic because few people actually enforced the rights they created understates their importance in contributing to a culture of rights. And, once the laws were on the books, the common view that people ought to do what the law says helped reshape social understandings about the rights the statutes protected. Legislatures, then, did not fall completely out of the picture. Nonetheless, their role was smaller, relative to the courts', at the end of the century than it had been at its outset.

One thing overshadowed all these discrete points: *Brown v Board of Education.* There the Supreme Court had faced up to the greatest challenge to the proposition that the United States Constitution was an instrument of justice, and by holding Jim Crow unconstitutional lodged rights-protection almost unshakably within the courts. Congress and the presidency, even when controlled by political liberals, had failed to do anything significant about Jim Crow. The Supreme Court did. That the Court's follow-through after *Brown* was shaky, and that the Court's actions on their own did little to bring about real desegregation, which occurred when the civil rights movement pushed Congress to enact the civil rights statutes of the 1960s, mattered little for the cultural authority the Court eventually garnered from what it had done in *Brown*. *Brown* brought into focus all the blurry ideas of rights and how courts could vindicate them that entered the legal culture since 1937 without being systematized. The Court's triumph, as it came to be seen, in *Brown* sharply limited the availability within US culture of alternative venues for vindicating rights.

THE 'BACKLASH' THESIS

Drawing on the experience following *Brown v Board of Education,* law professor Michael Klarman propounded the 'backlash' thesis.[71] Klarman argued that the vindication of civil rights after *Brown* took a complex path. On Klarman's account, the Court's decision pushed

---

[71] MJ Klarman, *From Jim Crow to Civil Rights: The Supreme Court and the Struggle for Racial Equality* (New York, Oxford University Press, 2004).

Southern politicians into a vigorous defense of segregation through programs that came to be known as 'massive resistance'. Responding to that resistance, the civil rights movement adopted increasingly confrontational tactics. Those tactics in turn provoked a violent response, which turned public opinion outside the South, previously indifferent to the civil rights struggle, into a factor strongly supporting civil rights claims. The response to the Supreme Court's decisions on abortion rights is sometimes said to illustrate a backlash as well. The decisions created or at least strengthened the movement against abortion rights, whose members became important in the Republican party's conservative coalition. President Reagan appointed critics of the Court's decisions to the Supreme Court and to the lower courts, with the long-term effect of eroding—though not yet overruling—the decisions' effect.

One important feature of the 'backlash' thesis is that it does *not* contend that controversial Supreme Court decisions always produce a backlash and undermine the very rights the Court sought to vindicate. Indeed, Klarman's account is one in which backlash occurred but, through the interaction between the Court's decisions and the backlash, actually supported the decisions, though not immediately. Klarman's later analysis of the gay rights movement was similarly qualified.[72] Early gay rights decisions in state courts provoked a political mobilization against those rights, but the Court's decision holding unconstitutional a federal statute, the Defense of Marriage Act, propelled lower courts into accepting marriage equality, a development that appears so far to have met with little real resistance.[73]

CONSTITUTIONAL RIGHTS IN THE TWENTY-FIRST CENTURY

By the end of the twentieth century, rights-based constitutionalism centered on the courts had essentially no serious competitors in the United States. Statutes protecting rights were important in part because they elicited judicial intervention. Overturning a series of Supreme Court decisions restricting the scope of national anti-discrimination law, Congress enacted the Civil Rights Restoration Act of 1991. The

---

[72] MJ Klarman, *From the Closet to the Altar: Courts, Backlash, and the Struggle for Same-Sex Marriage* (New York, Oxford University Press, 2013).

[73] *United States v Windsor* 133 SCt 2675 (2013).

term 'restoration' signaled the centrality of courts to the rights-based constitutionalism at the end of the century. Statutes were important as well because they sometimes led to the creation of bureaucracies in the executive branch and in corporations that took their mission to be the vindication of the rights created by the statutes. Even here, though, the bureaucrats' mission had purchase on the larger organization because they were operating within a culture in which judicial enforcement of other rights gave rights-claims an aura of presumptive legitimacy.

Rights-based constitutionalism had no necessary political valence, though. Modern liberalism was layered on to classical liberalism. Not only could conservatives call on classical liberalism to defend their positions and challenge their opponents' (as, indeed, could liberals), but even more, modern liberalism could be given conservative as well as liberal interpretations. Conservative constitutional theorists attacked affirmative action programs on several grounds, for example: Such programs violated requirements of formal equality, true, but they also were inconsistent with the achievement of substantive equality by 'white ethnics', a point specifically made by Justice Antonin Scalia, himself an Italian American.[74]

Conservative constitutional theory offered what turned out to be a supplement to modern liberalism's attention to autonomy. Conservatives argued—more in their polemics than in their judicial practice—that constitutional interpretation should rest on the original understandings of the Constitution's terms. Originalism became attractive because many of the Warren Court's innovations were not, and could not plausibly be, connected to original understandings. Warren Court decisions on criminal procedure, for example, were often expressly rooted in non-textual concerns about fairness under modern circumstances, and originalism offered an understandable alternative method to support opposition to the Warren Court's substantive results. Yet, the pull of precedent and the attractions of interpretive flexibility meant that conservative judges were no more consistently committed to originalism as an exclusive method of interpretation than were their adversaries opposed to originalism.[75]

---

[74] See, eg, A Scalia, 'The Disease as Cure: "In Order to Get Beyond Racism, We Must Take into Account Race"' (1979) *Washington University Law Quarterly* 147, 152.

[75] For a discussion, see ch 7.

What was absent was a serious constitutional theory giving priority to what in the Catholic tradition was called 'the common good'. At most, the common good was what was left over after individual rights, both liberal and conservative, had been respected. And, given the sweep of liberal and conservative claims about rights, the domain left to the common good was small indeed. That domain could have been larger, had an earlier tradition, in which rights-protection occurred outside the courts, remained vibrant. The most important institutional development over the course of the twentieth century, though, was the near disappearance of that tradition.

FURTHER READING

Cloward, RA and Piven, FF, *Poor Peoples' Movements: Why They Succeed, How They Fail* (New York, Pantheon Books, 1977) (a classic account of the welfare rights movement, with some comments on its legal arm).

Davis, MF, *Brutal Need: Lawyers and the Welfare Rights Movement, 1960–1973* (New Haven, Yale University Press, 1993).

Fischer, DH, *Liberty and Freedom* (New York, Oxford University Press, 2005) (an illustrated analytic history).

Kornbluh, FA, *The Battle for Welfare Rights: Politics and Poverty in Modern America* (Philadelphia, University of Pennsylvania Press, 2007) (with a narrower geographical focus than Davis).

Strum, P, *Women in the Barracks: The VMI Case and Equal Rights* (Lawrence, KS, University Press of Kansas, 2002) (uses the VMI case as a vehicle for examining women's rights litigation more broadly).

7

The Processes of Constitutional Change

————————

Formal Amendments – Substance – Constitutional Interpretation as a Mechanism of Constitutional Change – Interpretive Methods: An Introduction – Conclusion – Constitutional Moments and Constitutional Change – Constitutional Moments – Concluding Thoughts

S OMEONE WHO ATTEMPTED to understand constitutional change in the United States by reading the written Constitution's provision on amending the Constitution would be misled. The formal amendment process is only one, and almost certainly the least important, of several mechanisms of constitutional change. Constitutional interpretation accounts for a much larger portion of constitutional change. Yet, though interpretation may be the statistically dominant form of constitutional change, it is not the structurally dominant form. That form is the 'regime shift', described, as we will see, somewhat misleadingly by law professor Bruce Ackerman as involving occasional constitutional 'moments' after which the array of institutions in the government as a whole is dramatically different from what it had been earlier. And, in general, shifts in constitutional interpretation as a mechanism of constitutional change occur as a result of changes in the courts attendant upon regime shifts.

FORMAL AMENDMENTS

Processes

Article V of the Constitution sets out the formal amendment process. If supported by two-thirds of both houses of Congress, an amendment will be submitted to the states for ratification. A proposed amendment becomes part of the Constitution if it is ratified by three-quarters of the states.[1] There is no time limit set in the Constitution for ratification. Several amendments, by their own terms, specified that they had to be ratified within seven years, as they were.[2] The proposed Equal Rights Amendment dealing with gender equality was submitted to the states pursuant to congressional resolutions that set a similar time limit, but not embedded within the proposed amendment. The amendment secured ratifications from 35 states, three short of the needed three-quarters, when the seven years expired. Anticipating that outcome, Congress enacted an extension of the time period, the legality of which was challenged but not adjudicated. Efforts continue to adopt the Equal Rights Amendment, and questions about timeliness may arise again.

The Supreme Court found that constitutional challenges to ratifications generally presented political questions, rejecting a challenge to the Child Labor Amendment (which ultimately failed because it did not gain sufficient ratifications) based on the argument that not enough states had ratified the amendment within a 'reasonable' period.[3] The Secretary of State is formally charged with announcing that sufficient ratifications of proposed amendments have been obtained, and in 1992 he announced that an amendment initially proposed in 1789 had been ratified, becoming the Twenty-Seventh Amendment.[4] Although some scholars raised questions about the announcement, contending that a 'real' amendment requires agreement from three-quarters of the states

---

[1] Congress may specify whether the ratification occur by state legislatures or by conventions in the states; contemporary practice is to allow ratification by state legislatures. Article V provides an additional process, never used: if two-thirds of the states apply to Congress for a convention for proposing amendments, a convention will be called. This process allows states to get a chance to consider amendments that Congress on its own might not propose. A large number of theoretical questions are associated with the convention route to amendment: must the state applications take identical form? Once convened to consider specific amendments, may a convention propose others? May Congress prescribe rules for the convention? Because the convention route has never been used and seems unlikely to be used, these questions will remain unresolved.

[2] *See* Amend XVIII (alcohol prohibition), XX (altering the dates for the presidential inauguration), XXI (repeal of prohibition) and XXII (setting a limit of two terms for the president).

[3] *Coleman v Miller* 307 US 433 (1939).

[4] The Amendment provides that a salary increase for members of Congress cannot take effect until after an intervening election.

obtained within a reasonably short period, the Amendment's general acceptance establishes that there is no timeliness requirement for ratification.

A related point is that the question 'Are there unconstitutional constitutional amendments?', mooted in other constitutional systems such as India, has not arisen in the United States, and is quite unlikely to arise. Article V contains two substantive limitations on the amendment power. Article I prohibited Congress from prohibiting the 'migration or Importation of Such Persons as any of the States now existing shall think proper to admit'—that is, the interstate slave trade—before 1808. Article V bolstered that prohibition by barring any constitutional amendment before 1808 that would 'affect' that provision. In addition, Article V purports to prohibit a constitutional amendment that would deprive any state of 'its equal Suffrage in the Senate'. Scholars have debated whether such a limitation on the amendment power is possible either conceptually or as a matter of positive law. Conceptually, it is difficult to explain how the sovereign people could lack the power to eliminate the Senate or convert it to a body in which states have representation in proportion to their populations. And, as a matter of positive law, it is unclear why the people could not use the regular amendment process to amend Article V to eliminate this restriction, and then amend the Constitution to change the rules of representation in the Senate. Of course, given the role the Senate and the states play in the formal amendment process, such a course of action is completely unrealistic. Still, the existence in the written Constitution of two, and only two, substantive limitations on the amendment power suggests that there are no other substantive limitations on the amendment power.

SUBSTANCE

The formal amendments to the Constitution fall roughly into four groups. The first 10 amendments—the Bill of Rights—constitute the first group, and it is not clear that we should consider them as amendments rather than as fulfillments of the original Constitution. Opposition to the Constitution's adoption included a strongly expressed concern that the original Constitution lacked a Bill of Rights. To ensure ratification, the Constitution's supporters promised to introduce a Bill of Rights as amendments to the Constitution as soon as possible after ratification. James Madison compiled the suggestions for amendments that had been made during the ratification debates, added some he particularly favored, and pushed the Bill of Rights through the House of Representatives. Senate approval and ratification by the states followed quickly, and the Bill of Rights became effective in 1791.

Three amendments overturn Supreme Court decisions interpreting—or, as the nation saw it, misinterpreting—the Constitution. After the Court held in 1791 that the Constitution allowed states to be sued in federal court for failing to pay their debts, the Eleventh Amendment was added to rule out suits against the states.[5] The Sixteenth Amendment overturned a Supreme Court decision holding that the Constitution's ban on 'direct' taxes not apportioned among the states by population prohibited Congress from enacting a national income tax. And the Twenty-Sixth Amendment responded to a Supreme Court decision holding that, though Congress had the power to lower the minimum age for voting in *national* elections to 18, it had no such power with respect to *state* elections. This created an administrative nightmare, and Congress and the states responded quickly with an amendment establishing a national minimum voting age of 18.

Another set of amendments is basically technical improvements in the Constitution as a means of government. We have already seen how the Twelfth Amendment responded to a defect in the presidential selection process that came to light in the election of 1800. The Twentieth Amendment, adopted in 1933, shortened the time between a presidential election and the new president's inauguration, and similarly shortened the gap between congressional elections and the convening of a new Congress. Other amendments established a term limit for the president and created a complex system for dealing with a president's death or disability.

The remaining amendments, aside from the mistaken nationwide prohibition on alcohol in 1919 and its repeal 14 years later, all are fairly described as expanding the scope of American democracy. Three amendments adopted during Reconstruction eliminated slavery, provided all citizens but most notably the newly freed population with

---

[5] There is a large body of case law dealing with the precise scope of the Eleventh Amendment, which is badly drafted. The Amendment's text is directed at creating some sort of immunity of the states from suit in federal court, but its language is consistent with no sensible theory of sovereign immunity. For discussion, see ch 5 above.

a panoply of fundamental rights, and guaranteed that the right to vote would not be denied on the basis of race. The Seventeenth Amendment, ratified in 1913, provided for the direct rather than the indirect election of Senators. The Nineteenth (1920) guaranteed suffrage to women. An amendment adopted in 1961 gave residents of the District of Columbia, the nation's capitol, the right to vote in presidential elections, and one adopted in 1964 eliminated poll or head taxes as a reason for denying the right to vote in elections for national office.

Taken as a whole, the 27 formal amendments to the Constitution are a mix of technicalities and shifts toward greater democracy. The latter are symbolically important, and the Fourteenth Amendment in particular—one of the Reconstruction trio—provided the essential legal predicate for judicial decisions extending constitutional rights against invasions by state governments. We can also observe that the democracy-related amendments appear to occur in spurts—immediately after the Constitution's adoption, during Reconstruction, during the Progressive era, and in the late years of the New Deal-Great Society regime. As we will see, Bruce Ackerman uses the temporal compression of some periods of constitutional amendment as the basis for a different analysis of the processes of constitutional change in the United States. For now, though, the main point is that someone who read only the formal amendments would not understand the ways in which the US government in the twenty-first century differed from the one created in 1789.

CONSTITUTIONAL INTERPRETATION AS A MECHANISM OF CONSTITUTIONAL CHANGE

The world changes and constitutions must adjust to those changes. An old constitution that is difficult to amend formally is a prescription for disaster or a candidate for replacement. Formal amendments can deal with occasional and large problems, although even there one might find that the time it takes to deploy the formal amendment process too long.[6]

---

[6] The Twenty-Sixth Amendment's adoption probably can be taken to set the standard for speed in proposal and ratification. The Supreme Court issued its decision in *Oregon v Mitchell* 400 US 112 (1970), on 21 December 1970. The decision created serious problems for states in administering their election laws. The Amendment was approved in the Senate on 10 March 1971, and in the House on 23 March. Sufficient ratifications were obtained for the Amendment to become effective on 1 July 1971.

Formal amendments cannot deal with the routine updating that a constitution requires in the face of change.

The United States uses constitutional interpretation for that job. Updating takes two forms. In one, probably the more important, political actors—legislatures in the states, or Congress or the president—develop policies and means of administering them that are inconsistent with the original Constitution. Interpreting the Constitution to allow the political branches to innovate, the courts ratify the innovation. Notably, though, here the courts play a secondary role: The real updating is done by the political branches, with the courts letting them get away with it in the face of the written Constitution.

The long history of the Commerce Clause's interpretation examined in chapter five provides the best example of this form of political-judicial updating. There is little doubt that the national government operates within the states, regulating a wide range of activities because they are part of interstate commerce, far more extensively than the founding generation expected. And that is not merely because the scope of what they understood to be 'commerce among the several States' changed. Rather, Congress adopted, and the courts endorsed, a definition of 'commerce' that was significantly broader than the definition the founding generation used.

The second form of judicial updating gives the courts the primary role. Here the courts hold unconstitutional practices that would have been regarded as obviously constitutional when the written Constitution was adopted. Sometimes the Supreme Court has said that the specific constitutional provision being interpreted licenses updating. For example, according to the Court the Eighth Amendment's prohibition on cruel and unusual punishment embodies an 'evolving standard[] of decency that mark[s] the progress of a maturing society'.[7] Sometimes, using language bringing to mind legal philosopher Ronald Dworkin's distinction between general and abstract concepts on the one hand and specific conceptions on the other, it has said that the Constitution uses general terms, the specific applications of which may change as we come to understand better what the concepts mean. In 1937 the Supreme Court held that the Fourteenth Amendment's Equal Protection Clause was not violated by a state's use of a poll tax—a flat tax the payment of which was a prerequisite to voting. In 1964 the

---

[7] *Trop v Dulles* 356 US 86, 101 (1958) (opinion of Warren CJ).

Twenty-Fourth Amendment was added to the Constitution, barring states from denying the right to vote in elections for national office 'by reason of failure to pay any poll tax or other tax'. That left open the possibility of using failure to pay poll taxes as a reason for denying people the right to vote in elections for state and local offices. In 1966 the Supreme Court held that such a use of a poll tax did indeed violate the Equal Protection Clause. Writing for the Court, and overruling the 1937 decision, Justice William O Douglas explained that '[n]otions of what constitutes equal treatment for purposes of the Equal Protection Clause do change'.[8]

The pattern illustrated by the poll tax decision may illustrate a more general phenomenon associated with decisions striking down practices that the courts had previously upheld. The earlier decisions come to be thought grounded on premises that, though normatively acceptable at one point, are no longer normatively acceptable. A constitutional provision interpreted to allow legislatures to act, or to bar them from acting, is later interpreted to prohibit (or allow) the very same action, because of changes in the values the constitutional provision is understood to express.

An important opinion filed in a major abortion case in 1992 illustrates the role normative change plays in constitutional interpretation. The opinion discussed why its three authors thought it inappropriate to overrule the Court's basic decision on the right to choose in connection with abortion.[9] In the course of their discussion they wrote of two prior instances in which the Court had overruled highly controversial decisions. One was *Brown v Board of Education* (1954), which overruled the 1896 decision upholding racial segregation by law. The earlier decision, the justices said, rested on the factual assumption that facilities provided separately for whites and African Americans could be equal in quality; time had shown that that assumption was mistaken. Although most readers of *Brown* would conclude that the justices who joined the decision believed that the earlier decision was normatively indefensible, the fact-based account of the reasons for overruling was tenable. Less so for the other example the justices discussed. In 1937 the Supreme Court rejected what the justices called a 'line of cases identified with *Lochner v New York*'. The justices tried to assimilate that overruling to

---

[8] *Harper v Virginia Board of Elections* 383 US 663, 669 (1966).
[9] *Planned Parenthood of Southeastern Pennsylvania v Casey* 505 US 833 (1992).

Brown by saying that the *Lochner* line of cases 'rested on fundamentally false factual assumptions about the capacity of a relatively unregulated market to satisfy minimal levels of human welfare'. That is quite a revisionist interpretation of the *Lochner* line. More usually, it is said that they rest on an understanding of what the Constitution's guarantees of liberty and property mean, and that the 1937 decision rejected no factual assumptions that had proven false but rather rejected the normative account of liberty and property.

INTERPRETIVE METHODS: AN INTRODUCTION

The traditions of constitutional interpretation in the United States make it possible, and indeed relatively easy, to use interpretation as the vehicle for constitutional adaptation.[10] The interpretive traditions are decidedly eclectic. Interpretation relies on the words of the text as understood when they were made part of the Constitution, general propositions about how institutional arrangements promote constitutionalism, ideas about the values of democracy and individual autonomy, and much more. Chief Justice John Marshall's opinion for the Supreme Court in *McCulloch v Maryland* provides a useful introduction to the interpretive methods commonly used by the US Supreme Court.

An Introductory Case Study: *McCulloch v Maryland*

The issue in *McCulloch* was the constitutionality of the statute creating the Bank of the United States. No enumerated power specifically gave Congress the power to create a bank, and indeed the constitutional convention expressly considered whether to enumerate that power and decided against doing so. The issue before the Court, then, was whether the power to create a bank could be inferred from any of the other enumerated powers. The Court said that Congress did have the power to create the Bank. That answer, Marshall wrote, flowed from 'a fair construction of the whole instrument'.[11] Marshall said that it was

---

[10] The material on the following pages is drawn from M Tushnet, 'The United States: Eclecticism in the Service of Pragmatism' in J Goldsworthy (ed), *Interpreting Constitutions: A Comparative Study* (Cambridge, Cambridge University Press, 2006).

[11] *McCulloch v Maryland* 17 US 316 (1819).

'essential to just construction, that many words which import something excessive, should be understood in a more mitigated sense—in that sense which common usage justifies'. In construing constitutional terms, 'the subject, the context, the intention of the person using them, are all to be taken into view'.

Constitutions could not deal in detail with everything the governments they created would do:

> A constitution, to contain an accurate detail of all the subdivisions of which its great powers will admit, and of all the means by which they may be carried into execution, would partake of the prolixity of a legal code, and could scarcely be embraced by the human mind. It would probably never be understood by the public.

Instead, 'only its great outlines should be marked, its important objects designated, and the minor ingredients which compose those objects be deduced from the nature of the objects themselves'. So, Marshall concluded, 'In considering this question, then, we must never forget, that *it is a constitution we are expounding*'. Marshall supplemented this point with his observation a few pages later that the Constitution was 'intended to endure for ages to come, and, consequently, to be adapted to the various crises of human affairs'.

Marshall's opinion in *McCulloch* became the touchstone for everyone who defended the idea of a living Constitution. Marshall did not begin his discussion of whether Congress had the power to create the bank by citing any specific constitutional language. Instead, he observed that a national bank had been created by the first Congress after full discussion there and by Hamilton and Thomas Jefferson within the president's Cabinet. The longstanding judgment of the political branches, reflected in practice, should make 'a considerable impression' on the courts: 'It would require no ordinary share of intrepidity to assert that a measure adopted under these circumstances was a bold and plain usurpation.' Marshall then qualified his reliance on practice: 'These observations belong to the case; but they are not made under the impression that, were the question entirely new, the law would be found irreconcilable with the constitution.'

Marshall next turned to an exposition of the general theory of the Constitution's creation. Maryland's lawyers contended that the national government's powers had been delegated to it from the states, not from the people, and that the states therefore were 'truly sovereign'. Examining the Constitution's history, Marshall rejected the argument. The national government got its authority from the people of the states acting in special conventions called solely for the purpose of ratification, not from the standing state legislatures.[12]

Only after these points did Marshall even mention the constitutional text. He acknowledged that the text did not specifically say that Congress had the power to create a national bank. But, he noted, the Tenth Amendment, declaring that the powers not delegated to the national government were reserved to the states, 'omits the word "expressly"'. The list of enumerated powers defined the 'great outlines' of the national government's powers, leaving the 'minor ingredients' to be 'deduced from' the enumerated powers. Marshall pointed to the power to collect taxes, borrow money and raise and support armies and navies. A national bank, according to Marshall, was one of the 'usual means' of carrying out those enumerated powers. 'The exigencies of the nation may require that the treasure raised in the north should be transported to the south.' Without a national bank, 'these operations [would be] difficult, hazardous, and expensive'.

Maryland agreed that Congress has some choice of methods to implement its enumerated powers, but contended that the choice was limited by the final clause in the section enumerating Congress's powers, the Necessary and Proper Clause, which provides that Congress has the power 'To make all Laws which shall be necessary and proper for carrying into Execution the foregoing Powers'. Marshall's discussion of the clause began by observing that it was placed in the section of the Constitution granting Congress power, rather than in the section limiting that power, a point to which he returned later in the opinion, when he added that the clause's terms 'purport to enlarge, not to diminish the powers vested in the government. It purports to be an additional power, not a restriction on those already granted'.

Marshall continued by expounding on the ordinary meaning of the word *necessary*. According to Marshall, 'in the common affairs of the world' and 'in approved authors', the word 'frequently imports no more than that one thing is convenient, or useful, or essential to another'. It 'admits of all degrees of comparison', a point Marshall bolstered by pointing to another constitutional provision that prohibited states

---

[12] This rejects the proposition that the Constitution emanated from the states in their corporate capacities, but not the different theory, discussed earlier, that it emanated from the peoples of the several states coordinating their separate decisions.

from laying duties on imports 'except what may be absolutely necessary for executing its inspection laws'. Marshall then examined the effects of a restrictive interpretation of the Necessary and Proper Clause. Congress had the power to establish post offices and post roads, and based on that power it had made it a crime to steal from the mails. The criminal statute was 'essential to the beneficial exercise of the power, but not indispensably necessary to its existence'. Maryland objected that Marshall's argument that enumerated powers themselves gave Congress the power to implement them made the Necessary and Proper Clause redundant. Marshall replied that the clause might have been included out of a 'desire to remove all doubts respecting the right to legislate on that vast mass of incidental powers which must be involved in the constitution, if that instrument be not a splendid bauble'.

The case raised a second question. Maryland had imposed a tax on the operations of the national bank and, even if Congress had the power to create the bank, still Maryland's tax might be constitutionally permissible. Among the arguments Marshall developed against Maryland's position, one has continuing relevance. Maryland argued that its tax was permissible because people in other states, who benefited from the bank's existence, should be confident that Maryland would not impose a tax so large as to interfere with the bank's operations. Marshall replied, 'Would the people of any one State trust those of another with a power to control the most insignificant operations of their State government? We know they would not.' People have confidence in the governments in which they are represented, and '[i]n the legislature of the Union alone, are all represented. The legislature of the Union alone, therefore, can be trusted by the people with the power of controlling measures which concern all, in the confidence that it will not be abused'.

Marshall's idea here is that political representation is an important means by which the people guard against abusive exercises of power. Maryland's argument failed because people in other states, who might be affected by Maryland's actions, were not represented in that state's legislature. Political representation could not protect against an abusive tax. Marshall's idea supports a more general proposition about constitutional interpretation: Constitutional provisions should be interpreted so as to enhance the ability of the people to use their power as voters to protect them against over-reaching by legislatures.

McCulloch did not implicate one other approach to constitutional interpretation that already had arisen in the Supreme Court. Can judges go beyond the constitutional text and invoke unwritten principles of justice in deciding cases? Two Supreme Court justices discussed that question in *Calder v Bull* (1798). The case involved the constitutionality of a Connecticut statute authorizing the state courts to re-hear an already decided case invalidating a will. The claim was that this statute violated the federal Constitution's ban on state 'ex post facto' laws. The justices agreed that it did not, because the ban applied only to laws that made a crime out of something that was legal at the time it was done. In describing the point of constitutional limitations, Justice Samuel Chase said that the Constitution rested on 'certain vital principles' that limited government power—even if those principles were not set out in the Constitution itself:

> It is against all reason and justice, for a people to entrust a Legislature with SUCH powers; and, therefore, it cannot be presumed that they have done it … To maintain that our Federal, or State, Legislature possesses such powers, if they had not been expressly restrained; would, in my opinion, be a political heresy, altogether inadmissible in our free republican governments.

Chase gave as examples a statute that made a person the judge in his own case, and a statute that simply took property from one person and transferred it to another. Nothing found in the written Constitution as it stood in 1798 specifically made such statutes unconstitutional,[13] and yet to Chase they were.

Justice James Iredell disagreed. For Iredell, the Constitution did limit government, but only in the ways specified in its text:

> If … the Legislature of the Union, or the Legislature of any member of the Union, shall pass a law, within the general scope of their constitutional power, the Court cannot pronounce it to be void, merely because it is, in their judgment, contrary to the principles of natural justice.

Iredell continued by identifying a theme that would eventually come to predominate in theorizing about constitutional interpretation—the inability of anyone to identify the constraints natural justice (or, in later treatments, any other constitutional theory) placed on government. In

---

[13] The Fifth Amendment contains a due process clause and a provision that private property shall not be taken for public use without just compensation, which can be read to require that all takings be for public purposes. These provisions could readily be interpreted to make Chase's hypothetical statutes unconstitutional. Chase had state laws in mind, though, and early interpreters took the Fifth Amendment to restrict only the national government.

Iredell's terms, 'The ideas of natural justice are regulated by no fixed standard' and so those ideas provided no sound basis for judicial invalidation of a statute.

These early decisions use a number of interpretive techniques, all of which have been an important part of the practice of constitutional interpretation since then. A catalogue of interpretive techniques aids us in understanding how interpretation serves to update the Constitution. In essence, the availability of interpretive techniques that involve something other than the written text and original understanding makes updating both possible and inevitable.

Text: Ordinary Meaning

Interpretation of course begins with the constitutional text, and sometimes ends there. Many of the provisions setting out the structure of the national government are indisputably clear, the conventional examples being the provisions using numerical terms such as the one specifying that each state shall have two Senators, or the one setting forth the rule that a person must be 35 years old to be eligible for the presidency.

Occasionally even apparently transparent constitutional language can be overridden. A useful example is provided by the Emoluments Clause, which provides:

> No Senator or Representative shall, during the time for which he was elected, be appointed to any civil office under the authority of the United States, which shall have been created, or the emoluments whereof shall have been increased during such time.

Sometimes the following situation arises. Congress enacts a statute increasing the salaries of members of the president's Cabinet. During that same term of Congress, the president finds it politically useful to name a member of Congress to the Cabinet. To accommodate the president, Congress enacts a new statute returning the salary of the particular Cabinet position to its level at the start of the congressional term. This practice, which has become known as the 'Saxbe fix' after Ohio Senator and Attorney-General William Saxbe, has become uncontroversial, although the Supreme Court has never addressed its constitutionality. It is rather clearly in severe tension with the Constitution's language. The salary *was* increased during the affected person's term in Congress, and the fact that it was later decreased seems irrelevant in light of the Constitution's wording.

Text: Technical Meaning

The foregoing example involves interpretation according to the ordinary meaning of constitutional language. Some constitutional terms had technical meanings when they were inserted into the Constitution. The *Ex Post Facto* Clause at issue in *Calder v Bull* is an example. The core idea behind the clause is that there is something particularly unjust about changing the law to a person's disadvantage at a time when the person can do nothing to conform his or her conduct to the new law—after the fact almost literally. The injustice is not obviously different when the law takes away a person's property by changing the rules under which the property was already acquired, or when the law makes a person's completed actions illegal when they were lawful at the time they were done. Yet, in *Calder* the justices agreed that the *Ex Post Facto* Clause applied only to criminal statutes, not to the civil statute changing the distribution of property pursuant to a will.

Another, more complex example involves the Constitution's two Due Process Clauses. The ordinary meaning of those clauses would make them applicable to the procedures used to deprive people of property or liberty. Yet, by the time they were inserted into the Constitution, the term 'due process' had acquired an additional technical meaning. It was the modern version of the phrase 'law of the land' used in Magna Carta, and had come to mean that neither executive actions nor legislation could be unreasonable or arbitrary.[14] That is, the term 'due process' had come to incorporate some substantive limitations on government power.

Notably, interpretations that rely on technical meanings are inevitably originalist. The technical meaning at the time of adoption controls, not ordinary understanding (either then or at the time interpretation occurs).

Textual Structure

The overall structure of the constitutional text also provides the basis for interpreting particular provisions. *McCulloch* provides two examples of what Akhil Amar has recently called 'intratextualism'.[15]

---

[14] For a discussion, see JV Orth, *Due Process of Law* (Chapel Hill, University of North Carolina Press, 2003).

[15] AR Amar, 'Intratextualism' (1999) 112 *Harvard Law Review* 748.

By contrasting the word 'necessary' in the Necessary and Proper Clause with the phrase 'absolutely necessary' in the clause dealing with state inspection laws, Marshall was able to establish that the Constitution contemplated the possibility that necessity admitted of degrees. And, by observing that the Necessary and Proper Clause was included in the enumeration of Congress's powers, Marshall was able to undermine the state's argument that the clause should operate as a limitation on the other enumerated powers.

'Holistic' Interpretation

The relation between one constitutional provision and amendments added later has received some attention recently. The issue is whether an amendment not directed at a particular existing constitutional provision can be invoked to justify a new interpretation of that provision. In *United States v Morrison*, the Supreme Court held that a provision of the Violence Against Women Act was unconstitutional.[16] The provision gave a civil remedy in the national courts to victims of gender-motivated violence. Congress attempted to justify the provision by establishing that violence against women had a serious adverse impact on interstate commerce. The Court held that Congress lacked power under the Commerce Clause to enact the provision, because acts of violence against women were not themselves commercial in nature. Proponents of holistic interpretation argue that later adopted amendments, such as the Nineteenth Amendment guaranteeing women the right to vote, should be used to inform the interpretation of the Commerce Clause.[17] This approach, while attracting some academic support, has not yet worked its way into the Court's interpretive jurisprudence.

Text and Practice

The 'Saxbe fix' is little more than 100 years old. It indicates that long-standing practice can sometimes validate statutes that might otherwise be held unconstitutional. The Supreme Court has never been entirely

---

[16] 529 US 598 (2000).
[17] See, eg, VC Jackson, 'Holistic Interpretation: Fitzpatrick v Bitzer' (2001) 53 *Stanford Law Review* 1259.

clear about the relation between text and practice. Marshall opened his opinion in *McCulloch* by observing that the national bank had been in existence for many years, and took that practice to have some weight. He then immediately qualified his reliance on practice, specifically attempting to overcome the inference that he was relying on practice because otherwise Congress lacked the power to create the bank. The Court has been persistently ambivalent about the relation between text and practice. Justice William Rehnquist once wrote, 'Past practice does not, by itself, create power,' but that observation was preceded by a quotation from Justice Felix Frankfurter, that 'a systematic [and] unbroken practice … may be treated as a gloss' on specific constitutional terms—at least those terms that require glossing because their meaning is subject to fair dispute.[18]

Constitutional Structure

Professor Charles Black emphasized the importance of structural considerations in interpreting the Constitution.[19] Black's primary example was a 1965 case challenging the constitutionality of a state law barring members of the armed forces from voting in state elections, even though the soldiers satisfied the state's general requirement that only state residents could vote.[20] The Supreme Court held the statute unconstitutional as a violation of the Constitution's Equal Protection Clause. The case was a simple one from the standpoint of constitutional doctrine in 1965, although the application of the Equal Protection Clause to voting rights had been controversial earlier. Black argued that there was a simpler and better way to deal with the case. The state statute, according to Black, manifested a hostility to the national government and its employees that was inconsistent with the structural premises of the union: states could not treat national soldiers as an occupying or foreign force.

---

[18] *Dames & Moore v Regan* 453 US 654, 686 (1981). The Court divided over the relevance of practice to textual interpretation in *NLRB v Noel Canning*, 134 SCt 2550 (2014). The majority stated that 'in interpreting the Clause [at issue], we put significant weight upon historical practice,' whereas a separate opinion found the historical practice insufficient to overcome the text's seemingly obvious meaning.

[19] CL Black Jr, *Structure and Relationship in Constitutional Law* (Baton Rouge, Louisiana State University Press, 1969).

[20] *Carrington v Rash* 380 US 89 (1965).

Structural considerations have been important in cases dealing with the relation between the states and the nation. When California took advantage of a congressional statute that purported to authorize states to provide public assistance to recent migrants from another state at only the level the new residents had received in the states they had left, the Supreme Court invoked a constitutional right to travel protected by the Privileges and Immunities Clause to invalidate the statute.[21] Again, the holding was not doctrinally innovative. The Court took that clause as expressing an idea of national unity, to the effect that states were not allowed to treat migrants from other states as foreigners. The Privileges and Immunities Clause does indeed express that idea, but once again the Court could have relied on inferences from the structure of the national government to support its conclusion.

The Supreme Court has held that the constitutional structure bars Congress from requiring that states submit to suits in the national courts or in state courts, brought against them by their own citizens for violating substantive obligations Congress has the power to impose on the states.[22] The constitutional text is unavailing here, but the Court relied on the assumptions about state sovereignty held by the framing generation. Allowing Congress to require that states submit to suit would, according to the Court, be inconsistent with the combination of national and state sovereignty that characterized the government of the United States taken as a whole. In the Court's view, other remedies, such as suits by the national government to enforce its laws, or suits by individuals against officials rather than the state, are better means of enforcing national law while respecting the sovereignty the states retain in a national union.

Although structural analysis has been used most often to deal with questions implicating the federal structure of the United States, it can be used in cases implicating individual rights as well. Here the relevant structural feature, or pre-supposition, is the one Justice Chase alluded to in *Calder v Bull*, that all governments in the United States are limited governments. Justice Chase's argument is that not all the limitations on

---

[21] *Saenz v Roe* 526 US 48 (1999). The Privileges and Immunities Clause provides: 'No State shall make or enforce any law which shall abridge the privileges and immunities of citizens of the United States.'

[22] *Florida Prepaid Postsecondary Ed Expense Bd v College Savings Bank* 527 US 629 (1999); *Alden v Maine* 527 US 706 (1999).

government power are enumerated in the Constitution. The difficulty, common to all structuralist arguments, those dealing with federalism as well as individual rights, is to identify the precise content of the limitations on government power that the government's structure imposes. Notably, structuralist arguments are brought into play most often when there is little specific constitutional language to work with, which means that there is relatively little other material to impose discipline on the results offered via structuralist arguments. Structural arguments thus supplement other ones, and rarely stand on their own.

'Representation-Reinforcing Review'

Marshall's opinion in *McCulloch* rejected Maryland's tax on the national bank because the people of the nation as a whole, who benefited from the bank, were not represented in the legislature that imposed the tax, in contrast to Congress where, Marshall said, 'all are represented'. John Hart Ely gave this approach to constitutional interpretation its modern name, 'representation-reinforcing review'.[23] According to this approach, constitutional provisions should be interpreted so as to reinforce the nation's system of democratic representation. Doing so emphasizes the legitimacy of legislation that gets enacted in a fully democratic process and, conversely, emphasizes the questionable democratic legitimacy of laws enacted when we can identify some representational defect in the legislative process. For some advocates, the approach also has the advantage of focusing on what they believe to be relatively uncontroversial questions of process, relegating more controversial questions about the law's substance to the background.

Representation-reinforcing review draws on a general account of the democratic process, and may perhaps be better described as a theory of the constitution itself rather than as a method of constitutional interpretation. Still, ideas about the adequacy of representation have influenced some interpretations the Court has offered. Probably the best way to understand the theory of representation-reinforcing review is that it provides a general guideline applicable to all constitutional provisions, advising judges to apply particular constitutional provisions

---

[23] JH Ely, *Democracy and Distrust: A Theory of Judicial Review* (Cambridge, MA, Harvard University Press, 1980).

more aggressively when the judges can identify some representational defect in the processes that led to the challenged statute's enactment.

Ely derived his theory from the work of the Warren Court and from what has been called the most celebrated footnote in constitutional law,[24] footnote four of Justice Harlan Fiske Stone's opinion in *United States v Carolene Products* (1938).[25] The Court had little difficulty in upholding a congressional ban on the interstate shipment of filled milk, a low-cost substitute for whole milk, applying an extremely deferential standard for determining whether a statute violated the economic right of the filled milk producers to engage in ordinary commercial activity. Stone's footnote four said that a less deferential standard would be applied when the constitutional challenge rested on specific constitutional guarantees like those in the Bill of Rights rather than on what the Court took to be the generalities of the Due Process Clause. The footnote then turned to concerns about representation:

> It is unnecessary to consider now whether legislation which restricts those political processes which can ordinarily be expected to bring about repeal of undesirable legislation, is to be subjected to more exacting judicial scrutiny under the general prohibitions of the 14th Amendments than are most other types of legislation…
>
> Nor need we enquire whether similar considerations enter into the review of statues directed at particular religious … or national … or racial minorities; [or] whether prejudice against discrete and insular minorities may be a special condition, which tends seriously to curtail the operation of those political processes ordinarily to be relied upon to protect minorities, and which may call for a correspondingly more searching judicial inquiry… [26]

Exclusions from voting are good examples of the first category Stone's footnote identifies. The US Constitution protects the right to vote against denials based on a number of particular grounds, such as race, gender and youth, but it contains no general right to vote. The Supreme Court invoked representation-reinforcing ideas in subjecting exclusions from the franchise not covered by those particular provisions to exacting review under the Equal Protection Clause.[27] Also in

---

[24] LF Powell, 'Carolene Products Revisited' (1982) 82 *Columbia Law Review* 1087.

[25] 304 US 144 (1938).

[26] *Ibid* at 152 n 4.

[27] Eg *Kramer v Union Free Sch Dist* 395 US 621 (1969) (invalidating the denial of the right to vote in local school board elections to persons who neither owned property in the district nor had children enrolled in the district's schools).

this first category are laws suppressing speech: Those who would like to change the content of the law cannot do so if they are penalized for saying what they think. Such laws might well be covered by the specific guarantee of the First Amendment, but Stone's thought might be that representation-reinforcement concerns could be used to determine that Amendment's precise coverage in situations of interpretive ambiguity.

Stone's concern about laws based on prejudice against discrete and insular minorities seems to have been designed to address state laws discriminating against African Americans. When he wrote, African Americans were widely excluded from the franchise by formal and informal means, including physical coercion. Ely devoted a great deal of effort attempting to work out the implications of Stone's insight in situations where the 'discrete and insular minorities' had full access to the voting booth. Most commentators believe that Ely's efforts are not fully satisfactory. In some ways the deepest criticism is that, in situations of full enfranchisement, it is not discrete and insular minorities that are at a disadvantage, but dispersed majorities.[28] Consider the filled-milk case. Its primary beneficiaries are the well-organized special interest group of milk producers, who can raise funds to lobby Congress for the statute, while those who feel its burdens are low-income consumers who would be able to purchase more filled milk than whole milk, but are unable to organize themselves as an effective counter-lobby.[29]

Original Understanding

Reacting to what they perceived as the unjustified activism of the Supreme Court in the 1960s, political conservatives began to develop what they eventually called a jurisprudence of original intention. Reference to the framers' understandings had always been part of constitutional interpretation, but rarely were decisions justified solely by invoking original understanding. Modern political conservatives urged that only original understandings be used in constitutional

[28] The basic argument was made by B Ackerman, 'Beyond Carolene Products' (1985) 98 *Harvard Law Review* 713.

[29] Again, the full analysis is more complex, as it would have to take into account the ability of filled-milk producers to represent (virtually, to use the term common in political theory) the consumers.

interpretation. *District of Columbia v Heller* (2008), holding that the Constitution guarantees individuals a right to own ordinary weapons for purposes of self-protection, is widely regarded as the Court's most 'originalist' decision in generations, and as a vindication of originalism itself.[30]

After some mis-steps,[31] the jurisprudence of original understanding eventually settled on the proposition that the Constitution's terms should be interpreted by giving them the meaning they had among the general (or generally educated and politically attentive) public at the time they were inserted into the Constitution.[32] Supreme Court opinions rely on the dictionaries that were available in 1789, for example, to establish the meaning of words like 'arrest'.[33] Occasionally the jurisprudence of original understanding degenerates into bizarre disputes like one between Justices Antonin Scalia and David Souter over the proper way to read several sentences in the *Federalist Papers*,[34] but the difficulties with this form of originalism are more serious.

One problem echoes difficulties with versions of originalism that focus on intent rather than understanding. The nation's history made it clear that some constitutional arrangements were aimed at extending existing British practices, while others were aimed at repudiating those practices. Yet, without recourse to original intentions of some sort, it proved difficult indeed to explain why some words were to be interpreted as endorsing British practices, others as repudiating them. This reflected a deeper difficulty. The jurisprudence of original understanding attempted to reproduce the processes of legal reasoning of the late eighteenth century to determine what constitutional provisions mean. Yet, lawyers in the late eighteenth century agreed, more or less, on how

---

[30] 554 US 570 (2008).

[31] The mis-steps typically involved formulating the jurisprudence as one of original *intent*, which created large difficulties about identifying whose intent counted, about whether understandings about likely outcomes should count among the intentions or indeed should exhaust what counted as an intention, and, probably most important, about how to go about aggregating the intentions of many individuals.

[32] Most originalist scholarship focuses on the 1789 Constitution and the 1791 Bill of Rights, but originalism's interpretive principles are equally applicable to the Reconstruction Amendments.

[33] *Atwater v City of Lago Vista* 532 US 318, 330 (2001).

[34] *Printz v United States* 521 US 898, 911–12 (Scalia J, for the Court), 972–3 (Souter J, dissenting).

to engage in legal reasoning, but they disagreed, often quite substantially, about what the outcomes of that reasoning would be in particular instances. Words were understood to mean things because they fit into larger conceptions of the political order, but in the cases that interest today's interpreters, disagreements about those larger conceptions cascade down—in the eighteenth century no less than today—into disagreements about what an ordinary person would understand the words to mean. So, for example, everyone agreed that the states were to retain some sort of sovereignty within the new national government, but disagreement was pervasive over what the components of that sovereignty were.

The second difficulty with the jurisprudence of original understanding arises from changes in society, economy and the values held by the society. Slavery provides the most dramatic example. The 1789 Constitution and the 1791 Bill of Rights were written for a society in which slavery was well established in parts of the country, and legal almost everywhere else. Somehow people in the late eighteenth century were able to see in the Constitution's words, as they understood them, a charter for liberty from the British and from potential domestic tyrants, and yet were unable to see in those same words condemnation of slavery. Today it is trivially easy for an interpreter to give the original Constitution's words meanings that at least make slavery a constitutionally problematic institution, but that seemingly was not so in 1789 and 1791.

In discussions of the problem change poses for originalist approaches to constitutional interpretation, the term 'commerce' has been the one receiving most attention. As described in detail in chapter five, in the 1930s the Supreme Court adopted interpretations of that term that gave the national government essentially unrestricted power to enact statutes that regulated or banned activities that had even the slightest connection to interstate commerce. Those interpretations were in some tension with original understandings, and the results were inconsistent with the proposition, well established at the time of the Constitution's adoption, that the national government was one of limited powers. In the 1990s the Supreme Court began to rethink Commerce Clause doctrine. Its decisions were rather limited, though, because a return to original understandings threatened to make a great deal of the regulation adopted in the twentieth century unconstitutional.

Justice Clarence Thomas revived the idea that, as originally understood, commerce was distinguished from manufacturing and agriculture.[35] Were that idea to be adopted by the Court, national labor laws, national environmental laws, national anti-discrimination laws, and more might have come under a constitutional cloud. The Court was not prepared to take that step. Concurring in a decision that invalidated a national statute making it a crime to possess a gun near a school, Justice Anthony Kennedy, joined by Justice Sandra Day O'Connor, expressed concern about pushing the reconsideration of existing doctrine much beyond that point. The history of the Court's effort to limit the scope of the Commerce Clause, Kennedy wrote, gave him 'pause', but he emphasized that the Court's holding, while 'necessary', was 'limited'.[36]

How can original understandings be accommodated to the fact of change? The most popular solution uses the metaphor of *translation* to capture what needs to be done.[37] Today's interpreters should do what a good translator does: we should understand the powers the Constitution confers and the rights it protects as if the Constitution's words were translated from the eighteenth century into our modern language. A good translation preserves the original meaning, but makes the composition understandable and relevant to the reader unfamiliar with the original language.

The metaphor of translation preserves the shell of a jurisprudence of original understanding, but leaches out everything inside the shell; it seems to be originalist, but is not. Ordinarily we translate the Constitution's words first by identifying the principles those words embodied at the time they were written into the Constitution, and then by determining how those principles apply to contemporary problems. If Congress was given the power to regulate commerce among the states in 1789 to ensure that market transactions would be conducted according to the same rules through the nation, in order to ensure economic growth, we translate the term 'commerce' in a way that authorizes today's Congress to achieve the same goals.

The example illustrates the general problem with 'translation'. Conventionally called the 'level of generality' problem, it is that different interpreters will specify the principles underlying particular

---

[35] *United States v Lopez* 514 US 549, 590–91 (1995) (Thomas J, concurring).

[36] *Ibid* at 568 (Kennedy J, concurring).

[37] L Lessig, 'Understanding Changed Readings: Fidelity and Theory' (1995) 47 *Stanford Law Review* 395; 'Translating Federalism: United States v Lopez' (1995) 1995 *Supreme Court Rev* 125.

constitutional terms differently, some at an abstract level of generality, some at a more concrete level, and as a result will come up with different translations of the Constitution's original meaning. Contemporary disputes over affirmative action or positive discrimination illustrate the difficulty.

The Fourteenth Amendment bars states from denying the equal protection of the laws. The meaning of 'equal protection' is clear enough in core applications: states may not impose disadvantages on African Americans simply because of their race. What, though, is the principle of equality embodied in the Equal Protection Clause? It might be a principle of anti-subordination, making constitutionally questionable statutes that impose disabilities on African Americans but not affirmative action programs that are not designed or intended to perpetuate subordination or a caste system. Or, it might be a principle of color-blindness, according to which governments are barred from taking race into account in any way in their decisions. The color-blindness principle makes affirmative action programs constitutionally questionable.

The question of the provision's application to contemporary affirmative action programs arises precisely because we cannot tell from consulting the dictionaries used in 1868 what the provision's terms meant at the time. So, we have to have recourse to the principles that the provision was meant to write into the Constitution. Identifying those principles leads away from the meaning of the Constitution's words to the understandings held by people at the time. The latter inquiry is close to an intentionalist one: What principle did the people in 1868 intend to write into the Constitution? Unfortunately, with respect to almost every interesting controversy over the principles underlying particular constitutional provisions, we inevitably discover serious disagreement about what those principles were. Some people understood 'equal protection' to mean anti-subordination, others that it meant color-blindness. The effort to translate the earlier term into contemporary terms leads to the interpreter's reproducing the contemporary problems by discovering that, on the level of principle to which the translator must move, today's difficulties were present in the past.

Some version of a jurisprudence of original understanding remains an essential component of nearly all particular resolutions of interpretive controversies, but the effort in the 1980s to make such a jurisprudence the only component of constitutional interpretation failed.

Appeals to Justice

Several constitutional provisions employ terms that evoke moral judgments: 'due process' resonates with ideas about fairness, 'equal protection of the laws' with ideas of equality. In giving these general terms content in particular cases, the Supreme Court sometimes has suggested that the underlying moral judgments can be read into the Constitution.[38] The Court's equal protection jurisprudence, for example, requires that legislation treating one group differently from another must be justified by some relevant difference between the groups. Relevance necessarily has some normative component. This is true even in the ordinary case, and more dramatically so in cases involving so-called suspect classifications, where the Court requires extremely good reasons for laws that impose disadvantages on groups that have historically been subjected to adverse treatment.

Specific textual referents are not the only reason for importing the conclusions of moral reasoning into the Constitution. On the most general level, the Court—and even more, political leaders reflecting deeply on the nature of the Constitution, such as Abraham Lincoln during the Civil War—sometimes treat the Constitution as an expression of the nation's commitment to 'establish justice' and 'secure the blessings of liberty', in the Preamble's terms. The Preamble is not directly enforceable, but the concerns it expresses for justice and liberty easily inform the interpretation of specific, enforceable constitutional provisions.

The Court has relied on moral concepts to overcome the limitation that other interpretive approaches might impose on reaching conclusions that the justices believe correct. Revisiting the poll tax case is useful here. The poll tax was challenged as a violation of the Fourteenth Amendment's prohibition of laws that deny equal protection of the laws. Several obstacles stood in the way of invalidating the poll tax. When the Fourteenth Amendment was adopted, lawyers drew a sharp distinction between civil rights, which the Amendment was designed to protect, and political rights, which its framers thought it did not

---

[38] Commentators, most notably Ronald Dworkin, have gone further and argued that the conclusions drawn by those who engage in moral philosophy in a systematic way should be imported into the Constitution through the terms that invoke moral concepts.

protect. The right to vote was the quintessential political right, and so, it would seem, inequalities in the distribution of the right to vote would be unaffected by the adoption of the Equal Protection Clause. That conclusion is confirmed by the fact that Congress believed it necessary to propose another amendment, the Fifteenth, to guarantee the right to vote against denials on the basis of race, and by the fact that a separate provision in the Fourteenth Amendment sought to encourage states to distribute the franchise broadly by depriving them of seats in the House of Representatives in proportion to their denial of votes to males over the age of 21. Even more, the Supreme Court had rejected constitutional challenges to the poll tax in 1937. In the face of these obstacles, the Court nonetheless found the poll tax unconstitutional. Justice William O Douglas wrote: 'the Equal Protection Clause is not shackled to the political theory of a particular era' and that the Court has 'never been confined to historic notions of equality'. He concluded, 'Notions of what constitutes equal treatment for purposes of the Equal Protection Clause *do* change'.[39]

The Court's use of moral concepts in this way is explained best by combining the proposition that some constitutional provisions do appear to direct the courts to look to morality to give the provisions content, with the proposition that our understanding of morality is always imperfect. Notions of equality change because, it is said, we come to understand better what equality truly requires as we grapple with specific problems and reflect on the deep meaning of the Constitution's moral terms.

Yet, it is precisely the possibility that our *notions* of equality and other morally laden terms change that raises the most serious questions about the Court's reliance on such notions in interpreting the Constitution. Critics sometimes question the ability of Supreme Court justices, who are trained as ordinary lawyers, not moral or political philosophers, to engage in serious moral reflection—or, at least, more serious moral reflection than the legislators whose work they are reviewing engaged in. More important, though, is the persistent fact of moral disagreement even after serious reflection. What one person characterizes as a change responsive to deeper understanding of the underlying moral concept, another person characterizes as a willful departure from the concept's meaning in the service of a result driven by preference rather than morality.

---

[39] *Ibid* at 669.

These criticisms have real force, but they overstate the extent to which constitutional interpretation by the courts actually relies on the importation of conclusions from systematic moral theorizing. Commentators have urged the Court to do so, but the actual references to moral concepts in Supreme Court opinions are more often gestures in the direction of such concepts than reliance on them. And, to the extent that the Constitution itself gestures in the same direction, it is hard to fault the justices for doing so as well.

Precedent

The modal Supreme Court opinion is almost certainly one that deals almost entirely with the Court's own precedents, mentioning the Constitution's text only as a starting point and ignoring almost entirely the original understanding of the text's words. In one sense this is hardly surprising. The Court's precedents serve as glosses on the text. Ordinarily one can work one's way backwards through the precedents to an opinion at the foundation of the line of precedents that does deal to a substantial extent with text and original understanding, albeit that sometimes the older precedents are like Marshall's in *McCulloch*, dealing with the text by treating it as an exemplification of applied political theory. In addition, the Constitution's age makes precedents particularly important. The text has become so encrusted with precedent that looking past the precedents to the text might well disrupt practices deeply embedded in the constitutional system's on-going operation.

Precedent-based adjudication is a particular problem for those who believe that the only permissible basis for interpretation is the text as it was originally understood. Precedent matters, after all, only when it points in a direction different from the one indicated by the text or original understanding. The most devoted originalists do argue that erroneous precedents should simply be ignored,[40] but that is an eccentric position among US constitutionalists.

One reason for the rejection of such a purist position is that some of the Court's decisions seem rather clearly at odds with original understanding, and yet rejecting them is unthinkable in today's constitutional

[40] See, eg, G Lawson, 'The Constitutional Case Against Precedent' (1994) 17 *Harvard Journal of Law & Public Policy* 23.

culture. The primary example is *Brown v Board of Education,* holding segregation of the public schools unconstitutional.[41] The correctness of that decision is a fixed point, perhaps the only fixed point, in contemporary constitutional law. Yet, it is difficult to defend on originalist grounds.[42] Even originalists need some account of the proper role of precedent in constitutional adjudication if they are to agree that *Brown* should not be overruled.

The more important questions about the role precedent should play in constitutional interpretation involve the conditions for overruling erroneous precedents. The justices agree that it should be easier to overrule constitutional precedents than statutory ones. Mistaken interpretations of statutes, they say, can be rectified by ordinary legislative processes. Mistaken constitutional interpretations, in contrast, are embedded in the law unless they are overturned through the difficult process of constitutional amendment.

Sometimes the Court takes the position that precedents can be overruled simply because today's Court disagrees with them. *Lawrence v Texas,* holding unconstitutional state laws against homosexual sodomy, overruled a decision rendered 17 years earlier because, the Court said, the precedent 'was not correct when it was decided'.[43] Such an approach gives precedent no independent weight. Precedent has that weight only when the judge, considering the question as an original matter, would reach a decision different from the one indicated by a fair reading of the precedents—that is, precedent matters only when the precedent is, from the judge's point of view, mistaken.

In *Lawrence* the Court gestured toward other criteria, although its judgment that the precedent was wrong clearly played the largest role. The Court's opinion mentioned that the precedent misconstrued the nature of the constitutional claim presented, and that two later cases cast some doubt on the precedent's rationale. These are among the concerns the Court has mentioned in discussing the propriety of overruling a constitutional precedent.

---

[41]   347 US 483 (1954).

[42]   For one unsuccessful effort, see M McConnell, 'Originalism and the Desegregation Decisions' (1995) 81 *Virginia Law Review* 947.

[43]   *Lawrence v Texas* 539 US 558, 578 (2003).

The controversial joint opinion in *Planned Parenthood of Southeastern Pennsylvania v Casey* mentioned earlier contains a summary of the guidelines the justices said the Court uses:

> [The Court should consider] whether [the precedent] has been found unworkable; whether [the precedent] could be removed without serious inequity to those who have relied upon it or significant damage to the stability of the society governed by the rule in question; whether the law's growth in the intervening years has left [the precedent] a doctrinal anachronism discounted by society; and whether [the precedent's] premises of fact have so far changed … as to render its … holding somehow irrelevant or unjustifiable in dealing with the issue it addressed.[44]

The application of these guidelines is hardly mechanical. *Casey* involved the question of overruling the Supreme Court's basic abortion decision, *Roe v Wade*.[45] Discussing the reliance interest, the joint opinion's authors argued that reliance was established not by showing that specific individuals had relied on *Roe* and that their on-going expectations would be defeated by overruling that decision, but that 'for two decades of economic and social developments, people have organized intimate relationships and made choices that define their views of themselves and their places in society, in reliance on the availability of abortion in the event that contraception should fail. The ability of women to participate equally in the economic and social life of the Nation has been facilitated by their ability to control their reproductive lives.'[46] And, in dealing with changed factual premises, the opinion justified the overruling of *Lochner v New York*'s, which held that economic liberty enforced through the Due Process Clause made unconstitutional state laws requiring maximum hours, by referring to its 'fundamentally false factual assumptions about the capacity of a relatively unregulated market to satisfy minimal levels of human welfare', rather than by invoking the rather more obvious proposition that *Lochner* rested on normatively inappropriate assumptions about the relative freedom of workers and employers.

This discussion of the conditions for overruling or adhering to precedent should not obscure the more important point. Constitutional interpretation in the United States involves arguing about the

---

[44] *Planned Parenthood of Southeastern Pennsylvania v Casey* 505 US 833, 855 (1992) (joint opinion of O'Connor, Kennedy, and Souter JJ).

[45] 410 US 113 (1973).

[46] *Planned Parenthood* at 856.

implications of the Court's precedents far more than it involves any other interpretive approach.[47]

Non-US Law

Until the middle of the twentieth century, Supreme Court opinions referred routinely to the laws of other nations, although only occasionally in support of constitutional interpretations.[48] Justice Felix Frankfurter argued that the traditions of Anglo-American jurisdictions should inform constitutional interpretation in determining which features of the adversary system were so fundamental as to be applicable in state court proceedings, pursuant to the Fourteenth Amendment's Due Process Clause. A 1958 decision dealing with the interpretation of the Eighth Amendment's ban on cruel and unusual punishments said that the prohibition should be interpreted in light of 'evolving standards of decency', and implied that in determining what those standards were the courts could look to practices outside the United States.[49] Beyond that, references to non-United States law were rare.

In the 1990s some justices began to refer to non-United States law. Sometimes the references were mere observations about what other constitutional (or human rights) systems did with respect to the issue the Court was considering. These observations had the rhetorical effect of demonstrating that the Court's actions were not out of line with the legal standards applied elsewhere, but they were not an integral component of the Court's interpretation of the US Constitution provision at issue. A footnote in an opinion holding it unconstitutional to

---

[47] A final interpretive concern is the administrability of constitutional rules. Large swathes of American constitutional law do not involve interpreting the Constitution at all, at least directly. Instead, they are concerned with developing rules that allow the Constitution to be implemented in the nation's daily governance. (The term 'implemented' derives from RH Fallon Jr, *Implementing the Constitution* (Cambridge, MA, Harvard University Press, 2001).) Many constitutional rules such as the 'one person, one vote' rule for apportionments, discussed in ch 2 above, are linked to underlying constitutional text and values only by these considerations of administrability.

[48] For an overview, see VC Jackson, 'Ambivalent Resistance and Comparative Constitutionalism: Opening Up the Conversation On "Proportionality," Rights and Federalism' (1999) 1 *U Penn J Const L* 583, 584–93.

[49] *Trop v Dulles* 356 US 86 (1958).

impose the death penalty on people with mental retardation observed '[W]ithin the world community, the imposition of the death penalty for crimes committed by mentally retarded offenders is overwhelmingly disapproved', in a paragraph that began by asserting that the 'legislative judgment' of American states against such executions 'reflects a much broader social and professional consensus'.[50]

Other recent references to non-United States law are slightly more substantive. The Court relied on a judgment of the European Court of Human Rights to counter the argument made by Chief Justice Warren Burger in an earlier case to support his conclusion that consensual homosexual sodomy had been condemned by law 'throughout the history of Western civilization'.[51] And, in one of the Court's anti-commandeering cases, Justice Stephen Breyer in dissent noted that other federal systems, such as Germany's, not only had no anti-commandeering principle but affirmatively relied on subnational governments to implement national laws, because in those systems it was thought that using subnational governments in that way respected their autonomy.[52]

These references to non-United States law, mild though they were, provoked a substantial critical response from some justices and commentators. As Justice Scalia put it, 'it is American conceptions of decency that are dispositive', as he rejected the contention 'that the sentencing practices of other countries are relevant' to determining the constitutionality of imposing the death penalty on offenders who were aged 16 when they committed their crimes.[53] The critics had several concerns. First, they argued that the United States Constitution was a text that had been adopted by the people of the United States at a particular time, and lacked authoritative force unless it was interpreted only with reference to the understandings of the American people. Second, they believed that reference to non-United States law simply provided another resource for judges to use to overturn laws they disapproved of, when the other resources in US law failed to support that course of action. Finally, they noted that non-US law often arose in a particular institutional context that differed from the United States context in relevant ways, and that judges in the United States were unlikely to know enough about that context—or could spend their time more

[50] *Atkins v Virginia* 586 US 304, 316 n 21 (2002).
[51] *Lawrence* at 2480.
[52] *Printz v United States* 521 US 898, 976 (1997) (Breyer J, dissenting).
[53] *Stanford v Kentucky* 492 US 361, 369 n 1 (1989).

productively learning other things. Justice Breyer's reference to German federalism, for example, did not take into account the fact that the German länder had much more substantial representation in the German legislative process than American states do in the US national legislative process, a fact that plainly has some bearing on whether commandeering undermines or supports the autonomy of the subnational units.[54]

Despite these strictures, it seems likely that references to non-US law will increase gradually, as United States judges continue to participate in conversations—both in person and through the exchange of opinions—with judges of constitutional courts in other nations.

CONCLUSION

The eclecticism of constitutional interpretation in the United States guarantees that the courts will update the Constitution. The reason is simple. Consider a claim that Congress has exceeded the power granted it to regulate interstate commerce, because the activity it has regulated would not have been considered 'commerce' in 1789. Were the courts to use only originalist interpretive methods, no updating would occur. They would uphold or strike down the statute, but in either case the courts would follow that the original Constitution. Introduce some other interpretive method, though, and the picture changes. Eclecticism means that, at least sometimes, the several interpretive methods the courts use will come into conflict—and, in particular, that at least sometimes an originalist interpretation will lose out to an interpretation resting on another method. And that, finally, describes precisely what happens when a court updates the written Constitution.

CONSTITUTIONAL MOMENTS AND CONSTITUTIONAL CHANGE

Formal amendments and constitutional interpretation serve to update the Constitution on the molecular level, so to speak: After a formal

---

[54] D Halberstam, 'Comparative Federalism and the Issue of Commandeering' in K Nikolaïdis and R Howse (eds), *The Federal Vision: Legitimacy and Levels of Governance in the United States and the European Union* (New York, Oxford University Press, 2001), 213.

amendment or a new constitutional interpretation, the Constitution is different in one respect from what it was before. Sometimes, though, we can see—at least in retrospect—that large, 'molar' changes have occurred in the constitutional system. How do these more systemic changes come about?

We can approach an answer from two directions. First, we might consider how an entirely new constitution comes to replace an older one. Constitutional theorists argue that that type of transformation occurs when the people acting as a constituent power re-constitute the overall constitutional system. These theoretical formulations typically assume that these events are signaled by formal events such as the convening of a constituent assembly whose purpose is to write a new constitution. But such an assumption is not strictly speaking necessary. All that is required is that the people somehow come to think of themselves as acting outside of or above the ordinary politics of their legislatures.

CONSTITUTIONAL MOMENTS

This approach through constitutional theory is quite general, applicable in principle to constitutional transformation anywhere in the world. Bruce Ackerman has developed an alternative though analogous approach that rests on specific aspects of US history.[55] Like the constitutional theorists, Ackerman distinguishes between periods of ordinary politics and times of high constitutional deliberation and politics. For Ackerman, most political life occurs during extended periods of ordinary politics, which is, on his view, normatively valuable because people can devote most of their attention to their private pursuits and deal with politics only when and to the extent that politics affects their everyday lives. Occasionally, though, there are what Ackerman calls 'constitutional moments', in which the people shift their attention to higher lawmaking. And, importantly, when they do, they leave behind their quotidian concerns, the ones they deploy in ordinary politics, and deliberate more seriously and in a more detached way about fundamentals of the constitutional order.

---

[55] Ackerman's approach is developed in BA Ackerman, *We the People*, vols 1 and 2 (Cambridge, MA, Harvard University Press, 1991, 1998).

Ackerman argues that we can see a handful of constitutional moments in US history. Some look like times when constitutional change occurs through formal amendment, but, Ackerman argues, appearances are misleading. Consider the making of the Constitution itself. It came about when a convention was called to consider proposing amendments to the Articles of Confederation. According to the Articles, amendments could be adopted only by unanimous agreement of the states. The constitutional convention departed from its remit in two ways: Rather than proposing discrete amendments, it put forth an entirely new constitution; and, rather than seeking unanimous agreement to the new constitution's adoption, its framers said that it would come into effect when nine (not 13) states ratified it. Ackerman concludes from this that the Constitution's adoption occurred outside the bounds of the formal legal requirements then in place.

He makes a similar argument about what he identifies as the second constitutional moment in US history, which occurred during Reconstruction. Again there were formal amendments but, again, Ackerman argues, the formal amendments became legally effective even though they were not adopted in a manner that conformed to the requirements of the existing legal order. Here, the argument is quite complex. Southern states had purported to secede from the Union. Should their votes be counted when determining whether sufficient states had ratified a constitutional amendment? Having been defeated in the war, Southern states agreed to abolish slavery, and they were counted as members of the Union for purposes of ratifying the Thirteenth Amendment. The Fourteenth Amendment is a different matter. It was submitted to the states for ratification when Southern states were under military occupation. Congress insisted that the occupied states ratify the Fourteenth Amendment as a condition for their 're-admission' to the Union. Thus, though the Southern states were part of the Union for purposes of ratifying the Thirteenth Amendment, they somehow lost that status for purposes of ratifying the Fourteenth. And, even more, the southern states were coerced into ratifying the Fourteenth Amendment. It is hard to see how, as a matter of ordinary law and constitutional theory, coerced consent should count.

There are other details, but Ackerman's primary point is clear: the effect of constitutional moments is to bring about constitutional transformations on a relatively large scale even though the requirements for formal amendment have not been satisfied. One can quarrel, as critics have, with many details in Ackerman's account. He offers an overly schematic and formal set of criteria for determining when a constitutional moment occurs, for example. Yet, his basic insight—that constitutional transformation can occur outside the framework established by the formal amendment process, when the people are sufficiently mobilized—remains valid and valuable.

The real payoff from Ackerman's approach comes when he treats the New Deal as another constitutional moment. His approach helps us understand the New Deal in several ways. First, Ackerman argues that many scholars attempt to treat the New Deal in what he calls 'restorationist' terms—that is, as a period when the nation retrieved the true meaning of national power after an era in which that meaning had been distorted and abandoned. But, he points out, it is abundantly clear that the world of national power after the New Deal was dramatically different from anything that had come before—and, Ackerman argues, different even from the expansive visions of national power held by most of the most enthusiastic founders. Second, perhaps we can understand the Constitution's creation and its transformation during Reconstruction in terms of purely positive law and the formal amendment process. Replacing one constitution with another, we might think, can unproblematically involve departures from the amendment rules specified in the first constitution. And Ackerman's claims about the 'illegality' of the process by which the Reconstruction amendments became law, while more than plausible, are not so overwhelming that a critic might treat those amendments in purely positive-law terms. The New Deal is different because no formal amendment memorializes the New Deal transformation. If we are to regard the New Deal as a period in which substantial constitutional change occurred we are going to have to have at hand some account like Ackerman's. And, finally, it seems unquestionable that such a change did indeed occur during the New Deal.

Problems with Ackerman's Account

There remain difficulties with Ackerman's account. How are we to 'interpret' the constitutional changes brought about by constitutional moments? They need not be embodied in formal—even if procedurally flawed—constitutional amendments, so we have no language to work with. For example, should we regard such New Deal accomplishments as the national system of social assistance for the aged as protected against repeal by an unwritten constitutional amendment? The answer may not be as obvious as one might think. Efforts to change the social assistance system have met enormous political resistance, to the point where substantially altering the system might indeed require as much political support as would be required for a formal constitutional amendment.[56]

Perhaps more important, Ackerman's criteria for identifying constitutional moments seem a bit jury-rigged, with the principal goal of treating the New Deal as a constitutional moment but not, specifically, the Reagan Revolution of the 1980s and afterwards. Ackerman posits a sequence of events in which a political leader proposes substantial constitutional change, meets resistance from other political actors, and overcomes that resistance, after which the former opponents come into line. Identifying constitutional moments is a more interpretive enterprise than this rather formalist version suggests. What should matter is the degree to which a political leader mobilizes substantial public support behind a substantial change in the presuppositions of the governing order. On this more interpretive and less formalistic approach, the Progressive era, the civil rights era of the 1960s, and the Reagan Revolution are candidates for constitutional moments.

These examples, though, point to another difficulty with the specifics of Ackerman's presentation. His metaphor of constitutional 'moments' is powerful and does capture the idea of some sort of relatively intense popular commitment to substantial constitutional change. But it may be misleading to the extent that it suggests that popular mobilization can occur only for a short time before the people revert to their ordinary pursuits. Focusing on popular mobilization directly, we might more easily see periods rather than moments of constitutional transformation. In this light, we might see some formal constitutional amendments—the Reconstruction era amendments and those of the 1960s, for example—as part, but only part, of a larger form of constitutional change.

Seeing that constitutional moments actually occur over extended periods, during which politicians maneuver to mobilize the public for—and against—constitutional transformation allows us to understand 'constitutional hardball' in the United States.[57] Constitutional hardball

---

[56] For a suggestive argument along these lines, see EA Young, 'The Constitution Outside the Constitution' (2007) 117 *Yale Law Journal* 408.

[57] For a more extended discussion of constitutional hardball, see M Tushnet, 'Constitutional Hardball' (2004) 37 *John Marshall Law Review* 523.

consists of political claims and practices—legislative and executive initiatives—that are without much question within the bounds of existing constitutional doctrine and practice but that are nonetheless in some tension with existing *pre*-constitutional understandings.[58] It is *hardball* because its practitioners see themselves as playing for keeps in a special kind of way; they believe the stakes of the political controversy their actions provoke are quite high, and that their defeat and their opponents' victory would be a serious, perhaps permanent setback to the political positions they hold.

Consider again Skowronek's description of some political regimes as 'vulnerable'. Concerned with presidential leadership, Skowronek focuses on how a presidential candidate might present himself or herself as offering a reconstruction of a vulnerable constitutional order. But politicians might perceive vulnerability before the constitutional moment actually occurs. They will try to *build* popular support by testing the existing regime to identify points where it might be especially vulnerable. The tests occur when challengers raise questions about what had previously seemed stable practices of nearly constitutional dimension. The impeachment of President Clinton is a good example. The legal predicates for the impeachment were reasonable: Lying about activities not connected with the performance of a president's duties might be described as a 'high Crime [or] Misdemeanor', although the legal case for so interpreting the Impeachment Clause is hardly air-tight. Ordinarily, the president's opponents would have waited until the next election to mobilize against him, but, seeing his presidency as vulnerable—and perhaps as the last remaining redoubt of an already decayed New Deal constitutional order—President Clinton's opponents tested the limits of the Constitution. Ackerman's account of constitutional transformation through politics gives us some insight into these episodes of constitutional hardball.

Conclusion

If constitutional interpretation by the courts is the primary mechanism for updating the Constitution on a relatively small scale, popular

---

[58] By this I mean the 'go without saying' assumptions that underpin working systems of constitutional government. They are hard to identify outside of times of crisis precisely because they go without saying. (An alternative term would be 'conventions'.)

mobilization is the primary mechanism for large-scale constitutional transformation. Popular mobilization is of course a *political* phenomenon, and our examination of constitutional change must therefore return us to politics as the most important feature of US constitutionalism. Periods of constitutional transformation tend to coincide with the reconstructive presidencies discussed in chapter three: Lincoln and Reconstruction (after his assassination, a project carried on by his political heirs in Congress), Roosevelt and the New Deal, Reagan and the conservative resurgence of the late twentieth century. The coincidence is hardly accidental. Reconstructive presidents succeed by mobilizing the people behind their transformative programs. And, finally, when reconstruction succeeds, the president and his or her successors, whether 'affiliated' or 'pre-emptive,' staff the courts with judges imbued with the values associated with the constitutional transformation, which is why the courts translate older terms into the newer constitutional ones.

CONCLUDING THOUGHTS

The coexistence of judicial supremacy with a Bagehot-ian efficient Constitution is more than slightly odd. As we have seen, constitutional interpretation by the US courts is a mechanism for ensuring that the efficient Constitution works well as circumstances change and the written Constitution does not. Judicial supremacy is different. It rests on the strong claim by the courts that they are uniquely well-positioned to interpret the written Constitution, but the very existence of an efficient Constitution tells us to downplay the importance of the written Constitution, and thereby weakens the courts' claims of supremacy in developing the Constitution

Still, judicial supremacy is only one of several views about the proper location for constitutional interpretation. The role the courts have played in the US constitutional system has varied. The written Constitution creates the structures of politics in the United States, and it is politics—and more specifically the party system, and even more specifically the dynamics of presidential leadership—that has fueled constitutional development. The courts have tended to operate around the fringes of politics.[59] Sometimes they have articulated some of the

---

[59] See F Schauer, 'Foreword: The Court's Agenda—and the Nation's' (2006) 120 *Harvard Law Review* 4.

principles animating the then-dominant political order, sometimes they have temporarily resisted an emerging political order in the name of an older one, and sometimes they have pushed the dominant order's principles further than the political branches have been able to.

Early in the twenty-first century, some constitutional theorists were troubled by what they saw as the entrenchment of the Reagan Revolution in the Supreme Court even as that political order was either losing its grip on, or had never been able to consolidate its control of, the political branches. From their point of view, judicial supremacy made that entrenchment, if it truly were occurring, even more troublesome. The most notable contributions drew on US constitutional history for an account of popular constitutionalism.[60] The term was perhaps a bit misleading to the extent that it suggested giving normative priority to the constitutional interpretations proffered by the people themselves, either directly or through their representatives. In its best versions, the theory of popular constitutionalism was primarily descriptive rather than normative. It argued that constitutional development was driven by the people acting politically, and that we would be misled were we to focus too intensely on the courts' role.

Popular constitutionalism tells us little about the efficient Constitution's content, except that it will change regularly as one political order replaces another. And even the anxieties that pushed scholars to articulate popular constitutionalism as an account of the US Constitution may have been misplaced. If the Reagan Revolution has indeed run its course in the political branches, it is unlikely to entrench itself successfully in the courts for more than a few years. If displacement occurs, it may be through a crisis like that which occurred during the New Deal, or through more ordinary processes of replacement of older justices by newer ones, or through strategic calculations by sitting justices.

What US constitutional history shows, though, is that understanding the Constitution as it is requires us to pay relatively little attention to the written Constitution, somewhat more attention to the way in

[60] The most notable contribution is L Kramer, *The People Themselves: Popular Constitutionalism and Judicial Review* (New York, Oxford University Press, 2004). For an early version, lacking the historical detail, see M Tushnet, *Taking the Constitution Away from the Courts* (Princeton, Princeton University Press, 1999).

which the courts interpret the written Constitution, and a great deal of attention to the organization of politics by political parties under presidential leadership and to the principles that dominant parties and their presidents articulate. And so we end where we began: with the efficient Constitution rather than the written one.

FURTHER READING

Ackerman, BA, 'The Holmes Lectures: The Living Constitution,' (2007) 120 Harvard *L Rev* 1727 (a recent statement and application of Ackerman's approach).

Dworkin, RM, *Freedom's Law: The Moral Reading of the American Constitution* (Cambridge, MA, Harvard University Press, 1996).

Kyvig, D, *Explicit and Authentic Acts: Amending the US Constitution, 1776–1995* (Lawrence, KS, University Press of Kansas, 1996) (a history of successful and failed amendments).

Levinson, S (ed), *Responding to Imperfection: The Theory and Practice of Constitutional Amendment* (Princeton, Princeton University Press, 1995) (a collection of essays on the amendment process).

Magliocca, GN, *Andrew Jackson and the Constitution: The Rise and Fall of Generational Regimes* (Lawrence, KS, University Press of Kansas, 2007) (an interesting application of Ackerman's approach).

Scalia, A, *A Matter of Interpretation: Federal Courts and the Law* (Princeton, Princeton University Press, 1997) (a defense of textualism and originalism, with critical comments by respondents).

Index